TENT LIFE IN SIBERIA

George Kennan
1868

TENT LIFE
IN
SIBERIA

GEORGE KENNAN

INTRODUCTION BY LARRY MCMURTRY

PEREGRINE SMITH BOOKS, GIBBS M. SMITH, INC.

SALT LAKE CITY

Published by
Gibbs M. Smith, Inc.
P.O. Box 667
Layton, Utah 84041

Designed by Larry G. Clarkson

Printed and bound in the United States of America

LIBRARY OF CONGRESS CATALOGING-IN-PUBLICATION DATA

Kennan, George, 1845-1924.
Tent Life in Siberia

Reprint. Originally published:
New York: Putnam; London:
S. Low, Son & Marston, 1871.
With new introd.
1. Siberia, Eastern (R.S.F.S.R.)
—Description and travel.
2. Kennan George,
1845-1924. I. Title. DK755.K38
1986   957'.08   86-10016
ISBN 0-87905-254-6 (pbk.)

INTRODUCTION.

THE nineteenth century was to travel writing what the Elizabethan and Jacobean eras were to blank-verse drama: an unsurpassably flush time, in which a talent could be found equal to every opportunity.

George F. Kennan found his opportunity in Siberia and the result was *Tent Life in Siberia*, one of the most appealing classics of nineteenth century travel.

To the nineteenth century traveller, opportunity must have seemed infinite. Three centuries of incessant exploration by the great trading nations of Western Europe had left the oceans charted and the continents outlined. Almost every place had been discovered, but comparatively few had been described in the kind of detail that would satisfy the increasingly realistic appetites of the reading public.

The appetites had perhaps been stimulated by the growing realism of the novel. *Robinson Crusoe* succeeded in part because Defoe so ingeniously augmented the sparse detail of the ship-wreck narrative which seems to have been his principal source of inspiration.

In any event the nineteenth century produced traveller after traveller whose energies and descriptive powers were not inferior to those of the great novelists. The travellers' energies may even have been greater, for they had to travel as well as write, and at a time when the burdens of travel consisted of worse things than clogged freeways and crowded airports. The distinction between novelists and travel writers is itself delicate, for almost all the novelists travelled and wrote travel books, and not a few of the travellers wrote novels, though rarely good ones.

The great age of English travel writing begins with the African books of James Bruce and Mungo Park in the 1790s, and doesn't close until 1923, when Apsley Cherry-Garrard published the second volume of *The Worst Journey In The World*, his tragic masterpiece about the last Scott expedition.

During those one hundred and thirty years it seemed that virtually everyone who could move was on the seas or on the road. The naturalist-travellers (Bates, Wallace, Darwin) seemed to prefer South America. The more competitive sought the Northwest passage, or the source of the Nile. There was no region of the earth that didn't tempt someone, and all regions tempted that dervish of travellers, Richard Burton.

It is unfortunate that so few attempts have been made to study this literature as a genre. The best study to date, Paul Fussell's *Abroad* (1980), deals with English travel writing between the two world wars: the silver, not the golden, age.

America, of course, was one of the places most frequently travelled to by the Europeans. Some came to hunt (Prince Maximilian), some to lecture (Dickens), some came on business (Mrs. Trollope), and many just travelled and then wrote.

For the first thirty or forty years of the century Americans themselves mainly felt obliged to be concerned with staying alive. Often enough this required travel, sometimes rapid travel, but it didn't require writing. In books from the continent, native Americans and the indigenous people who would today be called Native Americans were alike unflatteringly drawn. When Americans began to write travel books they treated themselves as deprecatingly as they had been treated by the English or the French.

With travel so hard, writers, for literary purposes, frequently served as their own victims. A self-deprecating, comic style developed, in which the hardships of travel—many of them severe hardships—are treated with airy lightheartedness. In narrative after narrative, a comic tone prevails.

In nineteenth century America, genres didn't always separate neatly. John Lloyd Stephens' *Incidents of Travel in Yucatan* (1841) is a pure travel book, and a masterful one, but for its date it is a rarity. Cooper and Irving both brought travel into their fiction, and, one suspects, fiction into their travels. In *Omoo* and *Typee* Melville attempted to capitalize on the growing popularity of travel writing, but the books failed commercially and, in my view, aesthetically as well.

Other mixtures worked better, and classics that owed much of their flavor to travel began to emerge, with *Moby Dick* arguably the greatest of these. Others would include Thoreau's *A Week on the Concord and Merrimack Rivers*, Parkman's *The Oregon Trail*, Josiah Gregg's *Commerce On the Prairies*, and, of course, Mark Twain, who, in *Roughing It*, *Life on the Mississippi*, *The Innocents Abroad*, and various other books proved to have every gift that the travel-writer needs. He is vivid, idiomatic, ironic, witty, a skilled shaper of scenes, amused by awkward vicissitudes yet moved by the majesty of river, sky, and plain.

Above all, he is zestful. Without zest in the face of hardship, travel writing soon becomes little more than a record of misery.

This, in brief, is the context in which George Kennan (1845-1924) should be read.

Kennan may have lacked Twain's genius, but he was a match for him in the zest department, and, at his best, was just as witty. The funniest scenes in *Tent Life in Siberia*—for example, the description of the first night spent in a Korak *polog*—are as lively as anything in *Roughing It*. Indeed, the tone of the two books is so similar that Twain might have called his *Tent Life in the West*, while Kennan's could have been *Roughing It in Siberia*.

An argument could be made that the origins of black humor lie in travel writing, and *Tent Life in Siberia* would be an excellent book on which to base such a thesis. Young George Kennan, according to the article on him in *The Dictionary of American Biography*, had physical limitations which prevented him from seeing front line service in the Civil War. Whatever these were, they did not prevent him from tramping around northeastern Siberia for two years, in temperatures that reached sixty below and under conditions provocative of the blackest humor.

He was an accomplished telegrapher, and was hired at the age of twenty to assist in an enterprise that must, at the time, have seemed somewhat fantastical. The first Atlantic Cable had failed, and Western Union hoped to link America and Europe by a telegraph line that would run through Alaska, over the Bering Strait, and across Siberia to European Russia.

Kennan and a stalwart band left America in 1865 and travelled in Siberia for the better part of two years, surveying the unsurveyed wilderness and attempting to persuade the various native peoples they encountered to help them stick poles in the ground across which could be strung a magic wire whose clickety music would sing across continents.

Practically speaking, much of their time was spent trying to stay alive, a feat which required both extreme hardihood and the occasional miracle—the latter, in the form of the fortuitous encounter, being a facet rarely absent from good travel books.

Enroute to the West, the little group was taken aboard an American whaler, where they discovered, by perusing some old newspapers, that the Atlantic Cable had been successfully laid and the Russo-American telegraph abandoned.

George Kennan went on to become one of the most accomplished and trusted journalists of his day. When McKinley was shot, in 1901, Kennan was in charge of all telegraphic communications from the White House—the presidential press secretary of his day, as it were. He covered the eruption of Pelée, and the Spanish-American War.

Mother Russia had touched Kennan, though, as she was to touch his distinguished descendant, Ambassador George F. Kennan, in our own day. She called Kennan back more than once. In the mid-1880s, at the behest of an editor, he went back to Siberia to investigate the system of political exile. Inclined at first to vindicate the Romanovs, he ended by damning them. *Siberia and the Exile System* (2 vols, 1891) is the first great study of the Gulag, and it remains indispensable. It too, in its way, is a great travel book, one much more darkly toned than *Tent Life*. The sixteen months that he spent travelling amid the exiles almost broke Kennan's health.

Tent Life in Siberia is very much a young man's book: breezy, confident, irreverent, and wonderfully readable. It was published in 1870 and went through fourteen printings in its appealing binding (blue, green, or brown, with a Korak and his dog, sled, and yurt embossed on the cover). An expanded version was published in 1910.

Enduring travel books are rarely tragic: Cherry-Garrard's story of the Scott expedition is an exception. The explorers usually get home. The trip may in fact have been unmitigated hell, but in writing it up the author-explorer will usually make it seem like a happy jaunt, in which the nips bestowed upon the party by natives, beasts, or climate merely serve as a stimulant.

At this Kennan is superb. His wit never fails him, and he knows when something more than wit is merited. Prose *qua* prose, the greatest passage in the book is the description of an extraordinary display of the aurora borealis which occurred in February, 1867. In the copious annals of Arctic travel there is nothing to surpass Kennan's description of this display. It is the kind of writing that once would have been called sublime.

Like most good travel writers, George Kennan had a refreshing openness to experience. He approached his adventure with enthusiasm, and described it with a vividness and humor that immediately captured readers in the nineteenth century and, I think, will capture many in the twentieth, now that it is, at long last, available again.

LARRY MCMURTRY

PREFACE.

THE attempt which was made by the Western Union Telegraph Company, in 1865–6 and '7, to build an overland line to Europe viâ Alaska, Behring's Straits, and Siberia, was in some respects the most remarkable undertaking of the present century. Bold in its conception, and important in the ends at which it aimed, it attracted at one time the attention of the whole civilized world, and was regarded as the greatest telegraphic enterprise which had ever engaged American capital. Like all unsuccessful ventures, however, in this progressive age, it has been speedily forgotten, and the brilliant success of the Atlantic Cable has driven it entirely out of the public mind. Most readers are familiar with the principal facts in the history of this enterprise, from its organization to its ultimate abandonment; but only a few, even of its original projectors, know anything about the work which it accomplished in British Columbia, Alaska, and Siberia; the obstacles which were met and overcome by its exploring and working parties; and the contributions which it made to our knowledge of an hitherto untravelled, unvisited region. Its employés, in the course of two years, explored nearly six thousand miles of unbroken wilderness, extending from Vancouver's Island on the American coast to Behring's Straits, and from Behring's Straits to the Chinese frontier in Asia. The traces of their deserted camps may be found in the wildest mountain fastnesses of Kamtchatka, or the vast desolate plains of Northeastern Siberia, and throughout the gloomy pine forests of Alaska and British Columbia. Mounted on reindeer, they traversed the most rugged passes of the north Asiatic mountains; they floated in skin canoes down the great rivers of the north; slept in the smoky pologs of the Siberian Chookchees; and camped out upon desolate northern plains in temperatures of 50° and 60° below zero. The poles which they erected and the houses which they built now stand alone in an encircling wilderness,—the only results of their three years' labor and suffering, and the only monuments of an abandoned enterprise.

It is not my purpose to write a history of the Russo-American Telegraph. The success of its rival, the Atlantic Cable, has completely overshadowed its early importance, and its own failure has deprived it of all its interest for American readers. Though its history, however, be unimportant, the surveys and explorations which were planned and executed under its auspices have a value and an interest of their own, aside from the object for which they were undertaken. The territory which they covered is little known to the reading world, and its nomadic inhabitants have been rarely visited by civilized man. Only a few adventurous traders and fur-hunters have ever penetrated its almost unbroken solitudes, and it is not probable that civilized men will ever follow in their steps. The country holds out to the ordinary traveller no inducement commensurate with the risk and hardship which its exploration involves.

Two of the employés of the Russo-American Telegraph Company, Messrs. Whymper and Dall, have already published accounts of their travels in various parts of British Columbia and Alaska ; and believing that a history of the Company's explorations on the other side of Behring's Straits will possess equal interest, I have written the following narrative of two years' life in Northeastern Siberia. It makes no pretensions whatever to fulness of scientific information, nor to any very extraordinary researches of any kind. It is intended simply to convey as clear and accurate an idea as possible of the inhabitants, scenery, customs, and general external features of a new and comparatively unknown country. It is essentially a personal narrative of life in Siberia and Kamtchatka ; and its claim to attention lies rather in the freshness of the subject, than in any special devotion to science or skill of treatment.

CONTENTS.

CHAPTER   PAGE

I. The Russo-American Telegraph—The "Olga" sails from San Francisco for Kamtchatka and the Amoor.   1

II. The Voyage across the North Pacific.   10

III. Voyage continued—Petropavlovski.   22

IV. Petropavlovski.   30

V. Russian Language—Departure of the Amoor River Party.   40

VI. A Kamtchatkan Wedding—Start for the "Far North"   48

VII. Horseback Ride in Kamtchatka—The Mountains—Vegetation—Animal Life—The Villages—The People. .   56

VIII. "Jerusalem"—The Dwellings—A Kamtchatka Supper—Indian Summer—A "Jehu" Prayer—Hard Riding   67

IX. Malqua—Fine Scenery—Genul—A Bear Hunt—Pooschin.   78

X. Sherom—Boating—Milkova—Exciting Reception in the Character of "Emperor".   86

XI. The River, continued—Volcano Kloochay—A "Black Bath".   97

XII. Canoe Travel on the "Yolofka"—Volcanic Conversation—"Oh, Susanna!"—Talking "American"—Ride to Yolofka under Difficulties.   109

CONTENTS.

CHAPTER   PAG

XIII. A Chilly Lodging—Grand Scenery—Another Bear Hunt —Steeple-chase—Floating to Tigil 12%

XIV. Coast of the Okhotsk Sea—Lesnoi—Whale-boat and the Land Party—"Devil's Pass"—Samanka Mountains—Snow-storm—Wild Scene 133

XV. Gale continued—Famine imminent—Boating Party heard from—Return to Lesnoi 146

XVI. Kamtchadal Nights' Entertainments—The People—The Fish — Sables — Language — Music — Songs — Dog-sledges—Costume 154

XVII. Russian Doctoring—The Samanka Mountains—Encampment of Wandering Koraks—Dogs and Reindeer—Personals—Burrowing — "Pologs" — Korak Delicacies 166

XVIII. Other Traits of Wandering Koraks—Independence— Hospitality—Lodging—Breakfast—Reindeer Travel —Korak Notions of Distance—Mysterious Visitor. 181

XIX. Cheerless Travelling—Korak Marriage Ceremonies— Won't you take a Toadstool?—Monotonous Existence 195

XX. Korak Language—Religion—Customs, etc 206

XXI. River Penzhina—"25° below zero"—Kamenoi—Korak "Yourt"—Journey to Geezhega—"Pavoskas" Meekina—The "Settled Koraks" 221

XXII. Dog-driving—Reindeer Episode—Geezhega—The Governor and his Hospitality—Telegraphic Plans—The Author's Party sent to Anadyrsk 235

XXIII. Arctic Rambling in Winter—Malmofka—Night Scenes —Shestakova 250

CONTENTS.

CHAPTER   PAGE

XXIV. Dismal Lodgings—News from Col. Bulkley—Search for Lost Party of Americans—Curious Tree—Siberian "Poorga"—Storm.................. 261

XXV. Penzhina—Telegraph Poles—Arctic Temperature—Studying Astronomy—Arrival at Anadyrsk—A Priest's Hospitality......................... 273

XXVI. Anadyrsk—The Northern Outpost of Russian Life—Russian Christmas—A Ball—A Feast—Siberian Politeness.................................. 285

XXVII. Adventures in search of our Comrades............ 300

XXVIII. Adventures continued—Discovery of the Party...... 308

XXIX. Siberian Tribes and their Peculiarities—Ideas of Reading and the Arts............................. 320

XXX. An Arctic Aurora—Further Explorations—Arrival of our Comrades—Journey to the Okhotsk Sea..... 33*

XXXI. Social Life at Geezhega—Major Abasa's Expedition—Sudden Transformation from Winter to Summer—Customs of the People, etc.......... 343

XXXII. Weary Waiting—Mosquitoes—Arrival of a Russian Frigate.................................... 362

XXXIII. Arrival of Supply-Ships—Last Journey to the Arctic Circle—Korak Drivers—Famine at Anadyrsk.... 374

XXXIV. Bush Redivivus — Serious Dilemma — Starvation threatened—Eight Hundred Laborers hired—Enterprising American—A Wilderness............ 390

XXXV. Journey to Gamsk—Valley of the Viliga—A Storm—A perilous Pass............................. 406

XXXVI. Return to Geezhega—Arrival of the *Onward*—Orders to "Close up"—Beaten by the Atlantic Cable—Summary—Start for St. Petersburg—A Trip of more than 5,000 miles.

TENT LIFE IN SIBERIA

TENT LIFE IN SIBERIA.

CHAPTER I.

THE Russo-American Telegraph Company, or, as it was more properly called, the "Western Union Extension," was organized at New York in the summer of 1864. The idea of a line from America to Europe, by way of Behring's Straits, had existed for many years in the minds of several prominent telegraphers, and had been proposed by Perry McD. Collins, Esq., as early as 1857, when he made his trip across Northern Asia. It was never seriously considered, however, until after the failure of the first Atlantic cable, when the expediency of an overland line between the two continents began to be earnestly discussed. The plan of Mr. Collins, which was submitted to the Western Union Telegraph Company of New York as early as 1863, seemed to be the most practicable of all the projects which were suggested for inter-continental communication. It proposed to unite the telegraphic systems of America and Russia by a line through British Columbia, Russian America, and North-eastern Siberia, meeting the Russian lines at the mouth of the Amoor River on the Asiatic coast, and forming one continuous girdle of wire nearly round the globe.

This plan possessed many very obvious advantages. It called for no long cables. It provided for a line which would run everywhere overland, except for a short distance at Behring's Straits, and which could be easily repaired when injured by accident or storm. It promised also to extend its line eventually down the Asiatic coast to Pekin, and to develop a large and profitable business with China. All these considerations recommended it strongly to the favor of capitalists and practical telegraph men, and it was finally adopted by the Western Union Telegraph Co. in 1863. It was, of course, foreseen that the next Atlantic cable might succeed, and that such success would prove very damaging, if not fatal, to the prospects of the proposed overland line. Such an event, however, did not seem probable, and in view of all the circumstances, the company decided to assume the inevitable risk.

A contract was entered into with the Russian Government, providing for the extension of the latter's line through Siberia to the mouth of the Amoor River, and granting to the Company certain extraordinary privileges in Russian territory. Similar concessions were obtained in 1864 from the British Government ; assistance was promised by our own Congress ; and the " Western Union Extension Company " was immediately organized, with a nominal capital of $10,000,000. The stock was rapidly taken, principally by the stockholders of the original Western Union Company, and an assessment of five per cent was immediately made to provide funds for the prosecution of the work. Such was the faith at this time in the ultimate success of the enterprise, that its stock sold in two months for seventy-five dollars per share, with only one assessment of five dollars paid in.

In August, 1864, Col. Chas. S. Bulkley, formerly Superintendent of Military Telegraphs in the Department of the Gulf, was appointed Engineer-in-chief of the proposed line, and in December he sailed from New York for San Francisco, to organize and fit out exploring parties, and begin active operations.

Led by a desire of identifying myself with so novel and important an enterprise, as well as by a natural love of travel and adventure which I had never before been able to gratify, I offered my services as an explorer soon after the projection of the line. My application was favorably considered, and on the 13th of December I sailed from New York with the Engineer-in-chief, for the proposed headquarters of the company at San Francisco. Col. Bulkley, immediately after his arrival, opened an office in Montgomery street, and began organizing exploring parties to make a preliminary survey of the route of the line. No sooner did it become noised about the city that men were wanted to explore the unknown regions of British Columbia, Russian America, and Siberia, than the company's office was thronged with eager applicants for positions, in any and every capacity.

Adventurous Micawbers, who had long been waiting for something of this kind to turn up ; broken down miners, who hoped to retrieve their fortunes in new gold fields yet to be discovered in the north ; and returned soldiers thirsting for fresh excitement,—all hastened to offer their services as pioneers in the great work. Trained and skilled engi-

neers were in active demand; but the supply of only ordinary men, who made up in enthusiasm what they lacked
in experience, was unlimited.

Month after month passed slowly away in the selection,
organization, and equipment of parties, until at last, in June,
1865, the company's vessels were reported ready for sea.

The plan of operations, as far as it had then been decided
upon, was to land one party in British Columbia, near the
mouth of the Frazer River; one in Russian America, at
Norton's Sound; and one on the Asiatic side of Behring's
Straits, at the mouth of the Anadyr River. These parties,
under the direction respectively of Messrs. Pope, Kenni-
cott, and Macrae, were directed to push back into the interior, following as far as practicable the courses of the
rivers upon which they were landed; to obtain all possible
information with regard to the climate, soil, timber, and
inhabitants of the regions traversed; and to locate, in a
general way, a route for the proposed line.

The two American parties would have comparatively
advantageous bases of operations at Victoria and Fort St.
Michael; but the Siberian party, if left on the Asiatic coast
at all, must be landed near Behring's Straits, on the edge
of a barren, desolate region, nearly a thousand miles from
any known settlement. Thrown thus upon its own resources, in an unknown country, and among nomadic tribes
of hostile natives, without any means of interior transportation except canoes, the safety and success of this party
were by no means assured. It was even asserted by
many friends of the enterprise, that to leave men in such
a situation, and under such circumstances, was to abandon

them to almost certain death; and the Russian Consul at San Francisco wrote a letter to Colonel Bulkley, advising him strongly not to land a party on the Asiatic coast of the North Pacific, but to send it instead to one of the Russian ports of the Okhotsk Sea, where it could establish a base of supplies, obtain information with regard to the interior, and procure horses or dog-sledges for overland explorations in any desired direction.

The wisdom and good sense of this advice were apparent to all; but unfortunately the Engineer-in-chief had no vessel which he could send with a party into the Okhotsk Sea; and if men were landed at all that summer on the Asiatic coast, they must be landed near Behring's Straits.

Late in June, however, Col. Bulkley learned that a small Russian trading vessel, called the "Olga," was about to sail from San Francisco for Kamtchatka and the south-west coast of the Okhotsk Sea, and he succeeded in prevailing upon the owners to take four men as passengers to the Russian settlement of Nikolævsk, at the mouth of the Amoor River. This, although not as desirable a point for beginning operations as some others on the north coast of the sea, was still much better than any which could be selected on the Asiatic coast of the North Pacific; and a party was soon organized to sail in the "Olga" for Kamtchatka and the mouth of the Amoor. This party consisted of Major S. Abaza, a Russian gentleman who had been appointed superintendent of the work, and Generalissimo of the forces in Siberia; James A. Mahood, a civil engineer of reputation in California; R. J. Bush, who had just returned from three years' active service in the Carolinas; and myself,—not a very formidable force in point of numbers, nor a very remarkable one in point of experience, but strong in hope, self-reliance, and enthusiasm.

On the 28th of June we were notified that "the brig Olga" had nearly all her cargo aboard, and would have "*immediate dispatch.*"

This marine metaphor, as we afterward learned, meant only that she would sail some time in the course of the summer; but we, in our trustful inexperience, supposed that the brig must be all ready to cast off her moorings, and the announcement threw us into all the excitement and confusion of hasty preparation for a start. Dress coats, linen shirts, and fine boots were recklessly thrown or given away; blankets, heavy shoes, and over-shirts of flannel were purchased in large quantities; Ballard & Sharpes' rifles, revolvers, and bowie-knives of formidable dimensions gave our room the appearance of a disorganized arsenal; pots of arsenic, jars of alcohol, butterfly-nets, snake-bags, pill-boxes, and a dozen other implements and appliances of science about which we knew nothing, were given to us by our enthusiastic naturalists and packed away in big boxes; Vrangell's Travels, Gray's Botany, and a few scientific works were added to our small library; and before night we were able to report ourselves ready—armed and equipped for any adventure, from the capture of a new species of bug, to the conquest of Kamtchatka!

As it was against all precedent to go to sea without looking at the ship, Bush and I appointed ourselves an examining committee for the party, and walked down to the wharf where she lay. The Captain, a bluff Americanized German, met us at the gangway and guided us through the little brig from stem to stern. Our limited marine experience wouldn't have qualified us to pass an *ex cathedrâ* judgment upon the sea-worthiness of a mud scow; but Bush, with characteristic impudence and versatility of talent, discoursed learnedly to the Captain upon the beauty of his vessel's *"lines"* (whatever those were), her spread of canvas and build generally,—discussed the comparative merits of single and double topsails, and new patent yard-slings, and reefing-tackle, and altogether displayed such an amount of nautical learning that it completely crushed me and staggered even the Captain.

I strongly suspected that Bush had acquired most of his knowledge of sea terms from a cursory perusal of "Bowditch's Navigator," which I had seen lying on the office table, and I privately resolved to procure a compact edition of Marryat's sea tales as soon as I should go ashore, and just overwhelm him next time with such accumulated stores of nautical erudition that he would hide his diminished head. I had a dim recollection of reading something in Cooper's novels about a ship's dead heads and cat's eyes, or cat heads and dead eyes, I couldn't remember which, and, determined not to be ignored as an inexperienced landlubber, I gazed in a vague sort of way into the rigging, and made a few very general observations upon the nature of dead-eyes and spanker-booms. The Captain, however, promptly annihilated me by demanding categorically whether I had ever seen the spanker-boom jammed with the foretops'l-yard, with the wind abeam. I replied meekly that I believed such a catastrophe had never occurred under my immediate observation, and as he turned to Bush with a smile of commiseration for my ignorance I ground my teeth and went below to inspect the pantry. Here I felt more at home. The long rows of canned provisions, beef stock, concentrated milk, pie fruits, and a small keg, bearing the quaint inscription, "Zante cur.," soon soothed my perturbed spirit and convinced me beyond the shadow of a doubt that the "Olga" was stanch and sea-worthy, and built in the latest and most improved style of marine architecture.

I therefore went up to tell Bush that I had made a careful and critical examination of the vessel below, and that she would undoubtedly do. I omitted to state the nature of the observations upon which this conclusion was founded, but he asked no troublesome questions, and we returned to the office with a favorable report of the ship's build, capacity, and outfit.

On Saturday, July 1st, the "Olga" took in the last of her cargo, and was hauled out into the stream.

Our farewell letters were hastily written home, our final preparations made, and at nine o'clock on Monday morning we assembled at the Howard street wharf, where the steam-tug lay which was to tow us out to sea.

A large party of friends had gathered to bid us good-by; and the pier, covered with bright dresses and blue uniforms, presented quite a holiday appearance in the warm clear sunshine of a California morning.

Our last instructions were delivered to us by Colonel Bulkley, with many hearty wishes for our health and success; laughing invitations to "come and see us" were extended to our less fortunate comrades who were left behind; requests to send back specimens of the North Pole and the Aurora Borealis were intermingled with directions for preserving birds and collecting bugs; and amid a general confusion of congratulations, good wishes, cautions, bantering challenges, and tearful farewells, the steamer's bell rang. Dall, ever alive to the interests of his beloved science, grasped me cordially by the hand, saying, "Good-by, George. God bless you! Keep your eye out for land snails and skulls of the wild animals!"

Miss B—— said pleadingly, "Take care of my dear brother;" and as I promised to care for him as if he were my own, I thought of another sister far away, who, could she be present, would echo the request, "Take care of my dear brother." With waving handkerchiefs and repeated good-byes, we moved slowly from the wharf, and, steaming round in a great semicircle to where the "Olga" was lying, we were transferred to the little brig, which, for the next two months, was to be our home.

The steamer towed us outside the "heads" of the Golden Gate, and then cast off; and as she passed us on her way back, our friends gathered in a little group on the forward deck, with the Colonel at their head, and gave three generous cheers for the "First Siberian exploring party." We replied with three more,—our last farewell to civilization,—and silently watched the lessening figure of the steamer, until the white handkerchief which Arnold had tied to the backstays could no longer be seen, and we were rocking alone on the long swells of the Pacific.

CHAPTER II.

" He took great content and exceeding delight in his voyage, as who doth not as shall attempt the like."—BURTON.

AT SEA, 700 MILES N. W. OF SAN FRANCISCO.
Wednesday, July 12th, 1865.

TEN days ago, on the eve of our departure for the Asiatic coast, full of high hopes and joyful anticipations of pleasure, I wrote in a fair round hand on this opening page of my journal, the above sentence from Burton ; never once doubting, in my enthusiasm, the complete realization of those "future joys," which to "fancy's eye" lay in such "bright uncertainty," or suspecting that "a life on the ocean wave" was not a state of the highest felicity attainable on earth. The quotation seemed to me an extremely happy one, and I mentally blessed the quaint old Anatomist of Melancholy for providing me with a motto at once so simple and so appropriate. Of course "he took great content and exceeding delight in his voyage; " and the wholly unwarranted assumption that because "he" did, every one else necessarily *must*, did not strike me as being in the least absurd.

On the contrary, it carried all the weight of the severest logical demonstration, and I would have treated with contempt any suggestion of possible disappointment. My

ideas of sea life had been derived principally from glowing descriptions of poetical marine sunsets, of "summer
isles of Eden, lying in dark purple spheres of sea," and of
those "moonlight nights on lonely waters" with which
poets have for ages beguiled ignorant landsmen into
ocean voyages. Fogs, storms, and sea-sickness did not
enter at all into my conceptions of marine phenomena;
or if I did admit the possibility of a storm, it was only as
a picturesque, highly poetical manifestation of wind and
water in action, without any of the disagreeable features
which attend those elements under more prosaic circumstances. I had, it is true, experienced a little rough
weather on my voyage to California, but my memory had
long since idealized it into something grand and poetical;
and I looked forward even to a storm on the Pacific as
an experience not only pleasant, but highly desirable.
The illusion was very pleasant while it lasted; but—it is
over. Ten days of real sea life have converted the
"bright uncertainty of future joys" into a dark and decided certainty of future misery, and left me to mourn the
incompatibility of poetry and truth. Burton is a humbug, Tennyson a fraud, I'm a victim, and Byron and
Procter are accessaries before the fact. Never again
will I pin my faith to poets. They may tell the truth
nearly enough for poetical consistency, but their judgment is hopelessly perverted and their imagination is too
luxuriantly vivid for a truthful realistic delineation of sea
life. Byron's "London Packet" is a brilliant exception,
but I remember no other in the whole range of poetical
literature.

Our life since we left port has certainly been anything but poetical.

For nearly a week we suffered all the indescribable miseries of sea-sickness, without any alleviating circumstances whatever. Day after day we lay in our narrow berths, too sick to read, too unhappy to talk, watching the cabin lamp as it swung uneasily in its well-oiled gimbals, and listening to the gurgle and swash of the water around the after dead-lights, and the regular clank, clank of the blocks of the trisail sheet as the rolling of the vessel swung the heavy boom from side to side.

We all professed to be enthusiastic supporters of the Tapleyan philosophy — jollity under all circumstances; but we failed most lamentably in reconciling our practice with our principles. There was not the faintest suggestion of jollity in the appearance of the four motionless, prostrate figures against the wall. Sea-sickness had triumphed over philosophy ! Prospective and retrospective revery of a decidedly gloomy character was our only occupation. I remember speculating curiously upon the probability of Noah's having ever been sea-sick ; wondering how the sea-going qualities of the ark would compare with those of our brig, and whether she had our brig's uncomfortable way of pitching about in a heavy swell.

If she had—and I almost smiled at the idea—what an unhappy experience it must have been for the poor animals !

I wondered also if Jason and Ulysses were born with "sea legs," or whether they had to go through the same unpleasant process that we did to get them on.

Concluded finally that "sea legs," like some diseases, must be a diabolical invention of modern times, and that the ancients got along in some way without them. Then, looking intently at the fly-specks upon the painted boards ten inches from my eyes, I would recall all the bright anticipations with which I had sailed from San Francisco, and turn over, with a groan of disgust, to the wall.

I wonder if any one has ever written down on paper his sea-sick reveries. There are "Evening Reveries" "Reveries of a Bachelor," and "Sea-side Reveries" in abundance; but no one, so far as I know, has ever even attempted to do his Sea-sick Reveries literary justice. It is a strange oversight, and I would respectfully suggest to any aspiring writer who has the revery faculty, that there is here an unworked field of boundless extent. One trip across the North Pacific in a small brig will furnish an inexhaustible supply of material.

Our life thus far has been too monotonous to afford a single noticeable incident. The weather has been cold, damp, and foggy, with light head winds and a heavy swell; we have been confined closely to our seven by nine after-cabin; and its close stifling atmosphere, redolent of bilge-water, lamp-oil, and tobacco-smoke, has had a most depressing influence upon our spirits. I am glad to see, however, that all our party are up to-day, and that there is a faint interest manifested in the prospect of dinner; but even the inspiriting strains of the Faust march which the Captain is playing upon a wheezy old accordion, fail to put any expression of animation into the woe-begone faces around the cabin table. Mahood pretends that he is all

right, and plays checkers with the captain with an air of
assumed tranquillity which approaches heroism, but he is
observed at irregular intervals to go suddenly and unexpectedly on deck, and to return every time with a more
ghastly and rueful countenance. When asked the object
of these periodical visits to the quarter-deck, he replies,
with a transparent affectation of cheerfulness, that he only
goes up " to look at the compass and see how she's head-
ing." I am surprised to find that " looking at the compass" is attended with such painful and melancholy emotions as those expressed in Mahood's face when he comes
back ; but he performs the self-imposed duty with unshrink-
ing faithfulness, and relieves us of a great deal of anxiety
about the safety of the ship. The Captain seems a little neg-
ligent, and sometimes does not observe the compass once
a day ; but Mahood watches it with unsleeping vigilance.

BRIG OLGA, 800 MILES N. W. OF SAN FRANCISCO.
Sunday, July 16th, 1865.

The monotony of our lives was relieved night before
last, and our sea-sickness aggravated, by a severe gale of
wind from the north-west, which compelled us to lie to
for twenty hours under one close-reefed maintopsail.
The storm began late in the afternoon, and by nine o'clock
the wind was at its height and the sea rapidly rising. The
waves pounded like Titanic sledge-hammers against the
vessel's quivering timbers ; the gale roared a deep diapa-
son through the cordage ; and the regular thud, thud,
thud of the pumps, and the long melancholy whistling of the wind through the blocks, filled our minds

with dismal forebodings, and banished all inclination for sleep.

Morning dawned gloomily and reluctantly, and its first gray light, struggling through the film of water on the small rectangular deck-lights, revealed a comical scene of confusion and disorder. The ship was rolling and laboring heavily, and Mahood's trunk having in some way broken from its moorings, was sliding back and forth across the cabin floor. Bush's big meerschaum, in company with a corpulent sponge, had taken up temporary quarters in the crown of my best hat, and the Major's box of cigars revolved periodically from corner to corner in the close embrace of a dirty shirt. Sliding and rolling over the carpet in every direction were books, papers, cigars, brushes, dirty collars, stockings, empty wine-bottles, slippers, coats, and old boots; and a large box of telegraph material threatened momentarily to break from its fastenings and demolish everything. The Major, who was the first to show any signs of animation, rose on one elbow in bed, gazed fixedly at the sliding and revolving articles, and shaking his head reflectively, said : " It is a c-u-r-ious thing! It *is* a *c-u r*-ious thing!" as if the migratory boots and cigar-boxes exhibited some new and perplexing phenomena not to be accounted for by any of the known laws of physics. A sudden roll in which the vessel indulged at that particular moment gave additional force to the sentiment of the soliloquy; and with renewed convictions, I have no doubt, of the original and innate depravity of matter generally, and of the Pacific Ocean especially, he laid his head back upon the pillow.

It required no inconsiderable degree of resolution to
'turn out" under such unpromising circumstances; but
Bush, after two or three groans and a yawn, made the attempt to get up and dress. Climbing hurriedly down
when the ship rolled to windward, he caught his boots in
one hand and pants in the other, and began hopping about
the cabin with surprising agility, dodging or jumping over
the sliding trunk and rolling bottles, and making frantic
efforts to put both legs simultaneously into one boot. Surprised in the midst of this arduous task by an unexpected
lurch, he made an impetuous charge upon an inoffensive
washstand, stepped on an erratic bottle, fell on his head, and
finally brought up a total wreck in the corner of the room.
Convulsed with laughter, the Major could only ejaculate
disconnectedly, "I tell you—it is a—curious thing how
she—rolls!" "Yes," rejoined Bush savagely, as he rubbed one knee, "I should think it was! Just get up and
try it!" But the Major was entirely satisfied to see Bush
try it, and did nothing but laugh at his misfortunes. The
latter finally succeeded in getting dressed, and after some
hesitation I concluded to follow his example. By dint
of falling twice over the trunk, kneeling upon my heels,
sitting on my elbows, and executing several other
equally impracticable feats, I got my vest on inside out,
both feet in the wrong boots respectively, and staggered
up the companion-way on deck. The wind was still blowing a gale, and we showed no canvas but one close-reefed
maintopsail. Great massive mounds of blue water piled
themselves up in the concealment of the low hanging rain-
clouds, rushed out upon us with white foaming crests ten

feet above the quarter-deck, and broke into clouds of blinding, strangling spray over the forecastle and galley, careening the ship until the bell on the quarter-deck struck and water run in over the lee gunwale. It did not exactly correspond with my preconceived ideas of a storm, but I was obliged to confess that it had many of the characteristic features of the real phenomenon. The wind had the orthodox howl through the rigging, the sea was fully up to the prescribed standard, and the vessel pitched and rolled in a way to satisfy the most critical taste. The impression of sublimity, however, which I had anticipated was almost entirely lost in the sense of personal discomfort. A man who has just been pitched over a skylight by one of the ship's eccentric movements, or drenched to the skin by a burst of spray, is not in a state of mind to contemplate sublimity; and after going through a varied and exhaustive course of such treatment, any romantic notions which he may previously have entertained with regard to the ocean's beauty and sublimity are pretty much knocked and drowned out of him. Rough weather makes short work of poetry and sentiment. The "wet sheet" and "flowing sea" of the poet have a significance quite the reverse of poetical when one discovers the "wet sheet" in his bed and the "flowing sea" all over the cabin floor, and our experience illustrates not so much the sublimity as the unpleasantness and discomfort of a storm at sea.

BRIG OLGA, AT SEA, *July 27th*, 1865.

I used often to wonder, while living in San Francisco, where the chilling fogs that toward night used to drift in over Lone Mountain and through the Golden Gate, came from. I have discovered the laboratory. For the past two weeks we have been sailing continually in a dense wet gray cloud of mist, so thick at times as almost to hide the top-gallant yards, and so penetrating as to find its way even into our little after-cabin, and condense in minute drops upon our clothes. It rises, I presume, from the warm water of the great Pacific " Gulf Stream" across which we are passing, and whose vapor is condensed into fog by the cold north-west winds from Siberia. It is the most disagreeable feature of our voyage.

Our life has finally settled down into a quiet monotonous routine of eating, smoking, watching the barometer, and sleeping twelve hours a day. The gale with which we were favored two weeks ago afforded a pleasant thrill of temporary excitement and a valuable topic of conversation ; but we have all come to coincide in the opinion of the Major, that it was a " curious thing," and are anxiously awaiting the turning up of something else. One cold, rainy, foggy day succeeds another, with only an occasional variation in the way of a head wind or a flurry of snow. Time, of course, hangs heavily on our hands. We are waked about half-past seven in the morning by the second mate, a funny phlegmatic Dutchman, who is always shouting to us to "turn out" and see an imaginary whale, which he conjures up regularly before breakfast, and which invariably disappears before we can get on deck, as mysteriously as " Moby Dick." The whale, however, fails to " draw" after a time, and he resorts to an equally mysterious and eccentric sea serpent, whose wonderful appearance he describes in comical broken English, with the vain hope that we will crawl out into the raw foggy atmosphere to look at it. We never do. Bush opens his eyes, yawns, and keeps a sleepy watch of the breakfast table, which is situated in the Captain's cabin forward. I cannot see it from my berth, so I watch Bush. Presently we hear the hump-backed steward's footsteps on the deck above our heads, and, with a quick succession of little bumps, half a dozen boiled potatoes come rolling down the stairs of the companion-way into the cabin. They are the forerunners of breakfast. Bush watches the table, and I watch Bush more and more intently as the steward brings in the eatables; and by the expression of Bush's face, I judge whether it be worth while to get up or not. If he groans and turns over to the wall, I know that it is only hash, and I echo his groan and follow his example; but if he smiles and gets up, I do likewise, with the full assurance of fresh mutton-chops or rice-curry and chicken. After breakfast the Major smokes a cigarette and looks meditatively at the barometer, the Captain gets his old accordion and squeezes out the Russian National Hymn, while Bush and I go on deck to inhale a few breaths of pure fresh fog, and " chaff " the second mate about his sea serpent. In reading, playing checkers, fencing, and climbing about the rigging when the weather permits, we pass away the day, as we have already passed away twenty and must pass twenty more before we can hope to see land.

AT SEA, NEAR THE ALEUTIAN ISLANDS,
August 6th, 1865.

" Now would I give a thousand furlongs of sea for an
acre of barren ground, ling, heath, broom, furze, anything," except this wearisome monotonous waste of water !
Let Kamtchatka be what it will, we shall welcome it with
as much joy as that with which Columbus first saw the
flowery coast of San Salvador.   I am prepared to look
with complacency upon a sand bar and two spears of
grass, and would not even insist upon the grass if I could
only be sure of the sand bar.   We have now been thirty-
four days at sea without once meeting a sail or getting a
glimpse of land.

Our chief amusement lately has been the discussion of
controverted points of history and science, and wonderful
is the forensic and argumentative ability which these de-
bates have developed.   They are getting to be positively
interesting.   The only drawback to them is, that in the
absence of any decisive authority they never come to any
satisfactory conclusion.   We have now been discussing
for sixteen days the uses of a whale's " blow holes ;" and I
firmly believe that if our voyage were prolonged, like the
" Flying Dutchman's," to all eternity, we should never
reach any solution of the problem which would satisfy all
the disputants.   The Captain has an old Dutch History
of the World, in twenty-six folio volumes, to which he appeals as final authority in all questions under the heavens,
whether pertaining to Love, Science, War, Art, Politics,
or Religion ; and no sooner does he get cornered in a
discussion than he entrenches himself behind these pon-

derous folios, and keeps up a hot fire of terrific Dutch polysyllables until we are ready to make an unconditional surrender. If we venture to suggest a doubt as to the intimacy of the connection between a whale's "blow holes" and the History of the World, he comes down upon us with the most withering denunciations as wrong-headed sceptics who won't even believe what is *printed*—and in a Dutch History too! As the Captain dispenses the pie, however, at dinner, I have found it advisable to smother my convictions as to the veracity of his Teutonic historian, and join him in denouncing that pernicious heretic Bush, who is wise beyond what is written. Result—Bush gets only one small piece of pie, and I get two, which of course is highly gratifying to my feelings, as well as advantageous to the dispersion of sound historical learning!

I begin to observe at dinner an increasing reverence on Bush's part for Dutch Histories.

CHAPTER III.

Our voyage is at last drawing to a close, and after seven long weeks of cold, rainy, rough weather our eyes are soon to be gladdened again by the sight of land, and never was it more welcome to weary mariner than it will be to us. Even as I write, the sound of scraping and scrubbing is heard on deck, and proclaims our nearness to land. They are dressing the vessel to go once more into society. We were only 255 miles from the Kamtchatkan seaport of Petropavlovski last night, and if this favorable breeze holds we expect to reach there to-morrow noon. It has fallen almost to a dead calm, however, this morning, so that we may be delayed until Saturday.

At Sea, off the Coast of Kamtchatka.
Friday, August 18*th*, 1865.

We have a fine breeze this morning; and the brig, under every stitch of canvas that will draw, is staggering through the seas enveloped in a dense fog, through which even her top-gallant sails show mistily. Should the wind continue and the fog be dissipated we may hope to see land to night.

11 A.M.

I have just come down from the top-gallant yard, where for the last three hours I have been clinging uncomfortably to the backstays, watching for land, and swinging back and forth through the fog in the arc of a great circle as the vessel rolled lazily to the seas. We cannot discern any object at a distance of three ships' lengths, although the sky is evidently cloudless. Great numbers of gulls, boobies, puffin, fish-hawks, and solan-geese surround the ship, and the water is full of drifting medusæ.

NOON.

Half an hour ago the fog began to lift, and at 11.40 the Captain, who had been sweeping the horizon with a glass, shouted cheerily, "Land ho! Land ho! Hurrah!" and the cry was echoed simultaneously from stem to stern, and from the galley to the top-gallant yard. Bush, Mahood, and the Major started at a run for the forecastle; the little hump-backed steward rushed frantically out of the galley with his hands all dough, and climbed up on the bulwarks; the sailors ran into the rigging, and only the man at the wheel retained his self-possession. Away ahead, drawn in faint luminous outlines above the horizon, appeared two high conical peaks, so distant that nothing but the white snow in their deep ravines could be seen, and so faint that they could hardly be distinguished from the blue sky beyond. They were the mountains of Villeuchinski and Avatcha, on the Kamtchatkan coast, fully a hundred miles away. The Major looked at them through a glass long and eagerly, and then waving his hand proudly toward them, turned to us, and said with a burst of national enthusiasm, "You see before you my country—the great Russian Empire!" and then as the

fog drifted down again upon the ship, he dropped suddenly from his declamatory style, and with a look of disgust
exclaimed, " Chort zuiet shto etta takoi—it *is* a curious
thing ! fog, fog, nothing but fog ! "

In five minutes the last vestige of "the great Russian·
Empire" had disappeared, and we went below to dinner
in a state of joyful excitement, which can never be imagined by one who has not been forty-six days at sea in
the North Pacific.

4 P.M.

We have just been favored with another view of the
land.   Half an hour ago I could see from the top-gallant
yard, where I was posted, that the fog was beginning to
break away, and in a moment it rose slowly like a huge
gray curtain, unveiling the sea and the deep blue sky,
letting in a flood of rosy light from the sinking sun,
and revealing a picture of wonderful beauty.   Before us,
stretching for a hundred and fifty miles to the north and
south, lay the grand coast-line of Kamtchatka, rising abruptly in great purple promontories out of the blue sparkling sea, flecked here with white clouds and shreds of
fleecy mist, deepening in places into a soft quivering blue,
and sweeping backward and upward into the pure white
snow of the higher peaks.   Two active volcanoes, 10,000
and 16,000 feet in height, rose above the confused jagged
ranges of the lower mountains, piercing the blue sky with
sharp white triangles of eternal snow, and drawing the
purple shadows of evening around their feet.   The high
bold coast did not appear, in that clear atmosphere, to be

fifteen miles away, and it seemed to have risen suddenly like a beautiful mirage out of the sea. In less than five minutes the gray curtain of mist dropped slowly down again over the magnificent picture, and it faded gradually from sight, leaving us almost in doubt whether it had been a reality, or only a bright deceptive vision. We are enveloped now, as we have been nearly all day, in a thick clammy fog.

HABOR OF PETROPAVLOVSKI, KAMTCHATKA.
August 19*th*, 1865.

At dark last night we were distant, as we supposed, about fifteen miles from Cape Pavorotni, and as the fog had closed in again denser than ever, the Captain dared not venture any nearer. The ship was accordingly put about, and we stood off and on all night, waiting for sunrise and a clear atmosphere, to enable us to approach the coast in safety. At five o'clock I was on deck. The fog was colder and denser than ever, and out of it rolled the white-capped waves raised by a fresh south-easterly breeze. Shortly before six o'clock it began to grow light, the brig was headed for the land, and under foresail, jib, and topsails, began to forge steadily through the water. The Captain, glass in hand, anxiously paced the quarter-deck, ever and anon reconnoitering the horizon, and casting a glance up to windward to see if there were any prospect of better weather. Several times he was upon the point of putting the ship about, fearing to run on a lee shore in that impenetrable mist; but it finally lightened up, the fog disappeared, and the horizon line came out clear and

distinct. To our utter astonishment, not a foot of land
could be seen in any direction! The long range of blue
mountains which had seemed the previous night to be
within an hour's sail—the lofty snowy peaks—the deep
gorges and the bold headlands, had all

> "——melted into thin air,
> Leaving not a rack behind."

There was nothing to indicate the existence of land
within a thousand miles, save the number and variety of
the birds that wheeled curiously around our wake, and
flew away with a splattering noise from under our bows.
Many were the theories which were suggested to account
for the sudden disappearance of the high bold land. The
Captain attempted to explain it by the supposition that a
strong current, sweeping off shore, had during the night
carried us away to the south-east. Bush accused the mate
of being asleep on his watch, and letting the ship run over
the land, while the mate declared solemnly that he didn't
believe that there had been any land there at all; that it
was only a mirage. The Major said it was "pagánni,"
and "a curious thing," but did not volunteer any solution
of the problem. So there we were.

We had a fine leading wind from the S. E., and were
now going through the water at the rate of seven knots.
Eight o'clock, nine o'clock, ten o'clock, and still no appearance of land, although we had made since daylight
more than thirty miles. At eleven o'clock, however, the
horizon gradually darkened, and all at once a bold head-
land, terminating in a precipitous cliff, loomed up out of
a thin mist at a distance of only four miles. All was at

once excitement. The top-gallant sails were clewed up to reduce the vessel's speed, and her course was changed so that we swept round in a curve broadside to the coast, about three miles distant. The mountain peaks, by which we might have ascertained our position, were hidden by the clouds and fog, and it was no easy matter to ascertain exactly where we were.

Away to the left, dimly defined in the mist, were two or three more high blue headlands, but what they were or where the harbor of Petropavlovski might be, were questions which no one could answer. The Captain brought his charts, compass, and drawing instruments on deck, laid them on the cabin skylight, and began taking the bearings of the different headlands, while we eagerly scanned the shore with glasses, and gave free expressions to our several opinions as to our situation. The Russian chart which the Captain had of the coast, was fortunately a good one, and he soon determined our position, and the names of the headlands first seen. We were just north of Cape Pavorotni, about nine miles south of the entrance of Avatcha Bay. The yards were now squared, and we went off on the new tack before a steady breeze from the south-east. In less than an hour we sighted the high isolated rocks known as the "Three Brothers," passed a rocky precipitous island, surrounded by clouds of shrieking gulls and parrot-billed ducks, and by two o'clock were off "the heads" of Avatcha Bay, on which is situated the village of Petropavlovski. The scenery at the entrance more than equalled our highest anticipations. Green grassy valleys stretched away from openings in the rocky

coast until they were lost in the distant mountains; the
rounded bluffs were covered with clumps of yellow birch ;
and thickets of dark green chaparral, patches of flowers,
could be seen on the warm sheltered slopes of the hills ;
and as we passed close under lighthouse bluff, Bush shouted joyously, " Hurrah, there's clover ! " " Clover ! " exclaimed the Captain contemptuously, " There ain't any
clover in the Ar'tic regions ! " " How do you know,
you've never been there," retorted Bush caustically ; " it
looks like clover, and "—looking through a glass—" it *is*
clover ;" and his face lighted up as if the discovery of
clover had relieved his mind of a great deal of anxiety as
to the severity of the Kamtchatkan climate.   It was a sort
of vegetable exponent of temperature, and out of a little
patch of clover, Bush's imagination " developed," in a
style undreamt of by Darwin, the whole luxuriant Flora
of the temperate zone.

The very name of Kamtchatka had always been associated in our minds with everything barren and inhospitable, and we did not entertain for a moment the thought
that such a country could afford beautiful scenery and
luxuriant vegetation.   In fact, with us all it was a mooted
question whether anything more than mosses, lichens, and
perhaps a little grass maintained the unequal struggle for
existence in that frozen clime.   It may be imagined with
what delight and surprise we looked upon green hills
covered with trees and verdant thickets ; upon valleys
white with clover and diversified with little groves of silver-
barked birch ; and even the rocks nodding with wild roses
and columbine, which had taken root in their clefts as if

Nature strove to hide with a garment of flowers the evidences of past convulsions.

Just before three o'clock we came in sight of the village of Petropavlovki—a little cluster of red-roofed and bark-thatched log houses ; a Greek church of curious architecture, with a green painted dome ; a strip of beach, a half-ruined wharf, two whale-boats, and the dismantled wreck of a half-sunken vessel. High green hills swept in a great semicircle of foliage around the little village, and almost shut in the quiet pond-like harbor—an inlet of Avatcha Bay—on which it was situated. Under foresail and main-topsail we glided silently under the shadow of the encircling hills into this land-locked mill pond, and within a stone's throw of the nearest house the sails were suddenly clewed up, and with a quivering of the ship and a rattle of chain-cable our anchor dropped into the soil of Asia.

CHAPTER IV.

It has been well observed by Irving, that to one about to visit foreign countries a long sea voyage is an excellent preparative. To quote his own words, "The temporary absence of worldly scenes and employments produces a state of mind peculiarly fitted to receive new and vivid impressions." And he might have added with equal truth—favorable impressions. The tiresome monotony of sea life predisposes the traveller to regard favorably anything that will quicken his stagnating faculties and perceptions, and furnish new matter for thought, and the most commonplace scenery and circumstances afford him gratification and delight. For this reason one is apt, upon arriving after a long voyage in a strange country, to form a more favorable opinion of its people and scenery than his subsequent experience will sustain. But it seems to me particularly fortunate that our first impressions of a new country, which are most clear and vivid, and therefore most lasting, are also most pleasant, so that in future years a retrospective glance over our past wanderings will show the most cheerful pictures drawn in the brightest and most enduring colors. I am sure that the recollection of my first view of the mountains of Kamtchatka, the delight with which my eye drank in their "bright aërial tints," and the romance with which my ardent fancy invested them,

will long outlive the memory of the hardships I have endured among them, the snow-storms that have pelted me
on their summits, and the rains that have drenched me in
their valleys. Fanciful perhaps, but I believe true.

The longing for land which one feels after having been
five or six weeks at sea is sometimes so strong as to be
almost a passion. I verily believe that if the first land
we saw had been one of those immense barren moss
steppes which I afterward came to hold in such detestation, I should have considered it as nothing less than the
original site of the Garden of Eden. Not all the charms
which Nature has lavished upon the Vale of Tempe could
have given me more pleasure than did the little green
valley in which nestled the red-roofed and bark-covered
log-houses of Petropavlovski.

The arrival of a ship in that remote and unfrequented
part of the world is an event of no little importance; and
the rattling of our chain-cable through the hawse-holes
created a very perceptible sensation in the quiet village.
Little children ran bareheaded out of doors, looked at us
for a moment, and then ran hastily back to call the rest
of the household; dark-haired natives and Russian peasants, in blue shirts and leather pants, gathered in a group
at the landing; and seventy-five or a hundred half-wild
dogs broke out suddenly into a terrific chorus of howls in
honor of our arrival.

It was already late in the afternoon, but we could not
restrain our impatience to step once more upon dry
land; and as soon as the Captain's boat could be lowered, Bush, Mahood, and I went ashore to look at the town.

Petropavlovski is laid out in a style which is very irregular, without being at all picturesque. The idea of a street never seems to have suggested itself either to the original settlers or to their descendants; and the paths, such as they are, wander around aimlessly among the scattered houses, like erratic sheep-walks. It is impossible to go for a hundred yards in a straight line, in any direction, without either bringing up against the side of a house or trespassing upon somebody's back-yard; and in the night one falls over a slumbering cow, upon a fair average, once every fifty feet. In other respects it is rather a pretty village, surrounded as it is by high green hills, and affording a fine view of the beautiful snowy peak of Avatcha, which rises to a height of 11,000 feet directly behind the town.

Mr. Fluger, a German merchant of Petropavlovski, who had boarded us in a small boat outside the harbor, now constituted himself our guide; and after a short walk around the village, invited us to his house, where we sat in a cloud of fragrant cigar-smoke, talking over American war news, and the latest "on dit" of Kamtchatkan society, until it finally began to grow dark. I noticed, among other books lying upon Mr. F.'s table, "Life Thoughts," by Beecher, and "The Schönberg-Cotta Family," and wondered that the latter had already found its way to the far distant shores of Kamtchatka.

As new-comers, it was our first duty to pay our respects to the Russian authorities; and, accompanied by Mr. Fluger and Mr. Bollman, we called upon Captain Sutkovoi, the resident "Captain of the port." His house,

with its bright red tin roof, was almost hid by a large
grove of thrifty oaks, through which tumbled, in a succession of little cascades, a clear, cold mountain stream.
We entered the gate, walked up a broad gravelled path,
under the shade of the interlocking branches, and, without
knocking, entered the house. Captain S. welcomed us
cordially, and notwithstanding our inability to speak any
language but our own, soon made us feel quite at home.
Conversation however languished, as every remark had to
be translated through two languages before it could be
understood by the person to whom it was addressed ; and
brilliant as it might have been in the first place, it lost its
freshness in being passed around through Russian, German, and English to us.

I was surprised to see so many evidences of cultivated
and refined taste in this remote corner of the world, where
I had expected barely the absolute necessaries of life, or
at best a few of the most common comforts. A large
piano of Russian manufacture occupied one corner of the
room, and a choice assortment of Russian, German, and
American music testified to the musical taste of its owner.
A few choice paintings and lithographs adorned the walls,
and on the centre-table rested a handsome stereoscope
with a large collection of photographic views, and an unfinished game of chess, from which Capt. and Madame
Sutkovoi had risen at our entrance.

After a pleasant visit of an hour we took our leave, receiving an invitation to dinner on the following day.

It was not yet decided whether we should continue our
voyage to the Amoor River or remain in Petropavlovski

and begin our northern journey from there, so we still regarded the brig as our home and returned every night to
our little cabin. The first night in port was strangely
calm, peaceful, and quiet, accustomed as we had become
to the rolling, pitching, and creaking of the vessel, the
swash of water and the whistling of the wind. There was
not a zephyr abroad, and the surface of the miniature bay
lay like a dark mirror, in which were obscurely reflected
the high hills which formed its setting. A few scattered
lights from the village threw long streams of radiance
across the dark water, and from the black hillside on our
right was heard at intervals the faint lonely tinkle of a cow-
bell or the long melancholy howl of a wolf-like dog. I
tried hard to sleep ; but the novelty of our surroundings,
the thought that we were now in Asia, and hundreds of
conjectures and forecastings as to our future prospects
and adventures, put sleep for a long time at defiance.

The village of Petropavlovski which, although not the
largest, is one of the most important settlements in the
Kamtchatkan peninsula, has a population of perhaps two
or three hundred natives and Russian peasants, together
with a few German and American merchants, drawn thither
by the trade in sables. It is not fairly a representative
Kamtchadal town, for it has felt in no inconsiderable degree the civilizing influences of foreign intercourse, and
shows in its manners and modes of life and thought some
evidences of modern enterprise and enlightenment. It has
existed as a settlement since the early part of the eighteenth
century, and is old enough to have acquired some civilization of its own ; but age in a Siberian town is no criterion

of development, and Petropavlovski either has not attained the enlightenment of maturity, or has passed into its second childhood, for it is still in a benighted condition. Why it was and is called Petropavlovski—the village of St. Peter and St. Paul—I failed, after diligent inquiry, to learn. The sacred canon does not contain any epistle to the Kamtchatkans, much as they need it, nor is there any other evidence to show that the ground on which the village stands was ever visited by either of the eminent saints whose names it bears. The conclusion to which we are driven therefore is, that its inhabitants, not being distinguished for apostolic virtues, and feeling their need of saintly intercession, called the settlement after St. Peter and St. Paul, with the hope that those Apostles would feel a sort of proprietary interest in the place, and secure its final salvation without any unnecessary inquiries into its merits. Whether that was the idea of its original founders or not I cannot say; but such a plan would be eminently adapted to the state of society in most of the Siberian settlements where faith is strong, but where works are few in number and questionable in tendency.

The sights of Petropavlovski, speaking after the manner of tourists, are few and uninteresting. It has two monuments erected to the memory of the distinguished navigators Behring and La Perouse, and there are traces on its hills of the fortifications built during the Crimean war to repel the attack of the allied French and English squadrons; but aside from these, the town can boast of no objects or places of historical interest. To us, however, who had been shut up nearly two months in a close dark cabin, the village was attractive enough of itself, and early on the following morning we went ashore for a ramble on the wooded peninsula which separates the small harbor from Avatcha Bay. The sky was cloudless, but a dense fog drifted low over the hill tops and veiled the surrounding mountains from sight. The whole landscape was green as emerald and dripping with moisture, but the sunshine struggled occasionally through the gray cloud of vapor, and patches of light swept swiftly across the wet hillsides, like sunny smiles upon a tearful face. The ground everywhere was covered with flowers. Marsh violets dotted the grass here and there with blue; columbine swung its purple-hooded bells over the gray mossy rocks; and wild roses appeared everywhere in dense thickets, with their delicate pink petals strewn over the ground beneath them like a colored shadow.

Climbing up the slope of the steep hill between the harbor and the bay, shaking down little showers of water from every bush we touched, and treading under foot hundreds of dewy flowers, we came suddenly upon the monument of La Perouse. I hope his countrymen, the French, have erected to his memory some more tasteful and enduring token of their esteem than this. It is simply a wooden frame, covered with sheet iron, and painted black. It bears no date or inscription whatever, and looks more like the tombstone over the grave of a criminal, than a monument to keep fresh the memory of a distinguished navigator.

Bush sat down on a little grassy knoll to make a sketch of the scene, while Mahood and I wandered on up the hill toward the old Russian batteries. They are several in number, situated along the crest of the ridge which divides the inner from the outer bay, and command the approaches to the town from the west. They are now almost over-grown with grass and flowers, and only the form of the embrasures distinguishes them from shapeless mounds of earth. It would be thought that the remote situation and inhospitable climate of Kamtchatka would have secured to its inhabitants an immunity from the desolating ravages of war. But even this country has its ruined forts and grass-grown battle-fields; and its now silent hills echoed not long ago to the thunder of opposing cannon. Leaving Mahood to make a critical survey of the entrenchments—an occupation which his tastes and pursuits rendered more interesting to him than to me—I strolled on up the hill to the edge of the cliff from which the storming party of the Allies was thrown by the Russian gunners. No traces now remain of the bloody struggle which took place upon the brink of this precipice. Moss covers with its green carpet the ground which was torn up in the death-grap-ple; and the nodding bluebell, as it bends to the fresh sea-breeze, tells no story of the last desperate rally, the hand to hand conflict, and the shrieks of the overpowered as they were thrown from the Russian bayonets upon the rocky beach a hundred feet below.

It seems to me that it was little better than wanton cruelty in the Allies to attack this unimportant and isola-ted post, so far from the real centre of conflict. Could its capture have lessened in any way the power or re-sources of the Russian Government, or, by creating a diver-

sion, have attracted attention from the decisive struggle
in the Crimea, it would perhaps have been justifiable;
but it could not possibly have any direct or indirect influence upon the ultimate result, and only brought misery
upon a few inoffensive Kamtchadals who had never heard
of Turkey or the "Eastern Question," and whose first in-
timation of a war probably was the thunder of the enemy's
cannon and the bursting of shells at their very doors.
The attack of the Allied fleet, however, was signally re-
pulsed, and its Admiral, stung with mortification at being
foiled by a mere handful of Cossacks and peasants, committed suicide.   On the anniversary of the battle it is
still customary for all the inhabitants, headed by the priests,
to march in solemn procession round the town and over
the hill from which the storming party was thrown, chanting hymns of joy and praise for the victory.

After botanizing a while upon the battle-field, I was
joined by Bush, who had completed his sketch, and we
all returned, tired and wet, to the village.   Our appearance anywhere on shore always created a sensation among
the inhabitants.   The Russian peasants and native peasants whom we met removed their caps, and held them
respectfully in their hands while we passed; the windows of the houses were crowded with heads intent
upon getting a sight of the "Amerikanski Chinóvnikee;"
and even the dogs broke into furious barks and howls at
our approach.   Bush declared that he could not remember a time in his history when he had been of so much
consequence, and attracted such general attention as
now; and he attributed it all to the discrimination and

intelligence of Kamtchatkan society. Prompt and in
stinctive recognition of superior genius he affirmed to be
a characteristic of that people, and he expressed deep
regret that it was not equally so of some other people
whom he could mention. "No reference to an allusion
intended!"

CHAPTER V.

ONE of the first things which the traveller notices in any foreign land is the language, and it is especially noticeable in Kamtchatka, Siberia, or any part of the great Russian Empire. What the Russians did at the Tower of Babel to have been afflicted with such a complicated, contorted, mixed up, utterly incomprehensible language, I can hardly conjecture. I have thought sometimes that they must have built their side of the tower higher than any of the other tribes, and have been punished for their sinful industry by this jargon of unintelligible sounds, which no man could possibly hope to understand before he became so old and infirm that he could never work on another tower. However they came by it, it is certainly a thorn in the flesh to all travellers in the Russian Empire. Some weeks before we reached Kamtchatka I determined to learn, if possible, a few common expressions, which would be most useful in our first intercourse with the natives, and among them the simple declarative sentence, "I want something to eat." I thought that this would probably be the first observation which I should have to address to any of the inhabitants, and I determined to learn it so thoroughly that I should never be in danger of starvation from ignorance. I accordingly asked the Major one day what the equivalent expression was in Russian. He coolly replied that whenever I wanted any-

thing to eat, all that I had to do was to say, "Vashavwe-
sokeeblagarodiaee veeleekeeprevoskhodeetelstvoee takdal-
shai." I believe I never felt such a sentiment of reverential admiration for the acquired talents of any man as I
did for those of the Major when I heard him pronounce,
fluently and gracefully, this extraordinary sentence. My
mind was hopelessly lost in attempting to imagine the
number of years of patient toil which must have preceded
his first request for food, and I contemplated with astonishment the indefatigable perseverance which has borne him
triumphant through the acquirement of such a language.
If the simple request for something to eat presented such
apparently insurmountable obstacles to pronunciation,
what must the language be in its dealings with the more
abstruse questions of theological and metaphysical science? Imagination stood aghast at the thought.

I frankly told the Major that he might print out this
terrible sentence on a big placard and hang it around my
neck; but as for learning to pronounce it, I couldn't, and
didn't propose to try. I found out afterward that he had
taken advantage of my inexperience and confiding disposition by giving me some of the longest and worst words
in his barbarous language, and pretending that they
meant something to eat. The real translation in Russian
would have been bad enough, and it was wholly unnecessary to select peculiarly hard words.

The Russian language is, I believe, without exception,
the most difficult of all modern languages to learn. Its
difficulty does not lie, as would be supposed, in pronunciation. Its words are all spelled phonetically, and have

only a few sounds which are foreign to English; but its grammar is exceptionally involved and intricate. It has seven cases and three genders; and as the latter are dependent upon no definite principle whatever, but are purely arbitrary, it is almost impossible for a foreigner to learn them so as to give nouns and adjectives their proper terminations. Its vocabulary is very copious; and its idiom has a peculiarly racy individuality of its own, which can hardly be appreciated without a thorough acquaintance with the popular style of conversation among the Russian peasants.

The Russian, like all the Indo-European languages, is closely related to the ancient Sanscrit, and seems to have preserved unchanged, in a greater degree than any of the others, the old Vedic words. The first ten numerals, as spoken by a Hindoo a thousand years before the Christian era, would, with one or two exceptions, be understood by a modern Russian peasant.

During our stay in Petropavlovski we succeeded in learning the Russian for "Yes," "No," and "How do you do?" and we congratulated ourselves not a little upon even this slight progress in a language of such peculiar difficulty.

While upon this subject, I wish to say a few words with regard to the method which has been generally adopted by travellers and geographers of spelling Russian proper names in English letters. It consists briefly in using the English letter *j* indiscriminately to represent the Russian sounds *zh* and *ya*, the English *w* for the sounds of *v* and *f*, and the English *tch* and *stch* for the simple sound of *ch* in "chair."

How so senseless a custom originated I cannot imagine. There is no such letter in the Russian language as *W*, and no such sound as that of *w* in "wood;" and yet we have it used instead of *V* in all such words as Wrangell, Woronsof, Wolga, Wladimir, Pultowa, and werst, as if the compilers of our geographies were all lineal descendants of the elder Mr. Weller, and couldn't pronounce *V* otherwise than "we." What propriety is there in taking a Russian word which is pronounced Gee-zhee-ga and spelling it G-h-i-j-i-g-h-a, or in calling Kam-chat-ka Kam-skat-ka and spelling it K-a-m-s-t-c-h-a-t-k-a. The Russian sounds in those words are simple enough, and there is neither orthographical propriety nor common sense in the popular style of spelling and pronouncing them. I saw only a few days since the names of two prominent mountains in Kamtchatka spelled Klieutchiefskajia and Shieuvailitschinskajia, and I ask, who, in the name of Noah Webster, could ever pronounce them without getting half a dozen supplementary organs of speech? Had they been spelled as they should have been, Kloochefskiá and Soovail-itch-in'-skia, there would have been some hope of an approximation to their sound. I hope, for the sake of the rising generation, that our next geographical reform will be the adoption of some simple but comprehensive system of spelling foreign names in English letters, and that the orthography of Russian proper names will not be left, as it has hitherto been, to chance or individual caprice.

Our reception at Petropavlovski by both Russians and Americans was most cordial and enthusiastic, and the first three or four days after our arrival were spent in one con-

tinuous round of visits and dinners. On Thursday we
made an excursion on horseback to a little village called
Avatcha, ten or fifteen versts distant across the bay, and
came back perfectly charmed with the scenery, climate,
and vegetation of this beautiful peninsula. The road
wound around the slopes of grassy, wooded hills, above
the clear blue water of the bay, commanding a view of
the bold purple promontories which formed the gateway
to the sea, and revealing now and then, between the
clumps of silver birch, glimpses of long ranges of picturesque snow-covered mountains, stretching away along
the west coast to the white solitary peak of Vill-vó-chin-
ski, thirty or forty miles distant. The vegetation everywhere was almost tropical in its rank luxuriance. We
could pick handfuls of flowers almost without bending
from our saddles, and the long wild grass through which
we rode would in many places sweep our waists. Delighted to find the climate of Italy where we had anticipated the biting air of Labrador, and inspirited by the
beautiful scenery, we woke the echoes of the hills with
American songs, shouted, hallooed, and ran races on our
little Cossack ponies until the setting sun warned us that
it was time to return.

Upon the information which he obtained in Petropavlovski, Major Abasa formed a plan of operations for the
ensuing winter, which was briefly as follows : Mahood and
Bush were to go on in the " Olga" to the mouth of the
Amoor River, on the Chinese frontier, and making that
settlement their base of supplies, were to explore the
rough mountainous region lying west of the Okhotsk Sea

and south of the Russian seaport of Okhotsk. The Major
and I, in the meantime, were to travel northward with a
party of natives through the peninsula of Kamtchatka, and
strike the proposed route of the line about midway between Okhotsk and Behring's Straits. Dividing again here,
one of us would go westward to meet Mahood and Bush
at Okhotsk, and one northward to a Russian trading station called Anádirsk, about four hundred miles west of
the Straits. In this way we would cover the whole ground
to be traversed by our line, with the exception of the barren desolate region between Anádirsk and Behring's
Straits, which our chief proposed to leave for the present
unexplored. Taking into consideration our circumstances
and the smallness of our force, this plan was probably the
best which could possibly have been devised, but it made
it necessary for the Major and me to travel throughout the
whole winter without a single companion except our native teamsters. As I did not speak Russian, it would be
next to impossible for me to do this without an interpreter, and the Major engaged in that capacity a young
American fur trader, named Dodd, who had been living
seven years in Petropavlovski, and who was familiar with
the Russian language and the habits and customs of the
natives. With this addition our whole force numbered
five men, and was to be divided into three parties ; one
for the west coast of the Okhotsk Sea, one for the north
coast, and one for the country between the Sea and the
Arctic Circle. All minor details, such as means of transportation and subsistence, were left to the discretion of
the several parties. We were to live on the country,

travel with the natives, and avail ourselves of any and
every means of transportation and subsistence which the
country afforded. It was no pleasure excursion upon
which we were about to enter. The Russian authorities
at Petropavlovski gave us all the information and assistance in their power, but did not hesitate to express the
opinion that five men would never succeed in exploring
the eighteen hundred miles of barren, almost uninhabited
country, between the Amoor River and Behring's Straits.
It was not probable, they said, that the Major could get
through the peninsula of Kamtchatka at all that fall as he
anticipated, but that if he did, he certainly could not penetrate the great desolate steppes to the northward, which
were only inhabited by wandering tribes of Chookchis and
Koraks. The Major replied simply that he would show
them what we could do, and went on with his preparations.

On Saturday morning, August 26th, the " Olga" sailed
with Mahood and Bush for the Amoor River, leaving the
Major, Dodd, and me, at Petropavlovski, to make our
way northward through Kamtchatka.

As the morning was clear and sunny, I engaged a
boat and a native crew, and accompanied Bush and Mahood out to sea.

As we began to feel the fresh morning land-breeze, and
to draw out slowly from under the cliffs of the west coast,
I drank a farewell glass of wine to the success of the
" Amoor River Exploring Party," shook hands with the
Captain and complimented his Dutch History, and bade
good-by to the mates and men. As I went over the
side, the second mate seemed overcome with emotion at

the thought of the perils which I was about to encounter in that heathen country, and cried out in funny, broken English, " Oh, Mr. Kinney ! " (he couldn't say Kennan) "who's a g'un to cook for ye, and ye can't get no potatusses ? " as if the absence of a cook and the lack of potatoes were the summing up of all earthly privations. I assured him cheerfully that we could cook for ourselves, and eat roots : but he shook his head mournfully, as if he saw in prophetic vision the state of misery to which Siberian roots and our own cooking must inevitably reduce us. Bush told me afterward that on the voyage to the Amoor he frequently observed the second mate in deep and melancholy revery, and upon approaching him and asking him what he was thinking about, he answered, with a mournful shake of the head and an indescribable emphasis: " Poor Mr. Kinney ! *Poor* Mr. Kinney ! Poor Mr. Lemon ! " to use his own words. Notwithstanding the scepticism with which I treated his sea-serpent, he gave me a place in his rough affections, second only to " Tommy," his favorite cat, and the pigs.

As the " Olga " sheeted home her top-gallant sails, changed her course more to the eastward, and swept slowly out between the heads, I caught a last glimpse of Bush, standing on the quarter-deck by the wheel, and telegraphing some unintelligible words in the Morse alphabet with his arm. I waved my hat in response, and turning shoreward, with a lump in my throat, ordered the men to give way. The " Olga " was gone, and the last tie which connected us with the civilized world seemed severed.

CHAPTER VI.

OUR time in Petropavlovski, after the departure of the "Olga," was almost wholly occupied in making preparations for our northern journey through the Kamtchatkan peninsula. On Tuesday, however, Dodd told me that there was to be a wedding at the church, and invited me to go over and witness the ceremony. It took place in the body of the church, immediately after some sort of morning service, which had nearly closed when we entered. I had no difficulty in singling out the happy individuals whose fortunes were to be united in the holy bonds of matrimony. They betrayed their own secret by their assumed indifference and unconsciousness.

The unlucky (lucky?) man was a young, round-headed Cossack about twenty years of age, dressed in a dark frock coat trimmed with scarlet and gathered like a lady's dress above the waist, which, with a reckless disregard for his anatomy, was assumed to be six inches below his armpits. In honor of the extraordinary occasion he had donned a great white standing collar which projected above his ears, as the mate of the "Olga" would say "like fore to' gallant studd'n' s'ls." Owing to a deplorable lack of understanding between his cotton pants and his shoes they failed to meet by about six inches, and no provision had been made for the deficiency. The bride was comparatively an old woman—at least twenty years the young man's senior, and a *widow*. I thought with a sigh of the elder Mr. Weller's parting injunction to his son, "Bevare o' the vidders, Sammy—Bevare o' the vidders," and wondered what the old gentleman would say could he see this unconscious "wictim" walking up to the altar "and thinkin' in his 'art that it was all wery capital." The bride wore a dress of that peculiar style of calico known as "furniture prints," without trimming or ornaments of any kind. Whether it was cut "bias" or with "gores," I'm sorry to say I don't know, dress-making being as much of an occult science to me as divination. Her hair was tightly bound up in a scarlet silk handkerchief, fastened in front with a little gilt button. As soon as the church service was concluded the altar was removed to the middle of the room, and the priest, donning a black silk gown which contrasted strangely with his heavy cowhide boots, summoned the couple before him.

After giving to each three lighted candles tied together with blue ribbon, he began to read in a loud sonorous voice what I supposed to be the marriage service, paying no attention whatever to stops, but catching his breath audibly in the midst of a sentence and hurrying on again with ten-fold rapidity. The candidates for matrimony were silent, but the deacon, who was looking abstractedly out of a window on the opposite side of the church, interrupted him occasionally with doleful chanted responses.

At the conclusion of the reading they all crossed themselves devoutly half a dozen times in succession, and after asking them the decisive question the priest gave them each a silver ring. Then came more reading, at the end of which he administered to them a teaspoonful of wine out of a cup. Reading and chanting were again resumed and continued for a long time, the bridegroom and bride crossing and prostrating themselves continually, and the Deacon closing up his responses by repeating with the most astounding rapidity, fifteen times in five seconds, the words "Gáspodi pomeelui," "God have mercy upon us." He then brought in two large gilt crowns ornamented with medallions, and blowing off the dust which had accumulated upon them since the last wedding, he placed them upon the heads of the bridegroom and bride.

The young Cossack's crown was altogether too large, and slipped down over his head like a candle extinguisher until it rested upon his ears—eclipsing his eyes entirely. The bride's hair—or rather the peculiar manner in which it was "done up"—precluded the possibility of making a crown stay on her head, and an individual from among the spectators was detailed to hold it there. The priest then made the couple join hands, seized the groom's hand himself, and they all began a hurried march around the altar— the priest first, dragging along the Cossack, who, blinded by the crown, was continually stepping on his leader's heels, the bride following the groom, and trying to keep the crown from pulling her hair down, and lastly, the supernumerary stepping on the bride's dress and holding the gilt emblem of royalty in its place. The whole performance was so indescribably ludicrous, that I could not possibly keep my countenance in that sober frame which

befitted the solemnity of the occasion, and nearly scan-
dalized the whole assembly by laughing out aloud. Three
times they marched in this way around the altar, and the
ceremony was then ended. The bride and groom kissed
the crowns reverently as they took them off, walked
around the church, crossing themselves and bowing in
succession before each of the pictures of saints which
hung against the wall, and at last turned to receive the
congratulations of their friends. It was expected of
course that the *distinguished American*, of whose intelligence, politeness, and suavity, so much had been heard,
would congratulate the bride upon this auspicious occasion; but at least one distinguished but unfortunate
American didn't know how to do it. My acquirements in
Russian were limited to "Yes," "No," and "How do
you do?" and none of these expressions were fully equal
to the emergency. Desirous, however, of sustaining the
national reputation for politeness, as well as of showing my
good-will to the bride, I selected the last of the phrases
as probably the most appropriate, and walking solemnly,
and I fear awkwardly up, I asked the bride with a very
low bow, and in very bad Russian—how she did; she
graciously replied, "cherasvwechiano khorasho pakornashae
blagadoroo," and the distinguished American retired with
a proud consciousness of having done his duty. I was
not very much enlightened as to the state of the bride's
health; but, judging from the facility with which she
rattled off this tremendous sentence, we concluded that
she must be well. Nothing but a robust constitution and
the most excellent health would have enabled her to do it.

Convulsed with laughter, Dodd and I made our escape from the church and returned to our quarters. I have since been informed by the Major that the marriage ceremony of the Greek Church, when properly performed, has a peculiar impressiveness and solemnity ; but I shall never be able to see it now without having my solemnity overcome by the recollection of that poor Cossack, stumbling around the altar after the priest with his head extinguished in a crown !

From the moment when the Major decided upon the overland journey through Kamtchatka, he devoted all his time and energies to the work of preparation. Boxes covered with seal skin, and intended to be hung from pack-saddles, were prepared for the transportation of our stores ; tents, bear-skins, and camp equipage, were bought and packed away in ingeniously contrived bundles; and everything which native experience could suggest for lessening the hardships of out-door life was provided in quantities sufficient for two months' journey. Horses were then ordered from all the adjacent villages, and a special courier was sent throughout the peninsula by the route which we intended to follow, with orders to apprise the natives everywhere of our coming, and to direct them to remain at home with all their horses until after our party should pass.

Thus prepared, we set out on the 4th of September for the far north.

The peninsula of Kamtchatka, through which we were about to travel, is a long irregular tongue of land lying east of the Okhotsk Sea, between the fifty-first and sixty-second degrees of North latitude, and measuring in extreme length about seven hundred miles. It is almost entirely of volcanic formation, and the great range of rugged mountains by which it is longitudinally divided, comprises even now five or six volcanoes in a state of almost uninterrupted activity. This immense chain of mountains, which has never even been named, stretches from the fifty-first to the sixtieth degree of latitude in one almost continuous ridge, and at last breaks off abruptly into the Okhotsk Sea, leaving to the northward a high level steppe called the " dole " or desert, which is the wandering ground of the Reindeer Koraks. The central and southern parts of the peninsula are broken up by the spurs and foot hills of the great mountain range into deep sequestered valleys of the wildest and most picturesque character, and afford scenery which, for majestic and varied beauty, is not surpassed in all Northern Asia. The climate everywhere, except in the extreme north, is comparatively mild and equable, and the vegetation has an almost tropical freshness and luxuriance totally at variance with all one's ideas of Kamtchatka. The population of the peninsula I estimate from careful observation at about 5,000, and it is made up of three distinct classes—the Russians, the Kamchadals or settled natives, and the Wandering Koraks. The Kamchadals, who compose the most numerous class, are settled in little log villages throughout the peninsula, near the mouths of small rivers which rise in the central range of mountains, and fall into the Okhotsk Sea and the Pacific. Their principal occupations are fishing, fur trapping, and the cultivation of rye, turnips, cabbages, and po-

tatoes, which grow thriftily as far north as lat. 58°. Theii
largest settlements are in the fertile valley of the Kamtchatka River, between Petropavlovski and Kluche. The
Russians, who are comparatively few in number, are scattered here and there among the Kamtchadal villages, and
are generally engaged in trading for furs with the Kamchadals and the nomadic tribes to the northward. The
Wandering Koraks, who are the wildest, most powerful,
and most independent natives in the peninsula, seldom
come south of the 58th parallel of latitude, except for the
purpose of trade. Their chosen haunts are the great desolate steppes lying east of Penjinsk Gulf, where they
wander constantly from place to place in solitary bands,
living in large fur tents and depending for subsistence upon their vast herds of tamed and domesticated reindeer.
The government under which all the inhabitants of Kamtchatka nominally live is administered by a Russian officer
called an " Ispravnik " or local governor, who is supposed to settle all questions of law which may arise between
individuals or tribes, and to collect the annual " yassák "
or tax of furs, which is levied upon every male inhabitant
in his province. He resides in Petropavlovski, and owing
to the extent of country over which he has jurisdiction and
the imperfect facilities which it affords for getting about,
he is seldom seen outside of the village where he has his
head-quarters. The only means of transportation between the widely separated settlements of the Kamchadals
are pack-horses, canoes, and dog-sledges, and there is not
such a thing as a road in the whole peninsula. I may have
occasion hereafter to speak of "roads," but I mean by

the word nothing more than the geometrician means by a "line"—simple longitudinal extension without any of the sensible qualities which are popularly associated with it.

Through this wild, sparsely populated region, we purposed to travel by hiring the natives along our route to carry us with their horses from one settlement to another until we should reach the territory of the Wandering Koraks. North of that point we could not depend upon any regular means of transportation, but would be obliged to trust to "luck" and the tender mercies of the Arctic nomads.

CHAPTER VII.

I CANNOT remember any journey in my whole life which gave me more enjoyment at the time, or which is more pleasant in recollection, than our first horseback ride of 275 versts over the flowery hills and through the green valleys of Southern Kamtchatka, surrounded as we continually were by the wildest and most beautiful scenery in all Northern Asia, experiencing for the first time the novelty and adventurous excitement of camp life; and rejoicing in a newly-found sense of freedom and perfect independence, we turned our backs gaily on civilization, and rode away with light hearts into the wilderness, making the hills ring to the music of our songs and halloos.

Our party, aside from drivers and guides, consisted of four men. The Major Generalissimo of the forces and chief of Asiatic exploration, Dodd the young American, whom we had engaged in Petropavlovski, and myself. The biting sarcasm directed by Mithridates at the army of Lucullus—that if they came as ambassadors they were too many, if as soldiers too few—would have applied with equal force to our small party made up as it was of only four men; but strength is not always to be measured by numbers, and we had no fears that we should not be able to cope with any obstacles which might lie in our way. We could certainly subsist ourselves where a larger party would starve.

On Sunday, September 3d, our horses were loaded and dispatched in advance to a small village on the opposite side of the bay, where we intended to meet them with a whale-boat. On Monday the 4th we made our farewell calls upon the Russian authorities, drank an inordinate quantity of champagne to our own health and success, and set out in two whale-boats for Avatcha, accompanied by the whole American population of Petropavlovski. Crossing the bay under sprit-sail and jib, with a slashing breeze from the south-west, we ran swiftly into the mouth of the Avatcha River, and landed at the village to refresh ourselves for the fifteenth time with "fifteen drops," and take leave of our American friends, Pierce Hunter and Fronefield. Copious libations were poured out to the tutelary saint of Kamtchatkan explorers, and giving and receiving three hearty cheers, we pushed off and began to make our way slowly up the river with poles and paddles toward the Kamchadal settlement of Okoota.

Our native crew, sharing in the universal dissipation which had attended our departure, and wholly unaccustomed to such reckless drinking, were reduced by this time to a comical state of happy imbecility, in which they sang gurgling Kamchadal songs, blessed the Americans, and fell overboard alternately, without contributing in any marked degree to the successful navigation of our heavy whale-boat. Vushine, however, with characteristic energy hauled the drowning wretches in by their hair, rapped them over the head with a paddle to restore consciousness, pushed the boat off sand-bars, kept its head up stream, poled, rowed, jumped into the water, shouted, swore, and proved himself fully equal to any emergency.

It was considerably after noon when we left Petropavlovski, and, owing to the incompetency of our Kamtchadal crew, and the frequency of sand-bars, night overtook us on the river some distance below Okoota. Selecting a place where the bank was dry and accessible, we beached our whale-boat and prepared for our first bivouac in the open air. Beating down the high wet grass, Vushine pitched our little cotton tent, carpeted it with warm, dry bear-skins, improvised a table and a cloth out of an empty candle-box and a clean towel, built a fire, boiled tea, and in twenty minutes set before us a hot supper which would not have done discredit to the culinary skill of Soyer himself. After supper we sat by the fire smoking and talking until the long twilight died away in the west, and then rolling ourselves up in heavy blankets, we lay down on our bear-skins and listened to the low quacking of a half-awakened duck in the sedges, and the lonely cries of night-birds on the river, until at last we fell asleep.

Day was just breaking in the east when I awoke. The mist, which for a week had hung in gray clouds around the mountains, had now vanished, and the first object which met my eyes through the open door of the tent was the great white cone of Villoo-chin-ski gleaming spectrally through the grayness of the dawn. As the red flush in the east deepened, all nature seemed to awake. Ducks and geese quacked from every bunch of reeds along the shore; the strange wailing cries of sea-gulls could be heard from the neighboring coast; and from the clear, blue sky came down the melodious trumpeting of wild swans, as they flew inland to their feeding-places. I washed my face in the clear, cold water of the river, and waked Dodd to see the mountains. Directly behind our tent, in one unbroken sheet of snow, rose the colossal peak of Ko-rát-skoi, ten thousand five hundred feet in height, its sharp white summit already crimsoning with the rays of the rising sun, while the morning star yet throbbed faintly over the cool purple of its eastern slope. A little to the right was the huge volcano of Avatcha, with a long banner of golden smoke hung out from its broken summit, and the Roselskoi volcano puffing out dark vapor from three craters. Far down the coast, thirty miles away, stood the sharp peak of Villoóchinski, with the watch-fires of morning already burning upon its summit, and beyond it the hazy blue outlines of the coast range. Shreds of fleecy mist here and there floated up the mountain sides, and vanished like the spirits of the night-dews rising from earth to heaven in bright resurrection. Steadily the warm, rosy flush of sunrise crept down the snowy slopes of the mountains, until at last, with a quick sudden burst, it poured a flood of light into the valley, tinging our little white tent with a delicate pink, like that of a wild rose-leaf, turning every pendent dew-drop into a twinkling brilliant, and lighting up the still water of the river, until it became a quivering, flashing mass of liquid silver.

" I'm nɔt romantic, but, upon my word,
　　There are some moments when one can't help feeling
　As if his heart's chords were so strongly stirred
　　By things around him, that 'tis vain concealing
　　　A little music in his soul still lingers,
　　Whene'er the keys are touched by Nature's fingers."

I was just delivering the above quotation in impassioned style, when Dodd, who never allowed his enthusiasm for the beauties of Nature to interfere with a proper
regard for the welfare of his stomach, emerged from the
tent, and with a mock solemn apology for interrupting
my soliloquy, said that if I could bring my mind down to
the contemplation of material things, he would inform me
that breakfast was ready, and begged to suggest that the
little music in my soul be allowed to "linger," since it
could do so with less detriment than the said breakfast.
The force of this suggestion, seconded as it was by a
savory odor from the interior of the tent, could not be
denied. I went, but still continued between the spoon-
fuls of hot soup to "rave," as Dodd expressed it, about
the scenery. After breakfast the tent was struck, camp
equipage packed up, and taking seats in the stern-sheets
of our whale-boat, we pushed off and resumed our slow
ascent of the river.

The vegetation everywhere, untouched as yet by the
autumn frosts, seemed to have an almost tropical luxuriance. High wild grass, mingled with varicolored flowers,
extended to the very river's brink ; Alpine roses and cin-
quefoil grew in dense thickets along the bank, and dropped
their pink and yellow petals like fairy boats upon the sur-

face of the clear still water; yellow columbine drooped low over the river, to see its graceful image mirrored beside that of the majestic volcano; and strange black Kamtchatkan lilies, with downcast looks, stood here and there in sad loneliness, mourning in funeral garb some unknown flowery bereavement.

Nor was animal life wanting to complete the picture. Wild ducks, with long outstretched necks, shot past us continually in their swift level flight, uttering hoarse "quacks" of curiosity and apprehension; the "honking" of geese came to us, softened by distance, from the higher slopes of the mountains; and now and then a magnificent eagle, startled from his solitary watch on some jutting rock, expanded his broad-barred wings, launched himself into air, and soared upward in ever-widening circles until he became a mere moving speck against the white snowy crater of the Avatchinski volcano. Never had I seen a picture of such wild primitive loneliness as that presented by this beautiful fertile valley, encircled by smoking volcanoes and snow-covered mountains, yet green as the vale of Tempe, teeming with animal and vegetable life, yet solitary, uninhabited by man, and apparently unknown. About noon the barking of dogs announced our approach to a settlement, and turning an abrupt bend in the river, we came in sight of the Kamtchadal village of Okoota.

A Kamtchadal village differs in some respects so widely from an American frontier settlement, that it is worthy, perhaps, of a brief description. It is situated generally on a little elevation near the bank of some river or stream, surrounded by scattered clumps of poplar and yellow

birch, and protected by high hills from the cold northern
winds. Its houses, which are clustered irregularly together
near the beach, are very low, and are made of logs squared
and notched at the ends, and chinked with masses of dry
moss. The roofs are covered with a rough thatch of long
coarse grass, or with overlapping strips of tamarack bark,
and project at the ends and sides into wide overhanging
eaves. The window-frames, although occasionally glazed,
are more frequently covered with an irregular patchwork
of translucent fish-bladders, sewn together with thread
made of the dried and pounded sinews of the reindeer.
The doors are almost square, and the chimneys are nothing
but long straight poles, arranged in a circle and plastered
over thickly with clay. Here and there between the
houses stand half a dozen curious architectural quadrupeds
called "bologáns," or fish storehouses. They are simply
conical log-tents, elevated from the ground on four posts
to secure their contents from the dogs, and resemble as
much as anything small hay-stacks trying to walk away
on four legs. High square frames of horizontal poles
stand beside every house, filled with thousands of drying
salmon; and " an ancient and fish-like smell," which pervades the whole atmosphere, betrays the nature of the
Kamtchadals' occupation and of the food upon which they
live. Half a dozen dug-out canoes lie bottom upward on
the sandy shelving beach, covered with large neatly tied
seines; two or three long, narrow dog-sledges stand up on
their ends against every house, and a hundred or more
sharp-eared wolfish dogs, tied at intervals to long heavy
poles, lie panting in the sun, snapping viciously at the flies

and mosquitoes which disturb their rest. In the centre of the village, facing the west, stands, in all the glory of Kamtchatko-Byzantine architecture, red paint, and glittering domes, the omnipresent Greek church, contrasting strangely with the rude log-houses and conical "bologáns" over which it extends the spiritual protection of its resplendent golden cross. It is built generally of carefully-hewn logs, painted a deep brick red, covered with a green sheet-iron roof, and surmounted by two onion-shaped domes of tin, which are sometimes colored a sky-blue and spangled with golden stars. Standing with all its glaring contrasts of color among a few unpainted log-houses in a primitive wilderness, it has a strange picturesque appearance not easily described. If you can imagine a rough American backwoods' settlement of low log-houses, clustered round a gaily-colored Turkish mosque, half a dozen small haystacks mounted on high vertical posts, fifteen or twenty Titanic wooden gridirons similarly elevated and hung full of drying fish, a few dog-sledges and canoes lying carelessly around, and a hundred or more gray wolves tied here and there between the houses to long heavy poles, you will have a general but tolerably accurate idea of a Kamtchadal settlement of the better class. They differ somewhat in respect to their size and their churches; but the gray log-houses, conical "bologáns," drying fish, wolfish dogs, canoes, sledges, and fishy odors are all invariable features.

The inhabitants of these native settlements in Southern Kamtchatka are a dark swarthy race, considerably below the average stature of Siberian natives, and are very different in all their characteristics from the wandering tribes of Koraks and Chookchees who live farther north. The men average perhaps five feet three or four inches in height, have broad flat faces, prominent cheek bones, small and rather sunken eyes, no beards, long, lank, black hair, small hands and feet, very slender limbs, and a ten- dency to enlargement and protrusion of the abdomen. They are probably of Central Asiatic origin, but they cer- tainly have had no very recent connection with any other Siberian tribe with which I am acquainted, and are not at all like the Chookchees, Koraks, Gakoots, or Tungoos. From the fact of their living a settled instead of a wander- ing life, they were brought under Russian subjection much more easily than their nomadic neighbors, and have since experienced in a greater degree the civilizing influences of Russian intercourse. They have adopted almost univer- sally the religion, customs, and habits of their conquerors, and their own language, which is a very curious one, is already falling into disuse. It would be easy to describe their character by negatives. They are not independent, self-reliant, or of a combative disposition, like the northern Chookchees and Koraks ; they are not avaricious or dis- honest, except where those traits are the results of Rus- sian education ; they are not suspicious or distrustful, but rather the contrary ; and for generosity, hospitality, sim- ple good faith, and easy, equable good-nature under all circumstances, I have never met their equals. As a race they are undoubtedly becoming extinct. Since 1780 they have diminished in numbers more than one-half, and fre- quently recurring epidemics and famines will soon reduce them to a comparatively weak and unimportant tribe, which will finally be absorbed in the growing Russian population of the peninsula. They have already lost most of their distinctive customs and superstitions, and only an occasional sacrifice of a dog to some malignant spirit of storm or disease enables the modern traveller to catch a glimpse of their original paganism. They depend mainly for subsistence upon the salmon, which every summer run into these northern rivers in immense quantities to spawn, and are speared, caught in seines, and trapped in weirs by thousands. These fish, dried without salt in the open air, are the food of the Kamtchadals and of their dogs throughout the long, cold northern winter. During the summer, however, their bill of fare is more varied. The climate and soil of the river bottoms in Southern Kamtchatka admit of the cultivation of rye, potatoes, and turnips, and the whole peninsula abounds in animal life. Reindeer and black and brown bears roam everywhere over the mossy plains and through the grassy valleys; wild sheep and a species of ibex are not unfrequently found in the mountains; and millions upon millions of ducks, geese, and swans, in almost endless variety, swarm about every river and little marshy lake throughout the country. These aquatic fowls are captured in great multitudes while moulting, by organized "drives" of fifty or seventy-five men in canoes, who chase the birds in one great flock up some narrow stream, at the end of which a huge net is arranged for their reception. They are then killed with clubs, cleaned and salted for winter use. Tea and sugar have been introduced by the Russians, and have been received with great favor, the annual consumption now being more than 20,000 pounds of each in the Kamtchatkan peninsula alone. Bread is now made of rye, which the Kamtchadals raise and grind for themselves; but previous to the settlement of the country by the Russians, the only native substitute for bread was a sort of baked paste, consisting chiefly of the grated tubers of the purple Kamtchatkan lily. The only fruits in the country are berries and a species of wild cherry. Of the berries, however, there are fifteen or twenty different kinds, of which the most important are blueberries, "maróshkas," or yellow-cloud berries, and dwarf cranberries. These the natives pick late in the fall, and freeze for winter consumption. Cows are kept in nearly all the Kamtchadal settlements, and milk is always plenty. A curious native dish of sour milk, baked curds, and sweet cream, covered with powdered sugar and cinnamon, is worthy of being placed upon a civilized table.

It will thus be seen that life in a Kamtchatkan settlement, gastronomically considered, is not altogether so disagreeable as we have been led to believe. I have seen natives in the valley of the Kamtchatka as pleasantly situated, and enjoying as much comfort and almost as many luxuries, as nine-tenths of the settlers upon the frontiers of our western States and Territories.

CHAPTER VIII.

At Okoota we found our horses and men awaiting our arrival; and after eating a hasty lunch of bread, milk, and blueberries in a little native house, we clambered awkwardly into our saddles, and filed away in a long irregular line through the woods, Dodd and I taking the advance, singing "Bonnie Dundee."

We kept continually near the group of mountains which had presented so beautiful an appearance in the morning; but owing to the forest of birch and mountain ash which clothed the foot-hills, we caught only occasional glimpses between the tree-tops of their white snowy summits.

Just before sunset we rode into another little native village, whose ingeniously constructed name defied all my inexperienced attempts to pronounce it or write it down. Dodd was good-natured enough to repeat it to me fifteen or sixteen times; but as it sounded worse and more unintelligible every time, I finally called it Jerusalem, and let it go at that. For the sake of geographical accuracy I have so marked it down on my map; but let no future commentator point to it triumphantly as a proof that the lost tribes of Israel emigrated to Kamtchatka; I don't believe that they did, and I know that this unfortunate settlement, before I took pity on it and called it Jerusalem, was distinguished by a name so utterly barbarous that neither the Hebrew alphabet nor any other known to ancient literature could have begun to do it justice.

Tired by the unusual exercise of horseback riding, I entered Jerusalem at a walk, and throwing my bridle to a Kamtchadal in blue nankeen shirt and buckskin pants, who saluted me with a reverential bow, I wearily dismounted and entered the house which Vushine indicated as the one which we were to occupy.

The best room, which had been prepared for our reception, was a low bare apartment about twelve feet square, whose walls, ceiling, and floor of unpainted birch planks were scoured to a smooth snowy purity which would have been creditable even to the neat housewives of the Dutch paradise of Broek. An immense clay oven, neatly painted red, occupied one side of the room ; a bench, three or four rude chairs, and a table, were arranged with severe propriety against the other. Two windows of glass, shaded by flowery calico curtains, admitted the warm sunshine; a few coarse American lithographs hung here and there against the wall ; an air of perfect neatness, which prevailed everywhere, made us suddenly and painfully conscious of our own muddy boots and rough attire. No tools except axes and knives had been used in the construction of the house or of its furniture ; but the unplaned, unpainted boards had been diligently scrubbed with water and sand to a delicate creamy whiteness, which made amends for all rudeness of workmanship. There was not a plank in the floor from which the most fastidious need have hesitated to eat. The most noticeable peculiarity of this, as of all the other Kamtchadal houses which we saw in Southern

Kamtchatka, was the lowness of its doors. They seemed to have been designed for a race of beings whose only means of locomotion were hands and knees, and to enter them without making use of those means required a flexibility of spinal vertebræ only to be acquired by long and persevering practice. Vushine and Dodd, who had travelled in Kamtchatka before, experienced no difficulty in accommodating themselves to this peculiarity of native architecture; but the Major and I, during the first two weeks of our journey, bore upon the fore parts of our heads, bumps whose extraordinary size and irregularity of development would have puzzled even Spurzheim and Gall. If the abnormal enlargement of the bumps had only been accompanied by a corresponding enlargement of the respective faculties, there would have been some compensation for this disfiguration of our heads; but unfortunately "perception" might be suddenly developed by the lintel of a door until it looked like a goose-egg, without enabling us to perceive the very next beam which came in our way until after we had struck our heads against it.

The Cossack who had been sent through the peninsula as an avant-courier to notify the natives of our coming, had carried the most exaggerated reports of our power and importance, and elaborate preparations had been made by the Jerusalemites for our reception. The house which was to be honored by our presence had been carefully scrubbed, swept, and garnished; the women had put on their most flowery calico-dresses, and tied their hair up in their brightest silk handkerchiefs; most of the chil·

dren's faces had been painfully washed and polished with soap-water and wads of fibrous hemp; the whole village had been laid under contribution to obtain the requisite number of plates, cups, and spoons for our supper-table, and votive offerings of ducks, reindeers' tongues, blueberries, and clotted cream poured in upon us with a profusion which testified to the good-will and hospitality of the inhabitants, as well as to their ready appreciation of tired travellers' wants. In an hour we sat down, with appetites sharpened by the pure mountain air, to an excellent supper of cold roast duck, broiled reindeers' tongues, black bread and fresh butter, blueberries and cream, and wild rose petals crushed with white sugar into a rich delicious jam. We had come to Kamtchatka with minds and mouths heroically made up for an unvarying diet of blubber, tallow-candles, and train-oil; but imagine our surprise and delight at being treated instead to such Sybaritic luxuries as purple blueberries, cream, and preserved rose leaves! Did Lucullus ever feast upon preserved rose petals in his vaunted pleasure-gardens of Tusculum? Never! The original recipe for the preparation of celestial ambrosia had been lost before ever "Lucullus supped with Lucullus;" but it was rediscovered by the despised inhabitants of Kamtchatka, and is now offered to the world as the first contribution of the Hyperboreans to gastronomical science. Take equal quantities of white loaf sugar and the petals of the Alpine rose, add a little juice of crushed blueberries, macerate together to a rich crimson paste, serve in the painted cups of trumpet honeysuckles, and imagine yourself feasting with the gods upon the summit of high Olympus!

As soon as possible after supper I stretched myself out upon the floor under a convenient table, which answered practically and æsthetically all the purposes of a four-post bedstead, inflated my little rubber pillow, rolled myself up, à la mummy, in a blanket, and slept.

The Major, always an early riser, was awake on the following morning at daylight. Dodd and I, with a coincidence of opinion as rare as it was gratifying, regarded early rising as a relic of barbarism which no American, with a proper regard for the civilization of the nineteenth century, would demean himself by encouraging. We had therefore entered into a mutual agreement upon this occasion to sleep peacefully until the "caravan," as Dodd irreverently styled it, should be ready to start, or at least until we should receive a summons for breakfast. Soon after daybreak, however, a terrific row began about something, and with a vague impression that I was attending a particularly animated primary meeting in the Ninth Ward, I sprang up, knocked my head violently against a table-leg, opened my eyes in amazement, and stared wildly at the situation. The Major, in a scanty *déshabillé*, was storming furiously about the room, cursing our frightened drivers in classical Russian, because the horses had all stampeded during the night and gone, as he said with expressive simplicity, "Chort tolko znal kooda"—"the devil only knew where." This was rather an unfortunate beginning of our campaign; but in the course of two hours most of the wandering beasts were found, packs were adjusted, and after an unnecessary amount of profanity from the drivers, we turned our backs on Jerusalem and rode

slowly away over the rolling grassy foot-hills of the Avatch.
inski volcano.

It was a warm, beautiful Indian summer's day, and a
peculiar stillness and Sabbath-like quiet seemed to per-
vade all nature. The leaves of the scattering birches and
alders along the trail hung motionless in the warm sunshine, the drowsy cawing of a crow upon a distant larch
came to our ears with strange distinctness, and we even
imagined that we could hear the regular throbbing of the
surf upon the far-away coast. A faint murmurous hum
of bees was in the air, and a rich fruity fragrance came
up from the purple clusters of blueberries which our
horses crushed under foot at every step. All things
seemed to unite in tempting the tired traveller to stretch
himself out on the warm fragrant grass, and spend the
day in luxurious idleness, listening to the buzzing of the
sleepy bees, inhaling the sweet smell of crushed blueberries, and watching the wreaths of curling smoke which
rose lazily from the lofty crater of the great white volcano.
I laughingly said to Dodd that instead of being in Siberia
—the frozen land of Russian exiles—we had apparently
been transported by some magical Arabian Night's contrivance to the clime of the " Lotus Eaters," which would
account for the dreamy, drowsy influence of the atmosphere. " Clime of the Lotus Eaters be hanged ! " he
broke out impetuously, making a furious slap at his face ;
" the poet don't say that the Lotus Eaters were eaten up
themselves by such cursed mosquitoes as these, and
they're sufficient evidence that we're in Kamtchatka—
they don't grow as big as bumble-bees in any other coun-

try !" I reminded him mildly that according to Walton
—old Isaac—every misery we missed was a new mercy,
and that, consequently, he ought to be thankful for every
mosquito that didn't bite him. His only reply was that
"he wished he had old Isaac there." What summary
reprisals were to be made upon old Isaac I did not
know, but it was evident that Dodd did not approve of
his philosophy, or of my attempt at consolation, so I de-
sisted.

Maximof, the chief of our drivers, laboring under a vague
impression that, because everything was so still and quiet,
it must be Sunday, rode slowly through the scattered
clumps of silver birch which shaded the trail, chanting in
a loud, sonorous voice a part of the service of the Greek
Church, suspending this devotional exercise, occasionally,
to curse his vagrant horses in a style which would have
excited the envy and admiration of the most profane
trooper of the army in Flanders.

Oh ! let my pray-er be-e-e (*Here ! you pig ! Keep in
the road !*) set forth as the in-cense ; and let the lifting
up of my han-n-n-ds be—(*Get up ! you Korova ! You
old, blind, broken-legged son of the Evil Spirit ! Where
you going to !*)—an eve-n-ing sacrifice : let not my heart
be inclined to—(*Lie down again, will you ! Thwack !
Take that, you old sleepy-headed svenya proclatye !*)—any
e-vil thing ; let me not be occupied with any evil works
(*Akh ! What a horse ! Bokh s'neem !*). Set a watch before my mouth, and keep the do-o-o-r of my lips—(*Whoa !
You merzavitz ! What did you run into that tree for ?
Ecca voron ! Podletz ! Slepoi takoi ! Chort tibi vasmee !*)

—and Maximof lapsed into a strain of such ingenious and metaphorical profanity that my imagination was left to supply the deficiencies of my imperfect comprehension. He did not seem to be conscious of any inconsistency between the chanted psalm and the profane interjections by which it was accompanied; but, even if he had been fully aware of it, he probably would have regarded the chanting as a fair offset to the profanity, and would have gone on his way with serene indifference, fully assured that if he sang a sacred verse every time he swore, his celestial account must necessarily balance!

The road, or rather trail, from Jerusalem turned away to the westward, and wound around the bases of a range of low bare mountains, through a dense forest of poplar and birch. Now and then we would come out into little grassy openings, where the ground was covered with blueberries, and every eye would be on the lookout for bears; but all was still and motionless—even the grasshoppers chirping sleepily and lazily, as if they too were about to yield to the somnolence which seemed to overpower all nature.

To escape the mosquitoes, whose relentless persecution became almost unendurable, we rode on more briskly through a broad, level valley, filled with a dense growth of tall umbelliferous plants, trotted swiftly up a little hill, and rode at a thundering gallop into the village of Korak, amid the howling and barking of a hundred and fifty half-wild dogs, the neighing of horses, running to and fro of men, and a scene of general confusion.

At Korak we changed most of our horses and men, ate

an "al fresco" lunch under the projecting eaves of a
mossy Kamtchadal house, and started at two o'clock
for Malqua, another village, fifty or sixty miles distant,
across the water-shed of the Kamtchatka River. About
sunset, after a brisk ride of fifteen or eighteen miles, we
suddenly emerged from the dense forest of poplar, birch,
and mountain ash which had shut in the trail, and came
out into a little grassy opening, about an acre in extent,
which seemed to have been made expressly with a view
to camping out. It was surrounded on three sides by
woods, and opened on the fourth into a wild mountain
gorge, choked up with rocks, logs, and a dense growth
of underbrush and weeds. A clear, cold stream tumbled
in a succession of tinkling cascades down the dark ravine,
and ran in a sandy flower-bordered channel through the
grassy glade, until it disappeared in the encircling forest.
It was useless to look for a better place than this to
spend the night, and we decided to stop while we still
had daylight. To picket our horses, collect wood for a
fire, hang over our tea-kettles, and pitch our little cotton
tent, was the work of only a few moments, and we were
soon lying at full length upon our warm bear-skins, around
our towel-covered candle-box, drinking hot tea, discussing
Kamtchatka, and watching the rosy flush of sunset as it
slowly faded over the western mountains.

As I was lulled to sleep that night by the murmuring
plash of falling water, and the tinkling of our horses' bells
from the forest behind our tent, I thought that nothing
could be more delightful than camp life in Kamtchatka.

We reached Malqua on the following day, in a generally

exhausted and used-up condition. The road had been terribly rough and broken, running through narrow ravines blocked up with rocks and fallen trees, across wet mossy swamps, and over rugged precipitous hills, where we dared not attempt to ride our horses. We were thrown repeatedly from our saddles; our provision-boxes were smashed against trees, and wet through by sinking in swamps; girths gave way, drivers swore, horses fell down, and we all came to grief, individually and collectively. The Major, unaccustomed as he was to these vicissitudes of Kamtchatkan travel, held out like a Spartan; but I noticed that for the last ten miles he rode upon a pillow, and shouted at short intervals to Dodd, who, with stoical imperturbability, was riding quietly in advance: "Dodd! oh, Dodd! haven't we got most to that *con-found-ed* Malqua yet?" Dodd would strike his horse a sharp blow with a willow switch, turn half round in his saddle, and reply, with a quizzical smile, that we were "not most there yet, but would be soon!"—an equivocal sort of consolation which did not inspire us with much enthusiasm. At last, when it had already begun to grow dark, we saw a high column of white steam in the distance, which rose, Dodd and Vushine said, from the hot springs of Malqua; and in fifteen minutes we rode, tired, wet, and hungry, into the settlement. Supper was a secondary consideration with me *that* night. All I wanted was to crawl under a table where no one would step on me, and be let alone. I had never before felt such a vivid consciousness of my muscular and osseous system. Every separate bone and tendon in my body asserted its individual existence by a distinct and independent ache, and my back in twenty minutes was as inflexible as an iron ramrod. I felt a melancholy conviction that I never would measure five feet ten inches again, unless I could lie on some Procrustean bed and have my back stretched out to its original longitude. Repeated perpendicular concussions had, I confidently believed, "telescoped" my spinal vertebræ into each other, so that nothing short of a surgical operation would ever restore them to their original positions. Revolving in my mind such mournful considerations, I fell asleep under a table, without even pulling off my boots.

CHAPTER IX.

IT was hard work on the following morning to climb again into the saddle, but the Major was insensible to all appeals for delay. Stern and inflexible as Rhadamanthus, he mounted stiffly upon his feather pillow and gave the signal for a start. With the aid of two sympathetic Kamtchadals, who had perhaps experienced the misery of a stiff back, I succeeded in getting astride a fresh horse, and we rode away into the Genúl valley—the garden of Southern Kamtchatka.

The village of Malqua lies on the northern slope of the Kamtchatka River water-shed, surrounded by low barren granite hills, and reminded me a little in its situation of Virginia City, Nevada. It is noted chiefly for its hot mineral springs, but as we did not have time to visit these springs ourselves, we were compelled to take the natives' word for their temperature and their medicinal properties, and content ourselves with a distant view of the pillar of steam which marked their location.

North of the village opens the long narrow valley of Genul—the most beautiful as well as the most fertile spot in all the Kamtchatkan peninsula. It is about thirty miles in length, and averages three in breadth, and is bounded on both sides by chains of high snow-covered mountains, which stretch away from Malqua in a long vista of white ragged peaks and sharp cliffs, almost to the

head-waters of the Kamtchatka River. A small stream
runs in a tortuous course through the valley, fringed with
long wild grass four or five feet in height, and shaded
here and there by clumps of birches, willows, and alders.
The foliage was beginning already to assume the brilliant
colors of early autumn, and broad stripes of crimson,
yellow, and green ran horizontally along the mountain
sides, marking on a splendid chromatic scale the successive zones of vegetation as they rose in regular gradation
from the level of the valley to the pure glittering snows
of the higher peaks.

As we approached the middle of the valley just before
noon, the scenery assumed a vividness of color and grandeur of outline which drew forth the most enthusiastic exclamations of delight from our little party. For twenty-
five miles in each direction lay the sunny valley through
which the Genul River was stretched like a tangled chain
of silver, linking together the scattered clumps of birch
and thickets of alder, which at intervals diversified its
banks. Like the Happy Valley of Rasselas, it seemed to
be shut out from the rest of the world by impassable
mountains, whose snowy peaks and pinnacles rivalled in
picturesque beauty, in variety and singularity of form, the
wildest dream of eastern architect. Half down their sides
was a broad horizontal belt of dark green pines, thrown
into strong and beautiful contrast with the pure white
snow of the higher summits and the rich crimson of the
mountain ash which flamed below. Here and there the
mountains had been cleft asunder by some Titanic power,
leaving deep narrow gorges and wild ravines where the

sunlight could hardly penetrate, and the eye was lost in
soft purple haze.   Imagine with all this, a warm fragrant
atmosphere and a deep blue sky in which floated a few
clouds, too ethereal even to cast shadows, and you will
perhaps have a faint idea of one of the most beautiful
landscapes in all Kamtchatka.   The Sierra Nevadas may
afford views of more savage wildness, but nowhere in
California or Nevada have I ever seen the distinctive features of both winter and summer—snow and roses, bare
granite and brilliantly colored foliage—blended into so
harmonious a picture as that presented by the Genul
valley on a sunshiny day in early autumn.

Dodd and I devoted most of our leisure time during
the afternoon to picking and eating berries.   Galloping
furiously ahead until we had left the caravan several miles
behind, we would lie down in a particularly luxuriant
thicket by the river's bank, tie our horses to our feet, and
bask in the sunshine and feast upon yellow honeyed
"maroshkas" and the dark purple globes of delicious
blueberries, until our clothes were stained with crimson
spots, and our faces and hands resembled those of a couple
of Camanches painted for the war path.

The sun was yet an hour high when we approached the
native village of Genul.   We passed a field where men
and women were engaged in cutting hay with rude sickles,
returned their stare of amazement with unruffled serenity,
and rode on until the trail suddenly broke off into a river
beyond which stood the village.   Kneeling upon our saddles we succeeded in fording the shallow stream without
getting wet, but in a moment we came to another of about

the same size. We forded that, and were confronted by a
third. This we also passed, but at the appearance of the
fourth river the Major shouted despairingly to Dodd,
"Ay! Dodd! How many 'pagánni' rivers do we have to
wade through in getting to this beastly village?" "Only
one," replied Dodd composedly. "One! Then how
many times does this one river run past this one settlement?" "Five times," was the calm response. "You
see," he explained soberly, "these poor Kamtchadals
haven't got but one river to fish in, and that isn't a very
big one, so they have made it run past their settlement
five times, and by this ingenious contrivance they catch
five times as many salmon as they would if it only passed
once!" The Major was surprised into silence, and
seemed to be considering some abstruse problem. Finally
he raised his eyes from the pommel of his saddle, trans-
fixed the guilty Dodd with a glance of severe rebuke, and
demanded solemnly, "How many times must a given fish
swim past a given settlement, in order to supply the population with food, provided the fish is caught every time he
goes past?" This *reductio ad absurdum* was too much
for Dodd's gravity; he burst into a laugh, and digging his
heels into his horse's ribs, dashed with a great splatter into
the fourth arm or bend of the river, and rode up on the
other side into the village of Genul.

We took up our quarters at the house of the "Starosta,"
or head man of the village, and spread our bear-skins out
on the clean white floor of a low room, papered in a funny
way with odd copies of the London Illustrated News. A
colored American lithograph, representing the kiss of re-

conciliation between two offended lovers, hung against the
wall on one side, and was evidently regarded with a good
deal of pride by the proprietor, as affording incontestable
evidence of culture and refined taste, and proving his familiar acquaintance with American art, and the manners and
customs of American society.

Dodd and I, notwithstanding our fatigue, devoted the
evening entirely to literary pursuits; searching diligently
with tallow-candles over the wall and ceiling for consecutive numbers of the Illustrated News, reading court gossip from a birch plank in the corner, and obituaries of distinguished Englishmen from the back of a door.   By dint
of industry and perseverance we finished one whole side
of the house before bedtime, and having gained a vast
amount of valuable information with regard to the war in
New Zealand, we were encouraged to pursue our investi-
gations in the morning upon the three remaining sides
and the ceiling.   To our great regret, however, we were
obliged to start on our pilgrimage without having time to
find out how that war terminated, and we have never been
able to ascertain to this day !   Long before six o'clock we
were off with fresh horses for a long ride of ninety versts
to Pooschin.

The costumes of our little party had now assumed a
very motley and brigandish appearance, every individual
having discarded, from time to time, such articles of his
civilized dress as proved to be inconvenient or uncomfortable, and adopted various picturesque substitutes,
which filled more nearly the requirements of a barbarous
life.   Dodd had thrown away his cap, and tied a scarlet and

yellow handkerchief around his head. Vushine had ornamented his hat with a long streamer of crimson ribbon,
which floated gayly in the wind like a whip-pennant. A
blue hunting-shirt and a red Turkish fez had superseded my
uniform coat and cap. We all carried rifles slung across
our backs, and revolvers belted around our waists, and
were transformed generally into as fantastic brigands as
ever sallied forth from the passes of the Apennines to
levy black-mail upon unwary travellers. A timid tourist,
meeting us as we galloped furiously across the plain
toward Pooschin, would have fallen on his knees and pulled
out his purse without asking any unnecessary questions.

Being well mounted on fresh, spirited horses, the Major,
Dodd, Vushine, and I rode far in advance of the rest of
the party throughout the day. Late in the afternoon, as we
were going at a slashing rate across the level plain known
as the Kamtchatka Toondra, the Major suddenly drew his
horse violently back on his haunches, wheeled half round,
and shouted, "Medvaid! medvaid!" and a large black
bear rose silently out of the long grass at his very feet.

The excitement, I can conscientiously affirm, was terrific. Vushine unslung his double-barrelled fowling-
piece, and proceeded to pepper him with duck-shot;
Dodd tugged at his revolver with frantic energy, while his
horse ran away with him over the plain. The Major
dropped his bridle, and implored me by all I held sacred
not to shoot *him*, while the horses plunged, kicked, and
snorted in the most animated manner. The only calm
and self-possessed individual in the whole party was the
bear! He surveyed the situation coolly for a few sec-

onds, and then started at an awkward gallop for the woods. In an instant our party recovered its conjoint presence of mind, and charged with the most reckless heroism upon his flying footsteps, shouting frantically to "stop him!" popping away in the most determined and unterrified manner with four revolvers and a shot-gun, and performing prodigies of valor in the endeavor to capture the ferocious beast, without getting in his way or coming nearer to him than a hundred yards. All was in vain. The bear vanished in the forest like a flying shadow; and, presuming from his known ferocity and vindictiveness that he had prepared an ambuscade for us in the woods, we deemed it the better part of valor to abandon the pursuit. Upon comparing notes, we found that we had all been similarly impressed with his enormous size, his shagginess, and his generally savage appearance, and had all been inspired at the same moment with an irresistible inclination to take him by the throat and rip him open with a bowie-knife, in a manner so beautifully illustrated by the old geographies. Nothing but the fractiousness of our horses and the rapidity of his flight had prevented this desirable consummation. The Major even declared positively that he had seen the bear a long time before, and only rode over him "to scare him up," and said almost in the words of the redoubtable Falstaff, "that if we would do him honor for it, so; if not, we might scare up the next bear ourselves." Looking at the matter calmly and dispassionately afterward, I thought it extremely probable that if another bear didn't scare the Major up, he never would go out of his way to scare up another bear. We felt it to be our duty, however, to caution him against perilling the success of our expedition by such reckless exploits in the way of scaring up wild beasts.

Long before we reached Pooschin it grew dark; but our tired horses freshened up after sunset, with the cool evening air, and about eight o'clock we heard the distant howling of dogs, which we had already come to associate with hot tea, rest, and sleep. In twenty minutes we were lying comfortably on our bear-skins in a Kamtchadal house.

We had made sixty miles since daybreak; but the road had been good. We were becoming more accustomed to horseback riding, and were by no means so tired as we had been at Malqua. Only thirty versts now intervened between us and the head-waters of the Kamtchatka River, where we were to abandon our horses and float down two hundred and fifty miles on rafts or in native canoes.

A sharp trot of four hours over a level plain brought us on the following morning to Sherom, where rafts had already been prepared for our use.

It was with no little regret that I ended for the present my horseback travel. The life suited me in every respect, and I could not recall any previous journey which had ever afforded me more pure, healthy enjoyment, or seemed more like a delightful pleasure excursion than this. All Siberia, however, lay before us; and our regret at leaving scenes which we should never again revisit was relieved by anticipations of future adventures equally novel, and prospective scenery grander even than anything which we had yet witnessed.

CHAPTER X.

To a person of an indolent disposition there is some‧thing particularly pleasant in floating in a boat down a river. One has all the advantages of variety, and change of incident and scenery, without any exertion ; all the lazy pleasures—for such they must be called—of boat-life, without any of the monotony which makes a long sea voyage so unendurable. I think it was Gray who said that his idea of paradise was "To lie on a sofa and read eternally new romances of Marivaux and Crebillon." Could the author of the Elegy have stretched himself out on the open deck of a Kamtchadal boat, covered to a depth of six inches with fragrant flowers and freshly cut hay ; could he have floated slowly down a broad, tranquil river through ranges of snow-clad mountains, past forests glowing with yellow and crimson, and vast steppes waving with tall, wild grass ; could he have watched the full moon rise over the lonely, snowy peak of the Kloo-chef-skoi vol‧cano, bridging the river with a narrow trail of quivering light, and have listened to the flash of the boatman's pad‧dles, and the low melancholy song to which they kept time—he would have thrown Marivaux and Crebillon overboard, and have given a better example of the plea‧sures of paradise.

I know that I am laying myself open to the charge of exaggeration by thus praising Kamtchatkan scenery, and

that my enthusiasm will perhaps elicit a smile of amusement from the more experienced traveller who has seen
Italy and the Alps ; still, I am describing things as they
appeared to me, and do not claim that the impressions
which they made were those which should or would have
been made upon a man of more extensive experience
and wider observation. To use the words of a Spanish
writer, which I have somewhere read, " The man who has
never seen the glory of the sun cannot be blamed for
thinking that there is no glory like that of the moon ; nor
he who has never seen the moon, for talking of the unri-
valled brightness of the morning star." Had I ever sailed
down the Rhine, climbed the Matterhorn, or seen the
moon rise over the Bay of Naples, I should have taken
perhaps a juster and less enthusiastic view of Kamtchatka ;
but, compared with anything which I had previously seen
or imagined, the mountain landscapes of Southern and
Central Kamtchatka were superb.

At Sherom, thanks to the courier who had preceded us,
we found a boat or Kamtchatkan raft ready for our reception. It was composed of three large dug-out canoes
placed parallel to each other at distances of about three
feet, and lashed with seal-skin thongs to stout transverse
poles. Over these was laid a floor or platform about
ten feet by twelve, leaving room at the bow and stern of
each canoe for men with paddles, who were to guide and
propel the unwieldy craft in some unknown, but, doubt-
less, satisfactory manner. On the platform, which was
covered to a depth of six inches with freshly cut grass, we
pitched our little cotton tent, and transformed it with

bear-skins, blankets, and pillows into a very cosey substitute for a state-room. Rifles and revolvers were unstrapped from our tired bodies, and hung up against the tent poles; heavy riding boots were unceremoniously kicked off, and replaced by soft buckskin torbasses; saddles were stowed away in convenient nooks for future use; and all our things disposed with a view to the enjoyment of as much luxury as was compatible with our situation.

After a couple of hours' rest, during which our heavy baggage was transferred to another similar raft, we walked down to the sandy beach, bid "prash-chi-tia" to the crowd which had assembled to see us off, and swung slowly out into the current, the Kamtchadals on the shore waving hats and handkerchiefs until a bend in the river hid them from sight. The scenery of the upper Kamtchatka for the first twenty miles was comparatively tame and uninteresting, as the mountains were entirely concealed by a dense forest of pine, birch, and larch, which extended down to the water's edge. It was sufficient pleasure, however, at first, to lie back in the tent upon our soft bear-skins, watching the brilliantly colored and ever varying foliage of the banks, to sweep swiftly but silently around abrupt bends into long vistas of still water, startling the great Kamtchatkan eagle from his lonely perch on some jutting rock, and frightening up clouds of clamorous waterfowl, which flew in long lines down the river until out of sight. The navigation of the upper Kamtchatka is somewhat intricate and dangerous at night, on account of the rapidity of the current and the frequency of snags; and as soon as it grew dark our

native boatmen considered it unsafe to go on. We accordingly beached our rafts and went ashore to wait for
moonrise.

A little semicircle was cut in the thick underbrush at
the edge of the beach, fires were built, kettles of potatoes
and fish hung over to boil, and we all gathered around the
cheerful blaze to smoke, talk, and sing American songs
until supper-time. The scene to civilized eyes was
strangely wild and picturesque. The dark, lonely river
gurgling mournfully around sunken trees in its channel;
the dense primeval forest whispering softly to the passing
wind its amazement at this invasion of its solitude; the
huge flaming camp-fire throwing a red lurid glare over the
still water, and lighting up weirdly the encircling woods;
and the groups of strangely dressed men lounging carelessly about the blaze upon shaggy bear-skins—all made up
a picture worthy of the pencil of Rembrandt.

After supper we amused ourselves by building an immense bonfire of drift-wood on the beach, and hurling
blazing firebrands at the leaping salmon as they passed
up the river, and the frightened ducks which had been
roused from sleep by the unusual noise and light. When
nothing remained of our bonfire but a heap of glowing
embers, we spread our bear-skins upon the soft, yielding
sand by the water's edge, and lay staring up at the twinkling stars until consciousness faded away into dreams,
and dreams into utter oblivion.

I was waked about midnight by the splashing of rain in
my face and the sobbing of the rising wind in the tree-tops,
and upon crawling out of my water-soaked blankets found

that Dodd and the Major had brought the tent ashore, pitched it among the trees, and availed themselves of its shelter, but had treacherously left me exposed to a pelting rain-storm, as if it were a matter of no consequence whatever whether I slept in a tent or a mud-puddle! After mentally debating the question whether I had better go inside or revenge myself by pulling the tent down over their heads, I finally decided to escape from the rain first and seek revenge at some more propitious time. Hardly had I fallen asleep again when "spat" came the wet canvas across my face, accompanied by a shout to "get up! it was time to start;" and crawling out from under the fallen tent I walked sullenly down to the raft, revolving in my mind various ingenious schemes for getting even with the Major and Dodd, who had first left me out in the rain, and then waked me up in the middle of the night by pulling a wet tent down over my head. It was one o'clock in the morning—dark, rainy, and dismal—but the moon was charitably supposed to have risen, and our Kamtchadal boatman said that it was light enough to start. I didn't believe that it was, but my sleepily expressed opinions had no weight with the Major, and my protests were utterly ignored. Hoping in the bitterness of my heart that we *would* run against a snag, I lay down sullenly in the rain on the wet soaking grass of our raft, and tried to forget my misery in sleep. On account of the contrary wind we could not put up our tent, and were obliged to cover ourselves over as best we could with oil-cloth blankets and shiver away the remainder of the night.

About an hour after daylight we approached the Kam

tchadal settlement of " Milkova," the largest native village
in the peninsula. The rain had ceased, and the clouds
were beginning to break away, but the air was still cold
and raw. A courier, who had been sent down in a canoe
from Sherom on the previous day, had notified the inhabitants of our near approach, and the signal gun which we
fired as we came round the last bend of the river brought
nearly the whole population running helter-skelter to the
beach. Our reception was "a perfect ovation." The
"city fathers," as Dodd styled them, to the number of
twenty, gathered in a body at the landing and began bowing, taking off their hats, and shouting " zdrastuche."
While we were yet fifty yards from the shore, a salute was
fired from a dozen rusty flint-lock muskets, to the imminent
hazard of our lives, and a dozen natives waded into the
water to assist us in getting safely landed. The village
stood a short distance back from the river's bank, and the
natives had provided for our transportation thither two of
the worst-looking horses which I had seen in Kamtchatka.
Their equipments consisted of wooden saddles, modelled
after the gables of an angular house, stirrups about twelve
inches in length, patched up from discarded remnants of
seal-skin thongs, cruppers of bear-skin, and halters of walrus hide twisted around the animals' noses. The excitement which prevailed when we proceeded to mount was
unparalleled I believe in the annals of that quiet settlement. I don't know how the Major succeeded in getting
upon his horse, but I do know that a dozen long-haired
Kamtchadals seized Dodd and me, regardless of our remonstrances, hauled us this way and that until the strug-

gle to get hold of some part of our unfortunate persons resembled the fight over the dead body of Patroclus, and
finally hoisted us triumphantly into our saddles in a breathless and exhausted condition.   One more such hospitable
reception would forever have incapacitated us for the service of the Russo-American Telegraph Company!   I
had only time to cast a hurried glance back at the Major.
He looked like a frightened landsman straddling the end
of a studding-sail boom run out to leeward on a fast clip-
per, and his face was screwed up into an expression of
mingled pain, amusement, and astonishment, which evidently did not begin to do justice to his conflicting emotions.   I had no opportunity of expressing my sympathetic participation in his sufferings; for an excited native
seized the halter of my horse, three more with reverently
bared heads fell in on each side, and I was led away in
triumph to some unknown destination !   The inexpressible
absurdity of our appearance did not strike me with its full
force until I looked behind me just before we reached the
village.   There were the Major, Vushine, and Dodd,
perched upon gaunt Kamtchadal horses, with their knees
and chins on nearly the same level, half a dozen natives
in eccentric costumes straggling along by their sides at a
dog trot, and a large procession of bare-headed men and
boys solemnly bringing up the rear, punching the horses
with sharp sticks into a temporary manifestation of life and
spirit.   It reminded me faintly of a Roman triumph—the
Major, Dodd, and I being the victorious heroes, and the
Kamtchadals the captives, whom we had compelled to go
" sub jugum," and who now graced our triumphal entry

into the Seven-hilled City. I mentioned this fancy of mine
to Dodd, but he declared that one would have had to do
violence to his imagination to make "victorious heroes"
out of us on that occasion, and suggested "heroic victims" as equally poetical and more in accordance with
the facts. His severely practical mind objected to any
such fanciful idealization of our misery. The excitement
increased rather than diminished as we entered the village.
Our motley escort gesticulated, ran to and fro, and shouted out unintelligible orders in the most frantic manner;
heads appeared and disappeared with startling kaleido-
scopic abruptness at the windows of the houses, and three
hundred dogs contributed to the general confusion by
breaking out into an infernal canine peace jubilee which
fairly made the air quiver with sound. At last we stopped
in front of a large one-story log-house, and were assisted
by twelve or fifteen natives to dismount and enter. As
soon as Dodd could collect his confused faculties he demanded, "What in the name of all the Russian saints was
the matter with this settlement; was everybody insane?"
Vushine was ordered to send for the Starosta, or head man
of the village, and in a few moments he made his appearance, bowing with the impressive persistency of a Chinese
mandarin.

A prolonged colloquy then took place in Russian between the Major and the Starosta, broken by explanatory
commentaries in the Kamtchadal language, which did not
tend materially to elucidate the subject. An evident and
increasing disposition to smile gradually softened the stern
lines of the Major's face, until at last he burst forth into a

laugh of such infectious hilarity that, notwithstanding my
ignorance of the nature of the fun, I joined in with hearty
sympathy. As soon as he partially recovered his composure he gasped out, "The natives took you for the Emperor !"—and then he went off in another spasm of merriment which threatened to terminate either in suffocation
or apoplexy. Lost in bewilderment I could only smile
feebly until he recovered sufficiently to give me a more
intelligible explanation of his mirth. It appears that the
courier who had been sent from Petropavlovski to apprise
the natives throughout the peninsula of our coming, had
carried a letter from the Russian Governor giving the
names and occupations of the members of our party, and
that mine had been put down as "Yagor Kennan, Telegraphist and *Operator*." It so happened that the Starosta
of Milkova possessed the rare accomplishment of knowing
how to read Russian writing, and the letter had been handed over to him to be communicated to the inhabitants of
the village. He had puzzled over the unknown word
"telegraphist" until his mind was in a hopeless state of
bewilderment, but had not been able to give even the
wildest conjecture as to its probable meaning. "*Operator*," however, had a more familiar sound; it was not
spelled exactly in the way to which he had been accustomed, but it was evidently intended for "Imperator,"
the Emperor !—and with his heart throbbing with the excitement of this startling discovery, and his hair standing
on end from the arduous nature of his exegetical labors,
he rushed furiously out to spread the news that the Czar
of all the Russias was on a visit to Kamtchatka and would

pass through Milkova in the course of three days! The excitement which this alarming announcement created can better be imagined than described. The all-absorbing topic of conversation was, how could Milkova best show its loyalty and admiration for the Head of the Imperial Family, the Right Arm of the Holy Greek Church, and the Mighty Monarch of seventy millions of devoted souls? Kamtchadal ingenuity gave it up in despair! What could a poor Kamtchatkan village do for the entertainment of its august master? When the first excitement passed away, the Starosta was questioned closely as to the nature of the letter which had brought this news, and was finally compelled to admit that it did not say distinctly, "Alexander Nikolaivitch, *Imperator*," but "Yagor" something "*Operator*," which he contended was substantially the same thing, because if it didn't mean the Emperor himself it meant one of his most intimate relations, who was entitled to equal honor and must be treated with equal reverence. The courier had already gone, and had said nothing about the rank of the travellers whom he heralded, except that they had arrived at Petropavlovski in a ship, wore gorgeous uniforms of blue and gold, and were being entertained by the Governor and the Captain of the port. Public opinion finally settled down into the conviction that "*Op*-erator," etymologically considered, was first cousin to "*Im*-perator," and that it must mean some dignitary of high rank connected with the imperial family. With this impression they had received us when we arrived, and had, poor fellows, done their very best to show us proper honor and respect. It had been a severe ordeal to us, but it had proved in the most unmistakable manner the loyalty of the Kamtchadal inhabitants of Milkova to the reigning family of Russia.

The Major explained to the Starosta our real rank and occupation, but it did not seem to make any difference whatever in the cordial hospitality of our reception. We were treated to the very best which the village afforded, and stared at with a curiosity which showed that travellers through Milkova had hitherto been few and far between. After tasting experimentally various curiously compounded native dishes, and eating some more substantial bread and reindeer meat, we returned in state to the landing-place, accompanied by another procession, received a salute of fifteen guns, and resumed our **voyage down the river.**

CHAPTER XI.

THE valley of this river is unquestionably the most fertile part of the whole Kamtchatkan peninsula. Nearly all of the villages which we passed were surrounded by fields of rye and neatly fenced gardens; the banks everywhere were either covered with timber or waving with wild grass five feet in height; and the luxuriant growth in many places of flowers and weeds testified to the richness of the soil and the warm humidity of the climate. Primroses, cowslips, marsh violets, buttercups, wild roses, cinque-foil iris, and azure larkspur grow everywhere throughout the valley in the greatest abundance; and a peculiar species of umbelliferæ, with hollow-jointed stems, attains in many places a height of six feet, and grows so densely that its huge serrated leaves hide a man from sight at a distance of a few yards. All this is the growth of a single summer.

There are twelve native settlements between the head waters of the river and the Kloochefskoi volcano, and nearly all are situated in picturesque locations, and surrounded by gardens and fields of rye. Nowhere does the traveller see any evidences of the barrenness, sterility, and frigid desolation which have always been associated with the name of Kamtchatka.

After leaving our hospitable native friends and our imperial dignity at Milkova, on Monday morning, we floated slowly down the river for three days, catching distant glimpses of the snowy mountain ranges which bounded the valley, roaming through the woods in search of bears and wild cherries, camping at night on the river-bank among the trees, and living generally a wild, free, delightful life. We passed the native settlements of Keergánic, Márshoora, Schápina, and Tolbatchik, where we were received with boundless hospitality; and on Wednesday, September 13th, camped in the woods south of Kozerefski, only a hundred and twenty versts distant from the village of Kloocháy. It rained nearly all day Wednesday, and we camped at night among the dripping trees, with many apprehensions that the storm would hide the magnificent scenery of the lower Kamtchatka, through which we were about to pass. It cleared away, however, before midnight; and I was awakened at an early hour in the morning by a shouted summons from Dodd to get up and look at the mountains. There was hardly a breath of air astir, and the atmosphere had that peculiar crystalline transparency which may sometimes be seen in California. A heavy hoar-frost lay white on the boats and grass, and a few withered leaves dropped still and wavering through the still cool air from the yellow birch trees which overhung our tent. There was not a sound to break harshly upon the silence of dawn; and only the tracks of wild reindeer and prowling wolves on the smooth sandy beach showed that there was life in the quiet lonely wilderness around us. The sun had not yet risen, but the whole eastern heavens were glaring with yellow light, even up to the morning-star, which, although "paling its ineffectual fires," still maintained its position as a glittering outpost between the contending powers of night and day. Far away to the northeastward, over the yellow forest, in soft purple relief against the red sunrise, stood the high sharp peaks of Kloocháy, grouped around the central wedge-like cone of the magnificent Kloochefskoi volcano. Nearly a month before I had seen these noble mountains from the tossing deck of a little brig, seventy-five miles at sea; but I little thought that I should see them again from a lonely camp in the woods of the Kamtchatka River.

For nearly half an hour Dodd and I sat quietly on the beach, absent-mindedly throwing pebbles into the still water, watching the illumination of the distant mountains by the rising sun, and talking over the adventures which we had experienced since leaving Petropavlovski. With what different impressions had I come to look at Siberian life since I first saw the precipitous coast of Kamtchatka looming up out of the blue water of the Pacific!

Then it was an unknown, mysterious land of glaciers and snowy mountains, filled with possibilities of adventure, but lonely and forbidding in its uninhabited wildness. Now it was no longer lonely or desolate. Every mountain peak was associated with some hospitable village nestled at its feet; every little stream was connected with the great world of human interests by some pleasant recollection of camp life. The possibilities of adventure were still there, but the imaginary loneliness and desolation had vanished with one week's experience. I thought of the vague conceptions which I had formed in America

of this beautiful country, and tried to compare them with
the more recent impressions by which they had been
crowded out, but the effort was vain.   I could not surround myself again with the lost intellectual atmosphere
of civilization, nor reconcile those earlier anticipations
with this strangely different experience.   The absurd
fancies, which had seemed so vivid and so true only three
months before, had now faded away into the half-remem-
bered imagery of a dream, and nothing was real but the
tranquil river which flowed at my feet, the birch tree
which dropped its yellow leaves upon my head, and the
far-away purple mountains.

I was roused from my revery by the furious beating of
a tin mess-kettle, which was the summons to breakfast.
In half an hour breakfast was despatched, the tent struck,
camp equipage packed up, and we were again under
way.   We floated all day down the river toward Kloocháy, getting ever changing views of the mountains as they
were thrown into new and picturesque combinations by
our motion to the northward.   We reached Kozerefski at
dark, and, changing our crew, continued our voyage
throughout the night.   At daybreak on Friday we passed
Kristee, and at two o'clock in the afternoon arrived at
Kloochay, having been just eleven days out from Petropavlovski.

The village of Kloochay is situated in an open plain on
the right bank of the Kamtchatka River, at the very foot
of the magnificent Kloochefskoi volcano, and has nothing
to distinguish it from other Kamtchadal towns, except the
boldness and picturesque beauty of its situation.   It lies

exactly in the midst of the group of superb isolated peaks
which guard the entrance to the river, and is shadowed
over frequently by the dense, black smoke of two volcanoes.   It was founded early in the eighteenth century
by a few Russian peasants who were taken from their
homes in Central Russia, and sent with seeds and farm-
ing utensils to start a colony in far-away Kamtchatka.
After a long adventurous journey of six thousand miles
across Asia by way of Tobolsk, Irkootsk, Yakootsk, and
Kolyma, the little band of involuntary emigrants finally
reached the peninsula, and settled boldly on the Kamtchatka River, under the shadow of the great volcano.
Here they and their descendants have lived for more than
a hundred years, until they have almost forgotten how
they came there and by whom they were sent.   Notwithstanding the activity and frequent eruption of the two volcanoes behind the village, its location never has been
changed, and its inhabitants have come to regard with
indifference the occasional mutterings of warning which
come from the depths of the burning craters, and the
showers of ashes which are frequently sifted over their
houses and fields.   Never having heard of Herculaneum
or Pompeii, they do not associate any possible danger
with the fleecy cloud of smoke which floats in pleasant
weather from the broken summit of Kloochefskoi, or the
low thunderings by which its smaller, but equally dangerous, neighbor asserts its wakefulness during the long
winter nights.   Another century may perhaps elapse
without bringing any serious disaster upon the little village ; but after hearing the Kloochefskoi volcano rumble

at a distance of sixty miles, and seeing the dense volume₎
of black smoke which it occasionally emitted, I felt entirely satisfied to give its volcanic majesty a wide berth,
and wondered at the boldness of the Kamtchadals in
selecting such a site for their settlemeut.

The Kloochefskoi is one of the highest as well as one of
the most uninterruptedly active volcanoes in all the great
volcanic chain of the North Pacific.   Since the seven-
teenth century very few years have elapsed without an
eruption of greater or less violence, and even now, at irregular intervals of a few months, it bursts out into flame
and scatters ashes over the whole width of the peninsula
and on both seas.   The snow in winter is frequently so
covered with ashes for twenty-five miles around Kloochay
that travel upon sledges becomes almost impossible.
Many years ago, according to the accounts of the natives,
there was an eruption of terrible magnificence.   It began
in the middle of a clear, dark winter's night, with loud thunderings and tremblings of the earth, which startled the inhabitants of Kloochay from their sleep and brought them
in affright to their doors.   Far up in the dark winter's sky,
16,000 feet above their heads, blazed a column of lurid
flame from the crater, crowned by a great volume of fire-
lighted smoke.   Amid loud rumblings and dull reverberations from the interior the molten lava began to flow in
broad fiery rivers down the snow-covered mountain side,
until for half the distance to its base it was one glowing
mass of fire which lighted up the villages of Kristee, Kozerefski, and Kloochay like the sun, and illuminated the
whole country within a radius of twenty-five miles.   This

eruption is said to have scattered ashes over the peninsula for three hundred versts to a depth of one and a half inch !

The lava has never yet descended much, if any, below the snow line ; but I see no reason why it may not at some future time overwhelm the settlement of Kloochay and fill the channel of the Kamtchatka River with a fiery flood. The volcano, so far as I know, has never been ascended, and its reported height, 16,500 feet, is probably the approximative estimate of some Russian officer. It is certainly, however, the highest peak of the Kamtchatkan peninsula, and is more likely to exceed 16,000 feet than fall below it. We felt a strong temptation to try and scale its smooth snowy sides and peer over into its smoking crater ; but it would have been folly to make the attempt without two or three weeks' training, and we had not the time to spare. The mountain is nearly a perfect cone, and from the village of Kloochay it is so deceitfully foreshortened that the last 3,000 feet appear to be absolutely perpendicular. There is another volcano whose name, if it have any, I could not ascertain, standing a short distance south-east of the Kloochefskoi, and connected with it by an irregular broken ridge. It does not approach the latter in height, but it seems to draw its fiery supplies from the same source, and is constantly puffing out black coaly smoke, which an east wind drives in great clouds across the white sides of Kloochefskoi until it is sometimes almost hidden from sight.

We were entertained at Kloochay in the large comfortable house of the Starosta, or local magistrate of the vil-

lage. The walls of our room were gayly hung with figured
calico, the ceiling was covered with white cotton drill,
and the rude pine furniture was scoured with soap and
sand to the last attainable degree of cleanliness. A
coarsely executed picture, which I took to be Moses,
hung in a gilt frame in the corner; but the sensible prophet
had apparently shut his eyes to avoid the smoke of the
innumerable votive candles which had been burned in his
honor, and the expression of his face was somewhat marred in consequence. Table-cloths of American manufacture were spread on the tables, pots of flowers stood in
the curtained windows, a little mirror hung against the
wall opposite the door, and all the little fixtures and rude
ornaments of the room were disposed with a taste and a
view to general effect which the masculine mind may admire, but never can imitate. American art, too, had lent
a grace to this cottage in the wilderness, for the back of
one of the doors was embellished with pictorial sketches
of Virginian life and scenery from the skilful pencil of
Porte Crayon. I thought of the well-known lines of
Pope—

> "The things, we know, are neither rich nor rare,
> But wonder how the d—— they came there."

In such comfortable, not to say luxurious quarters as
these, we succeeded, of course, in passing away pleasantly
the remainder of the day.

At Kloochay we were called upon to decide what
route we would adopt in our journey to the northward.
The shortest, and in many respects the best, was that

usually taken by the Russian traders—crossing the central range of mountains to Tigil, by the pass of the
Yolofka, and then following up the west coast of the
peninsula to the head of the Okhotsk Sea. The only
objections to this were the lateness of the season and
the probability of finding deep snow in the mountain
passes. Our only alternative was to continue our journey from Kloochay up the eastern coast to a settlement
called Dranka, where the mountains sank into insignifi-
cant hills, and cross there to the Kamtchadal village of
Lesnoi, on the Okhotsk Sea. This route was considerably longer than the one by the Yolofka Pass, but its
practicability was much more certain.

After a great many prolonged consultations with sundry
natives, who were supposed tc know something about
the country, but who carefully avoided responsibility by
telling as little as possible, the Major concluded to try
the Yolofka Pass, and ordered canoes to be ready on
Saturday morning to carry us up the Yolofka Rver.

At the worst, we could only fail to get over the mountains, and there would be time enough then to return to
Kloochay, and try the other route before the opening of
winter.

As soon as we had decided the momentous question
of our route, we gave ourselves up to the unrestrained
enjoyment of the few pleasures which the small and
sedate village of Kloochay afforded. There was no
afternoon promenade where we could, as the Russians
say, "Show ourselves and see the people;" nor would
an exhibition of our dilapidated and weather-stained gar-

ments on a public promenade have been quite the proper
thing, had it been possible. We must try something else.
The only places of amusement of which we could hear
were the village bath-house and the church; and the
Major and I started out, late in the afternoon, with the
intention of "doing" these points of interest in the most
approved style of modern tourists. For obvious reasons
we took the bath-house first. Taking a steam-bath was
a very mild sort of dissipation; and if it were true that
"cleanliness was next to godliness," the bath-house certainly should precede the church. I had often heard
Dodd speak of the "black baths" of the Kamtchadals;
and without knowing definitely what he meant, I had a
sort of vague impression that these "black baths" were
taken in some inky fluid of Kamtchatkan manufacture, which possessed peculiar detersive properties. I
could think of no other reason than this for calling a
bath "black." Upon entering the "black bath," however, at Kloocháy, I saw my mistake, and acknowledged
at once the appropriateness of the adjective. Leaving
our clothes in a little rude entry, which answered the
purposes without affording any of the conveniences of a
dressing-room, we stooped to a low fur-clad door and
entered the bath-room proper, which was certainly dark
enough and black enough to justify the gloomiest, murki-
est adjective in the language. A tallow candle, which
was burning feebly on the floor, gave just light enough
to distinguish the outlines of a low, bare apartment, about
ten feet square, built solidly of unhewn logs, without a
single opening for the admission of air or light. Every

square inch of the walls and ceiling was perfectly black
with a sooty deposit from the clouds of smoke with which
the room had been filled in the process of heating.   A
large pile of stones, with a hollow place underneath for
a fire, stood in one end of the room, and a series of
broad steps, which did not seem to lead anywhere, occupied the other.   As soon as the fire had gone out the
chimney-hole had been closed and hermetically sealed,
and the pile of hot stones was now radiating a fierce dry
heat, which made *re*spiration a painful duty, and *per*-
spiration an unpleasant necessity.   The presiding spirit
of this dark, infernal place of torture soon made his
appearance in the shape of a long-haired, naked Kamtchadal, and proceeded to throw water upon the pile of
red-hot stones until they hissed like a locomotive, and
the candle burned blue in the centre of a steamy halo.
I thought it was hot before, but it was a Siberian winter
compared with the temperature which this manœuvre
produced.   My very bones seemed melting with fervent
heat.   After getting the air of the room as nearly as possible up to 212°, the native seized me by the arm, spread
me out on the lowest of the flight of steps, poured boiling
suds over my face and feet with reckless impartiality, and
proceeded to knead me up, as if he fully intended to
separate me into my original elements.   I will not attempt to describe the number, the variety, and the diabolical ingenuity of the tortures to which I was subjected
during the next twenty minutes.   I was scrubbed, rolled,
pounded, drenched with cold water and scalded with
hot, beaten with bundles of birch twigs, rubbed down

with wads of hemp which scraped like brick-bats, and finally left to recover my breath upon the highest and hottest step of the whole stairway. A douse of cold water finally put an end to the ordeal and to my misery; and groping my way out into the entry, I proceeded, with chattering teeth, to dress. In a moment I was joined by the Major, and we resumed our walk, feeling like disembodied spirits.

Owing to the lateness of the hour, we were compelled to postpone indefinitely our visit to the church; but we had been sufficiently amused for one day, and returned to the house satisfied, if not delighted, with our experience of Kamtchatkan black baths.

The evening was spent in questioning the inhabitants of the village about the northern part of the peninsula, and the facilities for travel among the wandering Koraks; and before nine o'clock we went to bed, in order that we might make an early start on the following morning.

CHAPTER XII.

THERE was a great variety in the different modes of transportation which we were compelled to adopt in our journey through Kamtchatka; and to this fact was attributable perhaps, in a great degree, the sense of novelty and freshness which during our three months' travel in the peninsula never entirely wore off. We experienced in turn the pleasures and discomforts of whale-boats, horses, rafts, canoes, dog sledges, reindeer sledges, and snow shoes; and no sooner did we begin to tire of the pleasures and ascertain the discomforts of one, than we were introduced to another.

At Kloochay we abandoned our rafts, and took Kamtchadal log canoes, which could be propelled more easily against the rapid current of the Yolofka River, which we had now to ascend. The most noticeable peculiarity of this species of craft, and a remarkable one it is, is a decided and chronic inclination to turn its bottom side upward and its upper side bottomward without the slightest apparent provocation. I was informed by a reliable authority that a boat capsized on the Kamtchatka, just previous to our arrival, through the carelessness of a Kamtchadal in allowing a jack-knife to remain in his right-hand pocket without putting something of a corresponding weight into the other; and that the Kamtchadal fashion of

parting the hair in the middle originated in attempts to
preserve personal equilibrium while navigating these
canoes.   I should have been somewhat inclined to doubt
these remarkable, and not altogether new stories, were it
not for the reliability and unimpeachable veracity of my
informant, Mr. Dodd.   The seriousness of the subject is
a sufficient guarantee that he would not trifle with my
feelings by making it the pretext for a joke.

We indulged ourselves on Saturday morning in a much
later sleep than was consistent with our duty, and it was
almost eight o'clock before we went down to the beach.

Upon first sight of the frail canoes, to which our desti-
nies and the interests of the Russian-American Telegraph
were to be intrusted, there was a very general expression
of surprise and dissatisfaction.   One of our party, with
the rapid à *priori* reasoning for which he was distinguished, came at once to the conclusion that a watery death
would be the inevitable termination of a voyage made in
such vessels, and he evinced a very marked disinclination
to embark.   It is related of a great warrior, whose Commentaries were the detestation of my early life, that
during a very stormy passage of the Ionian Sea he cheer-
ed up his sailors with the sublimely egotistical assurance
that they carried " Cæsar and his fortunes ; " and that,
consequently, nothing disastrous could possibly happen
to them.   The Kamtchatkan Cæsar, however, on this
occasion seemed to distrust his own fortunes, and the attempts at consolation came from the opposite quarter.
His boatman did not tell him, " Cheer up, Cæsar, a Kamtchadal and his fortunes are carrying you," but he *did* as-

sure him that he had navigated the river for several years, and had "never been drowned *once*." What more could Cæsar ask!—After some demur we all took seats upon bear-skins in the bottoms of the canoes, and pushed off.

All other features of natural scenery in the vicinity of Kloochay sink into subordination to the grand central figure of the Kloochefskoi volcano, the monarch of Siberian mountains, whose sharp summit, with its motionless streamer of golden smoke, can be seen anywhere within a radius of a hundred miles. All other neighboring beauties of scenery are merely tributary to this, and are valued only according to their capability of relieving and setting forth this magnificent peak, whose colossal dimensions rise in one unbroken sweep of snow from the grassy valleys of the Kamtchatka and Yolofka, which terminate at its base. "Heir of the sunset and herald of morning," its lofty crater is suffused with a roseate blush long before the morning mists and darkness are out of the valleys, and long after the sun has set behind the purple mountains of Tigil. At all times, under all circumstances, and in all its ever-varying moods, it is the most beautiful mountain I have ever seen. Now it lies bathed in the warm sunshine of an Indian summer's day, with a few fleecy clouds resting at the snow-line and checkering its sides with purple shadows; then it envelops itself in dense volumes of black volcanic smoke, and thunders out a hoarse warning to the villages at its feet; and finally, toward evening, it gathers a mantle of gray mists around its summit, and rolls them in convulsed masses down its sides, until it stands in the clear atmosphere a colossal "pillar of cloud," sixteen thousand feet in height, resting upon fifty square miles of shaggy pine forest.

You think nothing can be more beautiful than the delicate tender color, like that of a wild-rose leaf, which tinges its snows as the sun sinks in a swirl of red vapors in the west; but "visit it by the pale moonlight," when its hood of mist is edged with silver, when black shadows gather in its deep ravines, and white misty lights gleam from its snowy pinnacles—when the host of starry constellations seems to circle around its lofty peak, and the tangled silver chain of the Pleiades to hang upon one of its rocky spires—then say, if you can, that it is more beautiful by daylight.

We entered the Yolofka about noon. This river empties into the Kamtchatka from the north, twelve versts above Kloochay. Its shores are generally low and marshy, and thickly overgrown with rushes and reedy grass, which furnish cover for thousands of ducks, geese, and wild swans. We reached, before night, a native village called Hartchina, and sent at once for a celebrated Russian guide by the name of Nicolai Bragan, whom we hoped to induce to accompany us across the mountains.

From Bragan we learned that there had been a heavy fall of snow on the mountains during the previous week; but he thought that the warm weather of the last three or four days had probably melted most of it away, and that the trail would be at least passable. He was willing at all events to try and take us across. Relieved of a good deal of anxiety, we left Hartchina early on the morning of the 17th, and resumed our ascent of the river. On account of the rapidity of the current in the main stream we turned aside into one of the many "protoks" or arms into which the river was here divided, and poled slowly up for four hours. The channel was very winding and narrow, so that one could touch with a paddle the bank on either side, and in many places the birches and willows met over the stream, dropping yellow leaves upon our heads as we passed underneath. Here and there long scraggy tree-trunks hung over the bank into the water, logs green with moss thrust their ends up from the depths of the stream, and more than once we seemed about to come to a stop in the midst of an impassable swamp. Nicolai Alexandraitch, our guide, whose canoe preceded ours, sang for our entertainment some of the monotonous melancholy songs of the Kamtchadals, and Dodd and I made the woods ring in turn with the enlivening strains of " Kingdom coming" and " Upidee." When we tired of music we made an amicable adjustment of our respective legs in the narrow canoe; and lying back upon our bear-skins slept soundly, undisturbed by the splash of the water and the scraping of poles at our very ears. We camped that night on a high sandy beach over the water, ten or twelve miles south of Yolotka.

It was a warm still evening, and as we all sat on our bear-skins around the camp-fire, smoking and talking over the day's adventures, our attention was suddenly attracted by a low rumbling, like distant thunder, accompanied by occasional explosions. " What's that ? " demanded the Major quickly. " That," said Nicolai soberly, as he emptied his lungs of smoke, " is the Kloochefskoi

volcano talking to the peak of Soovailitch." "Nothing
private in the conversation, I suppose," observed Dodd
dryly; "he shouts it out loud enough." The reverberations
continued for several minutes, but the peak of Soovailitch
made no response. That unfortunate mountain had recklessly expended its volcanic energies in early life, and was
now left without a voice to answer the thundering shouts
of its mighty comrade. There was a time when volcanoes
were as numerous in Kamtchatka as knights around the
table of King Arthur, and the peninsula trembled to the
thunder of their shoutings and midnight jollity; but one
after another they had been suffocated with the fiery
streams of their own eloquence, until at last Kloochefskoi was left alone, calling to its old companions throughout the silent hours of long winter nights, but hearing no
response save the faint far-away echoes of its own mighty
voice.

I was waked early on the following morning by the
jubilant music of "Oh, Su-*sán*-na-a-a, don't ye cry for
me," and crawling out of the tent I surprised one of our
native boatmen in the very act of drumming on a frying-
pan and yelling out joyously,

> "Litenin' struck de telegraf,
> Killed two thousand niggers;
> Shut my eyes to hole my breff,
> Su-*sán*-na-a-a, don't ye cry!"

A comical skin-clad native, in the heart of Kamtchatka,
playing on a frying-pan and singing, "Oh, Susanna," like
an arctic negro minstrel, was too much for my gravity,
and I burst into a fit of laughter, which soon brought out

Dodd. The musician, who had supposed that he was ex-
ercising his vocal organs unheard, stopped suddenly, and
looked sheepishly around, as if conscious that he had been
making himself ridiculous in some way, but did not know
exactly how.

"Why, Andray," said Dodd, " I didn't know you could
sing in English."

" I can't, Bahrin," was the reply; " but I can sing a
little in *American*."

Dodd and I went off in another roar of laughter, which
puzzled poor Andray more and more.

"Where did you learn?" Dodd asked.

" The sailors of a whaling-ship learned it to me when I
was in Petropavlovski, two years ago; isn't it a good
song?" he said, evidently fearing that there might be
something improper in the sentiment.

" It's a capital song," Dodd replied reassuringly; " do
you know any more American words?"

" Oh yes, your honor!" (proudly) " I know 'dam yerize,'
'by 'm bye tomorry,' 'no savey John,' and 'goaty hell,'
but I don't know what they all mean."

It was evident that he didn't! His American education was of limited extent and doubtful utility; but not
even Cardinal Mezzofanti himself could have been more
proud of his forty languages than poor Andray was of
"dam yerize" and "goaty hell." If ever he reached
America, the blessed land which he saw in his happier
dreams, these questionable phrases would be his passports
to the first society.

While we had been talking with Andray, Vushine had

built a fire and prepared breakfast, and just as the sun peered into the valley we sat down on bear-skins around our little candle-box and ate some "selánka," or sour soup, upon which Vushine particularly prided himself, and drank tumbler after tumbler of steaming tea ; "selánka," hard bread and tea, with an occasional duck roasted before the fire on a sharp stick, made up our bill of fare while camping out. Only in the settlements did we enjoy such luxuries as milk, butter, fresh bread, preserved rose-leaves, and fish pies.

Taking our places again in the canoes after breakfast, we poled on up the river, shooting occasionally at flying ducks and swans, and picking as we passed long branches full of wild cherries which drooped low over the water. About noon we left the canoes to go around a long bend in the river, and started on foot with a native guide for Yolofka. The grass in the river bottom and on the plains was much higher than our waists, and walking through it was very fatiguing exercise ; but we succeeded in reaching the village about one o'clock, long before our canoes came in sight.

Yolofka, a small Kamtchadal settlement of half a dozen houses, is situated among the foot-hills of the great central Kamtchatkan range, immediately below the pass which bears its name, and on the direct route to Tigil and the west coast. It is the head of canoe navigation on the Yolofka river, and the starting-point for parties intending to cross the mountains. Anticipating difficulty in getting horses enough for our use at this small village, the Major had sent eight or ten overland from Kloocháy, and we found them there awaiting our arrival.

Nearly the whole afternoon was spent in packing the horses and getting ready for a start, and we camped for the night beside a cold mountain spring only a few versts away from the village.   The weather, hitherto, had been clear and warm, but it clouded up during the night, and we began the ascent of the mountains Tuesday morning, the 19th, in a cold, driving rain-storm from the north-west. The road, if a wretched footpath ten inches wide can be said in any metaphorical sense to *be* a road, was simply execrable.   It followed the track of a swollen mountain torrent, which had its rise in the melting snows of the summit, and tumbled in roaring cascades down a narrow, dark, precipitous ravine.   The path ran along the edge of this stream, first on one side, then on the other, and then in the water, around enormous masses of volcanic rock, over steep lava slopes, where the water ran like a mill-race through dense entangling thickets of trailing pine, into ragged heaps of fallen tree-trunks, and along narrow ledges of rock where it would be thought that a mountain sheep could hardly pass.   I would guarantee, with twenty men, to hold that ravine against the combined armies of Europe !   Our pack-horses rolled down steep banks into the stream, tore their loads off against tree trunks, stumbled, cut their legs and fell over broken volcanic rocks, took flying leaps across narrow chasms of roaring water, and performed feats which would have been utterly beyond the strength and endurance of any but Kamtchatkan horses.   Finally, in attempting to leap a distance of eight or ten feet across the torrent, I was thrown violently from the saddle, and my left foot caught firmly, just above the

instep, in the small iron stirrup. The horse scrambled up
the other side and started at a frightened gallop up the
ravine, dragging my body over the ground by one leg. I
remember making a desperate effort to protect my head,
by raising myself upon my elbows, but the horse kicked
me suddenly in the side, and I knew nothing more until I
found myself lying upon the ground with my foot still entangled in the broken stirrup, while the horse galloped
away up the ravine. The giving way of a single strap
had saved my skull from being crushed like an eggshell
against the jagged rocks. I was badly bruised and very
faint and dizzy, but no bones seemed to be broken, and I
got up without assistance. Thus far the Major had kept
his quick temper under strong control; but this was too
much, and he hurled the most furious invectives at poor
Nicolai for leading us over the mountains by such a horrible pass, and threatened him with the direst punishment
when we should reach Tigil. It was of no use for Nicolai to urge in self-defence that there *was* no other pass;
it was his business to *find* another, and not peril men's
lives by leading them into a God-forsaken ravine like this,
choked up with land slides, fallen trees, water, lava, and
masses of volcanic rock! If anything happened to any
member of our party in this cursed gorge, the Major
swore he would shoot Nicolai on the spot! Pale and
trembling with fright, the poor guide caught my horse,
mended my stirrup strap, and started on ahead to show
that he was not afraid to go where he asked us to follow.

I believe we must have jumped our horses across that
mountain torrent fifty times in an ascent of 2,000 feet, tc

avoid the rocks and land slides which appeared first on one side and then on the other. One of our pack-horses had given out entirely, and several others were nearly disabled, when, late in the afternoon, we finally reached the summit of the mountains, 4,000 feet above the sea. Before us, half hidden by gray storm-clouds and driving mist, lay a great expanse of level table-land, covered to a depth of eighteen inches with a soft dense cushion of Arctic moss, and holding water like an enormous sponge. Not a tree nor a landmark of any kind could be seen— nothing but moss and flying scud. A cold piercing wind from the north swept chilly storm-clouds across the desolate mountain top, and drove tiny particles of half-frozen rain into our faces with blinding, stinging force. Drenched to the skin by eight or nine hours' exposure to the storm, tired and weak from long climbing, with boots full of icy water, and hands numb and stiff from cold, we stopped for a moment to rest our horses and decide upon our course. Brandy was dealt out freely to all our men in the cover of a tin pail, but its stimulating influence was so counteracted by cold that it was hardly perceptible. The poor Starosta of Yolofka, with dripping clothes, blue lips, chattering teeth, and black hair plastered over his white cheeks, seemed upon the point of giving out. He caught eagerly at the pail cover full of brandy which the Major handed to him, but every limb was shaking spasmodically, and he spilled most of it in getting it to his mouth.

Fearing that darkness would overtake us before we could reach shelter, we started on toward a deserted, half-ruined " yourt," which Nicolai said stood near the west-

ern edge of this elevated plateau, about eight versts distant.   Our horses sank at every step to the knee in the
soft, spongy cushion of wet moss, so that we could travel
no faster than a slow walk, and the short distance of
eight versts seemed to be interminable.   After four more
dreary hours, spent in wandering about through gray
drifting clouds, exposed to a bitter north-west wind, and a
temperature of just 32°, we finally arrived in a half-
frozen condition at the yourt.   It was a low, empty hut,
nearly square in shape, built of variously sized logs, and
banked over with two or three feet of moss and grass-
grown earth, so as to resemble an outdoor cellar.   Half
of one side had been torn down by storm-besieged travellers for firewood ; its earthen floor was dank and wet with
slimy tricklings from its leaky roof; the wind and rain
drove with a mournful howl down through its chimney-
hole ; its door was gone, and it presented altogether a dismal picture of neglected dilapidation.   Nothing daunted,
Vushine tore down another section of the ruined side to
make a fire, hung over tea-kettles, and brought our provision boxes under such shelter as the miserable hut
afforded.   I never could ascertain where Vushine obtained the water that night for our tea, as there was no
available stream within ten miles, and the drippings of
the roof were thick and discolored with mud.   I have
more than a suspicion, however, that he squeezed it out
of bunches of moss which he tore up from the soaking
" toondra."   Dodd and I took off our boots, poured
about a pint of muddy water out of each, dried our feet,
and as the steam rose in clouds from our wet clothes,
began to feel quite comfortable.

Vushine was in high good humor. He had voluntarily assumed the whole charge of our drivers during the day, had distinguished himself by the most unwearied efforts in raising fallen horses, getting them over breakneck places, and cheering up the disconsolate Kamtchadals, and he now wrung the water out of his shirt, and squeezed his wet hair absent-mindedly into a kettle of soup, with a countenance of such beaming serenity and a laugh of such hearty good-nature that it was of no use for anybody to pretend to be cross, tired, cold, or hungry. With that sunny face irradiating the smoky atmosphere of the ruined "yourt," and that laugh ringing joyously in our ears, we made fun of our misery and persuaded ourselves that we were having a good time. After a scanty supper of "selánka," dried fish, hard bread, and tea, we stretched our tired bodies out in the shallowest puddles we could find, covered ourselves over with blankets, overcoats, oil-cloths, and bear-skins, and succeeded, in spite of our wet clothes and wetter beds, in getting to sleep.

CHAPTER XIII.

I AWOKE about midnight with cold feet and shivering limbs. The fire on the wet muddy ground had died away to a few smouldering embers, which threw a red glow over the black, smoky logs, and sent occasional gleams of flickering light into the dark recesses of the yourt. The wind howled mournfully around the hut, and the rain beat with intermittent dashes against the logs and trickled through a hundred crevices upon my already water-soaked blankets. I raised myself upon one elbow and looked around. The hut was deserted, and I was alone. For a moment of half-awakened consciousness I could not imagine where I was, or how I came in such a strange, gloomy situation; but presently the recollection of the previous day's ride came back, and I went to the door to see what had become of all our party. I found that the Major and Dodd, with all the Kamtchadals, had pitched tents upon the spongy moss outside, and were spending the night there, instead of remaining in the "yourt" and having their clothes and blankets spoiled by the muddy droppings of its leaky roof. The tents were questionable improvements; but I agreed with them in preferring clean water to mud, and gathering up my bedding I crawled in by the side of Dodd. The wind blew the tent down once during the night, and left us exposed for a few moments to the storm ; but it was repitched in defiance of the wind, ballasted with logs torn from the sides of the "yourt," and we managed to sleep after a fashion until morning.

We were a melancholy-looking party when we emerged from the tent at daylight. Dodd looked ruefully at his wet blankets, made a comical grimace as he felt of his water-soaked clothes, and then declared that

> " The weather was not what he knew it once—
> The nights were terribly damp;
> And he never was free from the rheumatiz'
> Except when he had the cramp ! "

In which poetical lament we all heartily sympathized if we did not join.

Our wet, low-spirited horses were saddled at daylight; and as the storm showed signs of a disposition to break away, we started again, immediately after breakfast, for the western edge of the high table-land which here formed the summit of the mountain range. The scenery from this point in clear weather must be magnificent, as it overlooks the Tigil valley and the Okhotsk Sea on one side, and the Pacific Ocean, the valleys of the Yolofka and the Kamtchatka, and the grand peaks of Soovailitch and Kloochefskoi on the other. We caught occasional glimpses, through openings in the mist, of the Yolofka River, thousands of feet below, and the smoke-plumed head of the distant volcano, floating in a great sea of bluish clouds ; but a new detachment of straggling vapors from the Okhotsk Sea came drifting across the mountain top, and, breaking furiously in our faces, blotted out everything except the mossy ground, over which plodded our tired, dispirited horses.

It did not seem possible that human beings could live, or would care to live, on this desolate plain of moss, 4,000 feet above the sea, enveloped half the time in drifting clouds, and swept by frequent storms of rain and snow. But even here the wandering Koraks herd their hardy reindeer, set up their smoky tent-poles, and bid contemptuous defiance to the elements. Three or four times during the day we passed heaps of reindeer's antlers, and piles of ashes surrounded by large circles of evergreen twigs, which marked the sites of Korak tents; but the band of wild nomades which had left these traces had long before disappeared, and was now perhaps herding its deer on the wind-swept shores of the Arctic Ocean.

Owing to the dense mist by which we were constantly surrounded, we could get no clear ideas as to the formation of the mountain range over which we were passing, or the extent and nature of this great plain of moss which lay so high up among extinct volcanic peaks. I only know that just before noon we left the "toondra," as this kind of moss steppe is called, and descended gradually into a region of the wildest, rockiest character, where all vegetation disappeared except a few stunted patches of trailing pine. For at least ten miles the ground was covered everywhere with loose slab-shaped masses of igneous rock, varying in size from five cubic feet to five hundred, and lying one upon another in the greatest disorder. The heavens at some unknown geological period seemed to have showered down huge volcanic paving-stones, until the earth was covered fifty feet deep with their broken fragments. Nearly all of these masses had two smooth flat sides, and resembled irregular slices of some black Plutonian pudding hardened into stone. I was not familiar enough with volcanic phenomena to be able to decide in what manner or by what agency the earth had been thus overwhelmed with loose rocky slabs; but it looked precisely as if great sheets of solidified lava had fallen successively from the sky, and had been shattered, as they struck the earth, into millions of angular slabs. I thought of Scott's description of the place where Bruce and the Lord of the Isles landed after leaving the Castle of Lorn, as the only one I had ever read which gave me an idea of such a scene.

We drank tea at noon on the west side of this rocky wilderness, and before night reached a spot where bushes, grass, and berries again made their appearance. We camped in a storm of wind and rain, and at daybreak on the 21st continued our descent of the western slope of the mountains. Early in the forenoon we were inspirited by the sight of fresh men and horses which had been sent out to meet us from a native village called "Sedónka," and exchanging our tired, lame, and disheartened animals for these fresh recruits, we pushed rapidly on. The weather soon cleared up warm and bright, the trail wound around among the rolling foot hills through groves of yellow birch and scarlet mountain ash, and as the sun gradually dried our water-soaked clothes, and brought a pleasant glow of returning circulation to our chilled limbs, we forgot the rain and dreary desolation of the mountain top and recovered our usual buoyancy of spirit.

I have once before, I believe, given the history of a bear hunt in which our party participated while crossing the Kamtchatka "toondra;" but as that was a mere skirmish, which did not reflect any great credit upon the individuals concerned, I am tempted to relate one more bear adventure which befell us among the foot hills of the Tigil mountains. It shall be positively the last.

Ye who listen with credulity to the stories of hunters, and pursue with eagerness the traces of bears; who expect that courage will rise with the emergency, and that the deficiencies of bravery will be supplied by the tightness of the fix, attend to the history of Rasselas, an inexperienced bear-slayer. About noon, as we were making our way along the edge of a narrow grassy valley, bordered by a dense forest of birch, larch, and pine, one of our drivers suddenly raised the cry of "medvaid," and pointed eagerly down the valley to a large black bear rambling carelessly through the long grass in search of blueberries, and approaching gradually nearer and nearer to our side of the ravine. He evidently had not yet seen us, and a party to attack him was soon made up of two Kamtchadals, the Major, and myself, all armed to the teeth with rifles, axes, revolvers, and knives. Creeping cautiously around through the timber, we succeeded in gaining unobserved a favorable position at the edge of the woods directly in front of his Bruinic majesty, and calmly awaited his approach. Intent upon making a meal of blueberries, and entirely unconscious of his impending fate, he waddled slowly and awkwardly up to within fifty yards. The Kamtchadals kneeled down, threw forward their long heavy rifles, fixed their sharp-pronged rests firmly in the ground, crossed themselves devoutly three times, drew a long breath, took a deadly and deliberate aim, shut their eyes, and fired. The silence was broken by a long fizzle, during which the Kamtchadals conscientiously kept their eyes shut, and finally a terrific bang announced the catastrophe, followed immediately by two more sharp reports from the rifles of the Major and myself. As the smoke cleared away I looked eagerly to see the brute kicking around in the agonies of death; but what was my amazement to find that instead of kicking around in the agonies of death, as a beast with any sense of propriety *would* after such a fusillade, the perverse animal was making directly for us at a gallop! Here was a variation introduced that was not down in the programme! We had made no calculations upon a counter-attack, and the ferocity of his appearance, as he came tearing through the bushes, left no room for doubt as to the seriousness of his intentions. I tried to think of some historic precedent which would justify me in climbing a tree; but my mind was in a state of such agitation that I could not avail myself of my extensive historical knowledge. "A man may know the seven portions of the Koran by heart, but when a bear gets after him he will not be able to remember his alphabet!" What we should have done in the last extremity will never probably be known. A shot from the Major's revolver seemed to alter the bear's original plan of operations, and, swerving suddenly to one side, he crashed through the bushes ten feet from the muzzles of our empty rifles, and disappeared in the forest. A careful examination of the leaves and grass failed to reveal any signs of blood, and we were reluctantly forced to the con- clusion that he escaped unscathed.

Hunting a bear with a Russian rifle is a very pleasant and entirely harmless diversion. The animal has plenty of time, after the gun begins to fizzle, to eat a hearty dinner of blueberries, run fifteen miles across a range of mountains into a neighboring province, and get comfort- ably asleep in his hole before the deadly explosion takes place !

It would have been unsafe for any one to suggest "bear- steaks" to the Major or me at any time during the suc- ceeding week.

We camped for the night under the huge spreading branches of a gnarled birch-tree, a few versts from the scene of our exploit, and early Friday morning were off for "Sedónka." When about fifteen versts from the village Dodd suggested a gallop, to try the mettle of our horses and warm our blood. As we were both well mounted, I challenged him to a steeple-chase as far as the settlement. Of all the reckless break-neck riding that we ever did in Kamtchatka, this was the worst. The horses soon became as excited as their riders, and tore through the bushes and leaped over ravines, logs, rocks, and swamps with a perfect frenzy. Once I was dragged from my saddle by the catching of my rifle against a limb, and several times we both narrowly escaped knocking our brains out against trees. As we approached the town we saw three or four Kamtchadals cutting wood a short distance ahead. Dodd gave a terrifying shout like a Sioux war-whoop, put spurs to his horse, and we came upon them like a thunderbolt. At the sight of two swarthy strangers in blue hunting-shirts, top-boots, and red caps, with pistols belted around their waists, and knives dangling at their girdles, charging down upon them like Mamelukes at the battle of the Pyramids, the poor Kamtchadals flung away their axes and fled for their lives to the woods. Except when I was dragged off my horse, we never once drew rein until our animals stood panting and foaming in the village. If you wish to draw a flash of excitement from Dodd's eyes, ask him if he remembers the steeple-chase to "Sedónka."

That night we floated down the Tigil River to Tigil, where we arrived just at dark, having accomplished in sixteen days a journey of eleven hundred and thirty versts.

My recollections of Tigil are somewhat vague and indefinite. I remember that I was impressed with the inordinate quantities of champagne, cherry cordial, white rum, and "vodka" which its Russian inhabitants were capable of drinking, and that Tigil was a somewhat less ugly village than the generality of Kamtchatkan towns, but nothing more. Next to Petropavlovski, however, it is the most important settlement in the peninsula, and is the trading centre of the whole west coast. A Russian supply steamer and an American trading vessel touch at the mouth of the Tigil river every summer, and leave large quantities of rye flour, tea, sugar, cloth, copper kettles, tobacco, and strong Russian "vodka," for distribution through the peninsula. The Brágans, Vorrebeóffs, and two or three other trading firms make it headquarters, and it is the winter rendezvous of many of the northern tribes of Chookchees and Koraks. As we should pass no other trading post until we reached the settlement of Gee-zhe-gá, at the head of the Okhotsk Sea, we determined to remain a few days at Tigil to rest and refit.

We were now about to enter upon what we feared would prove the most difficult part of our journey—both on account of the nature of the country and the lateness of the season. Only seven more Kamtchadal towns lay between us and the steppes of the wandering Koraks, and we had not yet been able to think of any plan of crossing these inhospitable wastes before the winter's snows should make them passable on reindeer sledges. It is difficult for one who has had no experience of northern life to get from a mere verbal description a clear idea of a Siberian moss steppe, or to appreciate fully the nature and extent of the obstacles which it presents to summer travel. It is by no means easy to cross, even in winter, when it is frozen and covered with snow; but in summer it becomes practically impassable. For three or four hundred square miles the eternally frozen ground is covered to a depth of two feet with a dense luxurious growth of soft, spongy Arctic moss, saturated with water, and sprinkled here and there with little hillocks of stunted blueberry bushes and clusters of Labrador tea. It never dries up, never becomes hard enough to afford stable footing. From June to September it is a great, soft, quaking cushion of wet moss. The foot may sink in it to the knee, but as soon as the pressure is removed it rises again with spongy elasticity, and no trace is left of the step. Walking over it is precisely like walking over an enormous wet sponge. The causes which produce this extraordinary, and apparently abnormal, growth of moss are those which exercise the most powerful influence over the development of vegetation everywhere,—viz., heat, light, and moisture,—and these agencies, in a northern climate, are so combined and intensified during the summer months as to stimulate some kinds of vegetation into almost tropical luxuriance. The earth thaws out in spring to an average depth of perhaps two feet, and below that point there is a thick, impenetrable layer of solid frost. The water produced by the melting of the winter's snows is prevented by this stratum of frozen ground from sinking any farther into the earth, and has no escape except by slow evaporation. It therefore saturates the cushion of moss on the surface, and, aided by the almost perpetual sunlight of June and July, excites it to a rapid and wonderfully luxuriant growth.

It will readily be seen that travel in summer, over a great steppe covered with soft elastic moss, and soaking with water, is a very difficult if not absolutely impracticable undertaking. A horse sinks to his knees in the spongy surface at every step, and soon becomes exhausted by the severe exertion which such walking necessitates. We had had an example of such travel upon the summit of the Yolofka pass, and it was not strange that we should look forward with considerable anxiety to crossing the great moss steppes of the Koraks in the northern part of the peninsula. It would have been wiser, perhaps, for us to have waited patiently at Tigil until the establishment of winter travel upon dog sledges; but the Major feared that the chief engineer of the enterprise might have landed a party of men in the dangerous region around Behring's Straits, and he was anxious to get where he could find out something about it as soon as possible. He determined, therefore, to push on at all hazards to the frontier of the Korak steppes, and then cross them on horses, if possible.

A whale-boat was purchased at Tigil, and forwarded with a native crew to Lesnoi, so that in case we failed to get over the Korak steppes we might cross the head of the Okhotsk Sea to Gee-zhe-gá by water before the setting in of winter. Provisions, trading goods, and fur clothes of all sorts were purchased and packed away in skin boxes, and every preparation made which our previous experience could suggest for rough life and bad weather.

CHAPTER XIV.

On Wednesday, September 27th, we again took the field, with two Cossacks, a Korak interpreter, eight or ten men, and fourteen horses. A little snow fell on the day previous to our departure, but it did not materially affect the road, and only served as a warning to us that winter was at hand, and we could not expect much more pleasant weather. We made our way as rapidly as possible along the coast of the Okhotsk Sea, partly on the beach under the cliffs, and partly over low wooded hills and valleys, extending down to the coast from the central mountain range. We passed the settlements of "Aminyana," "Wyumpelka," "Hucktaná," and "Polán," changing horses and men at every village, and finally, on the 3d of October, reached Lesnoi—the last Kamtchadal settlement in the peninsula. Lesnoi was situated, as nearly as we could ascertain, in lat. 59°20′, long. 160°25′, about a hundred and fifty versts south of the Korak steppes, and nearly two hundred miles in an air line from the settlement of Geezhe-gá, which for the present was our objective point.

We had hitherto experienced little difficulty in making our way through the peninsula, as we had been especially favored by weather, and there had been few natural obstacles to stop or delay our progress. Now, however, we

were about to enter a wilderness which was entirely uninhabited, and little known even to our Kamtchadal guides.
North of Lesnoi the great central range of the Kamtchatka mountains broke off abruptly into the Okhotsk
Sea, in a long line of tremendous precipices, and inter-
posed a great rugged wall between us and the steppes of
the wandering Koraks. This mountain range was very
difficult to pass with horses, even in midsummer, and was
of course infinitely worse now, when the mountain
streams were swollen by the fall rains into foaming torrents, and the storms which herald the approach of winter might be at any moment expected. The Kamtchadals
at Lesnoi declared positively that it was of no use to attempt to cross this range until the rivers should freeze
over and snow enough fall to permit the use of dog
sledges, and that they were not willing to risk fifteen or
twenty horses, to say nothing of their own lives, in any
such adventure. The Major told them, in language more
expressive than polite, that he didn't believe a word of
any such yarn ; that the mountains had to be crossed, and
that go they must and should. They had evidently never
had to deal before with any such determined, self-willed
individual as the Major proved to be, and after some consultation among themselves, they agreed to make the
attempt with eight unloaded horses, leaving all our baggage and heavy camp equipage at Lesnoi. This the
Major at first would not listen to ; but after thinking the
situation over he decided to divide our small force into two
parties—one to go around the mountains by water with
the whale-boat and heavy baggage, and one over the n

with twenty unloaded horses. The road over the mountains was supposed to lie near the sea-coast, so that the land party would be most of the time within signalling distance of the whale-boat, and in case either party met with any accident or found its progress stopped by unforeseen obstacles the other could come to its assistance. Near the middle of the mountainous tract, just west of the principal ridge, there was said to be a small river called the " Samanka," and the mouth of this river was agreed upon as a rendezvous for the two parties in case they lost sight of each other during storms or foggy weather. The Major decided to go with Dodd in the whale-boat, and gave me command of the land party, consisting of our best Cossack, Vushine, six Kamtchadals, and twenty light horses. Flags were made, a code of signals agreed upon, the heavy baggage transferred to the whale-boat and a large seal-skin canoe, and early on the morning of October 4th, I bade the Major and Dodd good-by at the beach, and they pushed off. We started up our train of horses as the boats disappeared around a projecting bluff, and cantered away briskly across the valley toward a gap in the mountains, through which we entered the "wilderness." The road for the first ten or fifteen versts was very good; but I was surprised to find that, instead of leading us along the sea-shore, it went directly back into the mountains away from the sea, and I began to fear that our arrangements for co-operation would be of little avail. Thinking that the whale-boat would not probably get far the first day under oars and without wind, we encamped early in a narrow valley between two parallel

ranges of mountains. I tried, by climbing a low mountain back of our tent, to get a sight of the sea; but we
were at least fifteen versts from the coast, and the view
was limited by an intervening range of rugged peaks,
many of which reach the altitude of perpetual snow. It
was rather lonely to camp that night without seeing
Dodd's cheerful face by the fireside, and I missed more
than I thought I should the lively sallies, comical stories,
and good-humored pleasantry which had hitherto brightened the long weary hours of camp life. If Dodd could
have read my thoughts that evening, as I sat in solitary
majesty by the fireside, he would have been satisfied that
his society was not unappreciated, nor his absence unfelt.
Vushine took especial pains with the preparation of my
supper, and did the best he could, poor fellow, to enliven
the solitary meal with stories and funny reminiscences of
Kamtchatkan travel; but the simple venison cutlets had
lost somehow their usual savor, and the Russian jokes
and stories I could not understand. After supper I lay
down upon my bear-skins in the tent, and fell asleep
watching the round moon rise over a ragged volcanic
peak east of the valley.

On the second day we travelled through a narrow
tortuous valley among the mountains, over spongy swamps
of moss, and across deep narrow creeks, until we reached
a ruined subterranean hut nearly half way from Lesnoi to
the Samanka River. Here we ate a lunch of dried fish
and hard bread, and started again up the valley in a heavy
rain-storm, surrounded on all sides by rocks, snow-capped
mountains, and extinct volcanic peaks. The road momen-

tarily grew worse. The valley narrowed gradually to a
wild rocky cañon, a hundred and fifty feet in depth, at
the bottom of which ran a swollen mountain torrent,
foaming around sharp black rocks, and falling over ledges
of lava in magnificent cascades. Along the black precipitous sides of this "Devil's Pass" there did not seem
to be footing for a chamois; but our guide said that he
had been through it many times before, and dismounting
from his horse he cautiously led the way along a narrow
rocky ledge in the face of the cliff which I had not before
noticed. Over this we carefully made our way, now
descending nearly to the water's edge, and then rising again
until the roaring stream was fifty feet below, and we could
drop stones from our outstretched arms directly into the
boiling, foaming waters. Presuming too much upon the
sagacity of a sure-footed horse, I carelessly attempted the
passage of the ravine without dismounting, and came near
paying the penalty of my rashness by a violent death.
About half way through, where the trail was only eight or
ten feet above the bed of the torrent, the ledge, or a portion of it, gave way under my horse's feet, and we went
down together in a struggling mass upon the rocks in the
channel of the stream. I had taken the precaution to
disengage my feet from the treacherous iron stirrups, and
as we fell I threw myself toward the face of the cliff so as
to avoid being crushed by my horse. The fall was not
a very long one, and I came down uppermost, but narrowly escaped having my head broken by my animal's hoofs
as he struggled to regain his feet. He was somewhat cut
and bruised, but not seriously hurt, and tightening the

saddle-girth I waded along through the water, leading him after me until I was able to regain the path. Then climbing into the saddle again, with dripping clothes and somewhat shaken nerves, I rode on.

Just before dark we reached a point where further progress in that direction seemed to be absolutely cut off by a range of high mountains which ran directly across the valley. It was the central ridge of the Samanka mountains. I looked around with a glance of inquiring surprise at the guide, who pointed directly over the range, and said that there lay our road. A forest of birch extended about half way up the mountain side, and was succeeded by low evergreen bushes, trailing pine, and finally by bare black rocks rising high over all, where not even the hardy reindeer moss could find soil enough to bury its roots. I no longer wondered at the positive declaration of the Kamtchadals, that with loaded horses it would be impossible to cross, and began even to doubt whether it could be done with light horses. It looked very dubious to me, accustomed as I was to rough climbing and mountain roads. I decided to camp at once where we were, and obtain as much rest as possible, so that we and our horses would be fresh for the hard day's work which evidently lay before us. Night closed in early and gloomily, the rain still falling in torrents, so that we had no opportunity of drying our wet clothes. I longed for a drink of brandy to warm my chilled blood, but my pocket flask had been forgotten in the hurry of our departure from Lesnoi, and I was obliged to content myself with the milder stimulus of hot tea. My bedding having been wrapped up in an oil-cloth blanket, was fortunately dry, and crawling feet first, wet as I was, into my bear-skin bag, and covering up warmly with heavy blankets, I slept in comparative comfort.

Vushine waked me early in the morning with the announcement that it was snowing. I rose hastily and putting aside the canvas of the tent looked out. That which I most dreaded had happened. A driving snow-storm was sweeping down the valley, and Nature had assumed suddenly the stern aspect and white pitiless garb of winter. Snow had already fallen to a depth of three inches in the valley, and on the mountains, of course, it would be deep, soft, and drifted. I hesitated for a moment about attempting to cross the rugged range in such weather; but my orders were imperative to go on at least to the Samanka River, and a failure to do so might defeat the object of the whole expedition. Previous experience convinced me that the Major would not let a storm interfere with the execution of his plans; and if he should succeed in reaching the Samanka River and I should not, I would never recover from the mortification of the failure, nor be able to convince him that Anglo-Saxon blood was as good as Slavonic. I reluctantly gave the order therefore to break camp, and as soon as the horses could be collected and saddled we started for the base of the mountain range. Hardly had we ascended two hundred feet out of the shelter of the valley before we were met by a hurricane of wind from the northeast, which swept blinding, suffocating clouds of snow down the slope into our faces until earth and sky seemed

mingled and lost in a great white whirling mist. The
ascent soon became so steep and rocky that we could
no longer ride our horses up it. We therefore dismounted, and wading laboriously through deep soft drifts,
and climbing painfully over sharp jagged rocks, which cut
open our seal-skin boots, we dragged our horses slowly
upward. We had ascended wearily in this way perhaps a
thousand feet, when I became so exhausted that I was compelled to lie down. The snow in many places was drifted
as high as my waist, and my horse refused to take a step
until he was absolutely dragged to it. After a rest of a
few moments we pushed on, and after another hour of hard
work we succeeded in gaining what seemed to be the
crest of the mountain, perhaps 2,000 feet above the sea.
Here the fury of the wind was almost irresistible. Dense
clouds of driving snow hid everything from sight at a distance of a few steps, and we seemed to be standing on a
fragment of a wrecked world enveloped in a whirling
tempest of stinging snow-flakes. Now and then a black
volcanic crag, inaccessible as the peak of the Matterhorn,
would loom out in the white mist far above our heads, as
if suspended in mid-air, giving a startling momentary
wildness to the scene; then it would disappear again in
flying snow, and leave us staring blindly into vacancy.
A long fringe of icicles hung round the visor of my cap,
and my clothes, drenched with the heavy rain of the previous day, froze into a stiff crackling armor of ice upon my
body. Blinded by the snow, with benumbed limbs and
clattering teeth, I mounted my horse and let him go where
he would, only entreating the guide to hurry and get

down somewhere off from this exposed position. He tried in vain to compel his horse to face the storm. Neither shouts nor blows could compel him to turn round, and he was obliged finally to ride along the crest of the mountain to the eastward. We went down into a comparatively sheltered valley, up again upon another ridge higher than the first, around the side of a conical peak where the wind blew with great force, down into another deep ravine and up still another ridge, until I lost entirely the direction of our route and the points of the compass, and had not the slightest idea where we were going. I only knew that we were half frozen and in a perfect wilderness of mountains.

I had noticed several times within half an hour that our guide was holding frequent and anxious consultations with the other Kamtchadals about our road, and that he seemed to be confused and in doubt as to the direction in which we ought to go. He now came to me with a gloomy face, and confessed that we were lost. I could not blame the poor fellow for losing the road in such a storm, but I told him to go on in what he believed to be the direction of the Samanka River, and if we succeeded in finding somewhere a sheltered valley we would camp and wait for better weather. I wished to caution him also against riding accidentally over the edges of precipices in the blinding snow, but I could not speak Russian enough to make myself understood.

We wandered on aimlessly for two hours, over ridges, up peaks, and down into shallow valleys, getting deeper and deeper apparently into the heart of the mountains but finding no shelter from the storm. It became evident that something must be done, or we should all freeze to death. I finally called the guide, told him I would take the lead myself, and, opening my little pocket compass, showed him the direction of the sea-coast. In that direction I determined to go until we should come out somewhere. He looked in stupid wonder for a moment at the little brass box with its trembling needle, and then cried out despairingly, "Oh, Bahrin!" "How does the come-*páss* know anything about these *proclatye* mountains? the come-*páss* never has been over this road before. I've travelled here all my life, and, God forgive me, I don't know where the sea is!" Hungry, anxious, and half-frozen as I was, I could not help smiling at our guide's idea of an inexperienced compass which had never travelled in Kamtchatka, and could not therefore know anything about the road. I assured him confidently that the "come-*páss*" was "shipka masteer," or a great expert at finding the sea in a storm; but he shook his head mournfully, as if he had little faith in its abilities, and refused to go in the direction which I indicated. Finding it impossible to make my horse face the wind, I dismounted, and, compass in hand, led him away in the direction of the sea, followed by Vushine, who, with an enormous bear-skin wrapped around his head, looked like some wild animal. The guide, seeing that we were determined to trust in the compass, finally concluded to go with us. Our progress was necessarily very slow, as the snow was deep, our limbs chilled and stiffened by their icy covering, and a hurricane of wind blowing in our faces. About the middle of the afternoon, however, we came suddenly out upon the very brink of a storm-swept precipice, a hundred and fifty feet in depth, against the base of which the sea was hurling tremendous green breakers with a roar that drowned the rushing noise of the wind. I had never imagined so wild and lonely a scene. Behind and around us lay a wilderness of white, desolate peaks, crowded together under a gray, pitiless sky, with here and there a patch of trailing pine, or a black pinnacle of trap-rock, to intensify by contrast the ghastly whiteness and desolation of the weird snowy mountains. In front, but far below, was the troubled sea, rolling mysteriously out of a gray mist of snowflakes, breaking in thick sheets of clotted froth against the black cliff, and making long reverberations, and hollow, gurgling noises in the subterranean caverns which it had hollowed out. Snow, water, and mountains, and in the foreground a little group of ice-covered men and shaggy horses, staring at the sea from the summit of a mighty cliff! It was a simple picture, but it was full of cheerless, mournful suggestions. Our guide, after looking eagerly up and down the gloomy precipitous coast in search of some familiar landmark, finally turned to me with a brighter face, and asked to see that compass. I unscrewed the cover and showed him the blue quivering needle still pointing to the north. He examined it curiously, but with evident respect for its mysterious powers, and at last said that it was truly "shipka masteer," and wanted to know if it always pointed toward the sea! I tried to explain to him its nature and use, but I could not make him understand, and he walked away

firmly believing that there was something uncanny and
supernatural about a little brass box that could point
out the road to the sea in a country where it had never
before been!

We pushed on to the northward throughout the afternoon, keeping as near the coast as possible, winding around among the thickly-scattered peaks and
crossing no less than nine low ridges of the mountain
range.

I noticed throughout the day the peculiar phenomenon
of which I had read in Tyndall's "Glaciers of the Alps"
—the blue light which seemed to fill every footprint and
little crevice in the snow. The hole made by a long
slender stick was fairly luminous with what appeared to
be deep blue vapor. I never saw this singular phenomenon so marked at any other time during nearly three
years of northern travel.

About an hour after dark we rode down into a deep,
lonely valley, which came out, our guide said, upon the
sea-beach near the mouth of the Samanka River. Here
no snow had fallen, but it was raining heavily. I thought
it hardly possible that the Major and Dodd could have
reached the appointed rendezvous in such a storm; but I
directed the men to pitch the tent, while Vushine and
I rode on to the mouth of the river to ascertain whether
the whale-boat had arrived or not. It was too dark to see
anything distinctly, but we found no traces of any human
beings having ever been there, and returned disappointed
to camp. We were never more glad to get under a tent,
eat supper, and crawl into our bear-skin sleeping-bags,

than after that exhausting day's work. Our clothes had been either wet or frozen for nearly forty-eight hours, and we had been fourteen hours on foot and in the saddle, without warm food or rest.

CHAPTER XV.

EARLY on Saturday morning we moved on to the mouth of the valley, pitched our tent in a position to command a view of the approaches to the Samanka River, ballasted its edges with stones to keep the wind from blowing it down, and prepared to wait two days, according to orders, for the whaleboat. The storm still continued, and the heavy sea, which dashed sullenly all day against the black rocks under our tent, convinced me that nothing could be expected from the other party. I only hoped that they had succeeded in getting safely landed somewhere before the storm began. Caught by a gale under the frowning wall of rock which stretched for miles along the coast, the whaleboat, I knew, must either swamp with all on board, or be dashed to pieces against the cliffs. In either case not a soul could escape to tell the story.

That night Vushine astonished and almost disheartened me with the news that we were eating the last of our provisions. There was no more meat, and the hard bread which remained was only a handful of water-soaked crumbs. He and all the Kamtchadals, confidently expecting to meet the whaleboat at the Samanka River, had taken only three days' food. He had said nothing about it until the last moment, hoping that the whaleboat would arrive or something turn up; but it could no longer be

concealed. We were three days' journey from any settlement, and without food. How we were to get back to
Lesnoi I did not know, as the mountains were probably
impassable now, on account of the snow which had fallen
since we crossed, and the weather did not permit us to
indulge a hope that the whaleboat would ever come.
Much as we dreaded it, there was nothing to be done but
to attempt another passage of the mountain range, and
that without a moment's delay. I had been ordered to
wait for the whaleboat two days; but circumstances, I
thought, justified a disobedience of orders, and I directed
the Kamtchadals to be ready to start for Lesnoi early the
next morning. Then, writing a note to the Major, and
enclosing it in a tin can, to be left on the site of our camp,
I crawled into my fur bag to sleep and get strength for
another struggle with the mountains.

The following morning was cold and stormy, and the
snow was still falling in the mountains, and heavy rain in
the valley. We broke camp at daylight, saddled our
horses, distributed what little baggage we had among
them, as equally as possible, and made every preparation
for deep snow and hard climbing.

Our guide, after a short consultation with his comrades,
now came to me and proposed that we abandon our plan
of crossing the mountains as wholly impracticable, and
try instead to make our way along the narrow strip of
beach which the ebbing tide would leave bare at the foot
of the cliffs. This plan, he contended, was no more dangerous than attempting to cross the mountains, and was
much more certain of success, as there were only a few

points where at low water a horse could not pass with
dry feet. It was not more than thirty miles to a ravine on the south side of the mountain range, through
which we could leave the beach and regain our old
trail at a point within one hard day's ride of Lesnoi.
The only danger was in being caught by high water
before we could reach this ravine, and even then we
might save ourselves by climbing up on the rocks,
and abandoning our horses to their fate.   It would
be no worse for them than starving and freezing to
death in the mountains.   Divested of its verbal plausi-
bility, his plan was nothing more nor less than a grand
thirty-mile race with a high tide along a narrow beach,
from which all escape was cut off by precipitous cliffs one
and two hundred feet in height.   If we reached the ravine
in time, all would be well ; but if not, our beach would be
covered ten feet deep with water, and our horses, if not
ourselves, would be swept away like corks.   There was
a recklessness and dash about this proposal which made
it very attractive when compared with wading laboriously
through snow-drifts, in frozen clothes, without anything to
eat, and I gladly agreed to it, and credited our guide with
more sense and spirit than I had ever before seen exhibited by a Kamtchadal.   The tide was now only beginning to ebb, and we had three or four hours to spare before it would be low enough to start.   This time the
Kamtchadals improved by catching one of the dogs which
had accompanied us from Lesnoi, killing him in a cold-
blooded way with their long knives, and offering his lean
body as a sacrifice to the Evil Spirit, in whose jurisdiction

these infernal mountains were supposed to be. The poor
animal was cut open, his entrails taken out and thrown
to the four corners of the earth, and his body suspended
by the hind legs from the top of a long pole set perpendicularly in the ground. The Evil Spirit's wrath, however, seemed implacable, for it stormed worse after the
performance of these propitiatory rites than it did before.
This did not weaken at all the faith of the Kamtchadals in
the efficacy of their atonement. If the storm did not
abate, it was only because an unbelieving American with
a diabolical brass box called a " come-*páss*" had insisted
upon crossing the mountains in defiance of the "*genius
loci*" and all his tempestuous warnings. One dead dog
was no compensation at all for such a sacrilegious violation of the Evil Spirit's clearly expressed wishes! The
sacrifice, however, seemed to relieve the natives' anxiety
about their own safety; and much as I pitied the poor
dog thus remorselessly murdered, I was glad to see the
manifest improvement which it worked in the spirits of
my superstitious comrades.

About ten o'clock, as nearly as I could estimate the
time without a watch, our guide examined the beach and
said we must be off; we would have between four and
five hours to reach the ravine. We mounted in hot haste,
and set out at a swinging gallop along the beach, overshadowed by tremendous black cliffs on one side, and
sprinkled with salt spray from the breakers on the other.
Great masses of green, slimy sea-weed, shells, water-
soaked drift-wood, and thousands of medusæ, which had
been thrown up by the storm, lay strewn in piles along

the beach ; but we dashed through and over them at a mad gallop, never drawing rein for an instant except to pick our way between enormous masses of rock, which in some places had caved away from the summit of the cliff and blocked up the beach with gray barnacle-encrusted fragments as large as freight-cars.

We had got over the first eighteen miles in splendid style, when Vushine, who was riding in advance, stopped suddenly, with an abruptness which nearly threw him over his horse's head, and raised the familiar cry of "medvaide! medvaide! dva." Bears they certainly seemed to be, making their way along the beach a quarter of a mile or so ahead ; but how bears came in that desperate situation, where they must inevitably be drowned in the course of two or three hours, we could not conjecture. It made little difference to us, however, for the bears were there and we must pass. It was a clear case of breakfast for one party or the other. There could be no dodging or getting around, for the cliffs and the sea left us a narrow road. I slipped a fresh cartridge into my rifle and a dozen more into my pocket ; Vushine dropped a couple of balls into his double-barrelled fowling-piece, and we crept forward behind the rocks to get a shot at them, if possible, before we should be seen. We were almost within rifle range when Vushine suddenly straightened up with a loud laugh, and cried out, "loode"—"they are people." Coming out from behind the rocks, I saw clearly that they were. But how came people there ? Two natives, dressed in fur coats and pants, approached us with violent gesticula tions, shouting to us in Russian not to shoot, and holding

up something white, like a flag of truce. As soon as
they came near enough one of them handed me a wet,
dirty piece of paper, with a low bow, and I recognized
him as a Kamtchadal from Lesnoi. They were messengers
from the Major ! Thanking God in my heart that the other
party was safe, I tore open the note and read hastily :—

"Sea Shore, 15 versts from Lesnoi, October 4th. Driven ashore
here by the storm. Hurry back as fast as possible.

"S. ABAZA."

The Kamtchadal messengers had left Lesnoi only one
day behind us, but had been detained by the storm and
bad roads, and had only reached on the previous night
our second camp. Finding it impossible to cross the
mountains on account of the snow, they had abandoned
their horses, and were trying to reach the Samanka River
on foot by way of the sea-beach. They did not expect to
do it in one tide, but intended to take refuge on high
rocks during the flood, and resume their journey as soon
as the beach should be left bare by the receding water.
There was no time for any more explanations. The
tide was running in rapidly, and we must make twelve
miles in a little over an hour, or lose our horses. We
mounted the tired, wet Kamtchadals on two of our spare
animals, and were off again at a gallop. The situation
grew more and more exciting as we approached the
ravine. At the end of every projecting bluff the water
was higher and higher, and in several places it had already
touched with foam and spray the foot of the cliffs. In
twenty minutes more the beach would be impassable.

Our horses held out nobly, and the ravine was only a short distance ahead—only one more projecting bluff intervened. Against this the sea was already beginning to break, but we galloped past through several feet of water, and in five minutes drew rein at the mouth of the ravine. It had been a hard ride, but we had won the race with a clear ten minutes to spare, and were now on the south side of the snowy mountain range, less than sixty miles from Lesnoi. Had it not been for our guide's good sense and boldness we would still have been floundering through the snow, and losing our way among the bewildering peaks, ten miles south of the Samanka River. The ravine up which our road lay was badly choked with massive rocks, patches of trailing pine, and dense thickets of alder, and it cost us two hours more hard work to cut a trail through it with axes.

Before dark, however, we had reached the site of our second day's camp, and about midnight we arrived at the ruined "yourt" where we had eaten lunch five days before. Exhausted by fourteen hours' riding without rest or food, we could go no farther. I had hoped to get something to eat from the Kamtchadal messengers from Lesnoi, but was disappointed to find that their provisions had been exhausted the previous day. Vushine scraped a small handful of dirty crumbs out of our empty bread-bag, fried them in a little blubber, which I suppose he had brought to grease his gun, and offered them to me; but, hungry as I was, I could not eat the dark, greasy mass, and he divided it by mouthfuls among the Kamtchadals.

The second day's ride without food was a severe trial of

my strength, and I began to be tormented by a severe gnawing, burning pain in my stomach. I tried to quiet it by eating seeds from the cones of trailing pine and drinking large quantities of water; but this afforded no relief, and I became so faint toward evening that I could not sit in my saddle.

About two hours after dark we heard the howling of dogs from Lesnoi, and in twenty minutes rode into the settlement, dashed up to the little log-house of the Starosta, and burst in upon the Major and Dodd as they sat at supper. Our long ride was over.

Thus ended our unsuccessful expedition to the Samanka Mountains—the hardest journey I ever experienced in Kamtchatka.

Two days afterward, the anxiety and suffering which the Major had endured in a five days' camp on the sea-beach during the storm, brought on a severe attack of rheumatic fever, and all thoughts of further progress were for the present abandoned. Nearly all the horses in the village were more or less disabled, our Samanka mountain guide was blind from inflammatory erysipelas, brought on by exposure to five days of storm, and half my party unfit for duty. Under such circumstances, another attempt to cross the mountains before winter was impossible. Dodd and the Cossack Meroneff were sent back to Tigil after a physician and a new supply of provisions, while Vushine and I remained at Lesnoi to take care of the Major.

CHAPTER XVI.

AFTER our unsuccessful attempt to pass the Samanka Mountains, there was nothing for us to do but wait patiently at Lesnoi until the rivers should freeze over, and snow fall to a depth which would enable us to continue our journey to Gee-zhe-ga on dog-sledges. It was a long, wearisome delay, and I felt for the first time, in its full force, the sensation of exile from home, country, and civilization. The Major continued very ill, and would show the anxiety which he had felt about the success of our expedition by talking deliriously for hours of crossing the mountains, starting for Geezhega in the whaleboat, and giving incoherent orders to Vushine, Dodd, and myself, about horses, dog-sledges, canoes, and provisions. The idea of getting to Geezhega before winter filled his mind, to the exclusion of everything else. His sickness made the time previous to Dodd's return seem very long and lonesome, as I had absolutely nothing to do except to sit in a little log-room, with opaque fish-skin windows, and pore over Shakespeare and my Bible, until I almost learned them by heart. In pleasant weather I would sling my rifle across my back and spend whole days in roaming over the mountains in pursuit of reindeer and foxes ; but I rarely met with much success. One deer and a few Arctic ptarmigan were my only trophies. At night I would sit on the transverse section of a log in our

little kitchen, light a rude Kamtchadal lamp, made with a
fragment of moss and a tin-cup full of seal oil, and listen
for hours to the songs and guitar-playing of the Kamtchadals, and to the wild stories of perilous mountain adventure which they delighted to relate. I learned during
these Kamtchatkan Nights' Entertainments many interesting particulars of Kamtchadal life, customs, and peculiarities, of which I had before known nothing; and, as I
shall have no occasion hereafter to speak of this curious,
little-known people, I may as well give here what account
I can of their language, music, amusements, superstitions,
and mode of life.

The people themselves I have already described as a
quiet, inoffensive, hospitable tribe of semi-barbarians, remarkable only for honesty, general amiability, and comical reverence for legally-constituted authority. Such an
idea as rebellion or resistance to oppression is wholly foreign to the Kamtchadal character *now*, whatever it may
have been in previous ages of independence. They will
suffer and endure any amount of abuse and ill-treatment,
without any apparent desire for revenge, and with the
greatest good-nature and elasticity of spirit. They are as
faithful and forgiving as a dog. If you treat them well,
your slightest wish will be their law; and they will do
their best in their rude way to show their appreciation of
kindness, by anticipating and meeting even your unexpressed wants. During our stay at Lesnoi the Major
chanced one day to inquire for some milk. The Starosta
did not tell him that there was not a cow in the village,
but said that he would try and get some. A man was

instantly despatched on horseback to the neighboring settlement of Kinkill, and before night he returned with a
champagne bottle under his arm, and the Major had milk
that evening in his tea. From this time until we started
for Geezhega—more than a month—a man rode twenty
miles every day to bring us a bottle of fresh milk. This
seemed to be done out of pure kindness of heart, without
any desire or expectation of future reward ; and it is a
fair example of the manner in which we were generally
treated by all the Kamtchadals in the peninsula.

The settled natives of Northern Kamtchatka have generally two different residences, in which they live at different seasons of the year. These are respectively called
the "zimnia" or winter settlement, and the "letova" or
summer fishing station, and are from one to five miles
apart. In the former, which is generally situated under
the shelter of timbered hills, several miles from the sea-
coast, they reside from September until June. The "letova" is always built near the mouth of an adjacent river
or stream, and consists of a few "yourts" or earth-cov-
ered huts, eight or ten conical "bologans" mounted on
stilts, and a great number of wooden frames on which fish
are hung to dry. To this fishing station the inhabitants
all remove early in June, leaving their winter settlement
entirely deserted. Even the dogs and the crows abandon
it for the more attractive surroundings and richer pickings
of the summer "bologans." Early in July the salmon
enter the river in immense numbers from the sea, and are
caught by the natives in gill-nets, baskets, seines, weirs,
traps, and a dozen other ingenious contrivances—cut open,

cleaned and boned by the women, with the greatest skill and celerity, and hung in long rows upon horizontal poles to dry. A fish, with all the confidence of an inexperienced sea life, enters the river as a sailor comes ashore, intending to have a good time ; but before he fairly knows what he is about, he is caught in a seine, dumped out upon the beach with a hundred more equally unsophisticated and equally unfortunate sufferers, split open with a big knife, his backbone removed, his head cut off, his internal arrangements scooped out, and his mutilated remains hung over a pole to simmer in a hot July sun. It is a pity that he cannot enjoy the melancholy satisfaction of seeing the skill and rapidity with which his body is prepared for a new and enlarged sphere of usefulness ! He is no longer a fish. In this second stage of passive unconscious existence he assumes a new name, and is called a "Yoókala."

It is astonishing to see in what enormous quantities and to what great distances these fish ascend the Siberian rivers. Dozens of small streams which we passed in the interior of Kamtchatka, seventy miles from the seacoast, were so choked up with thousands of dying, dead, and decayed fish, that we could not use the water for any purpose whatever. Even in little mountain brooks, so narrow that a child could step across them, we saw salmon eighteen or twenty inches in length still working their way laboriously up stream, in water which was not deep enough to cover their bodies. We frequently waded in and threw them out by the dozen with our bare hands. They change greatly in appearance as they ascend a river. When they first come in from the sea their scales

are bright and hard, and their flesh fat and richly colored;
but as they go higher and higher up stream, their scales
lose their brilliancy and fall off, their flesh bleaches out
until it is nearly white, and they become lean, dry, and
tasteless.   For this reason all the fishing stations in
Kamtchatka are located, if possible, at or near the mouth
of some river.   To the instinct which leads the salmon
to ascend rivers for the purpose of depositing its spawn,
is attributable the settlement of all Northeastern Siberia.   If it were not for the abundance of fish, the whole
country would be uninhabited and uninhabitable, except
by the Reindeer Koraks.   As soon as the fishing season
is over, the Kamtchadals store away their dried "yookala" in "bologans," and return to their winter-quarters
to prepare for the fall catch of sables.   For nearly a month
they spend all their time in the woods and mountains,
making and setting traps.   To make a sable trap, a
narrow perpendicular slot, fourteen inches by four in
length and breadth, and five inches in depth, is cut in
the trunk of a large tree, so that the bottom of the slot
will be about at the height of a sable's head when he
stands erect.   The stem of another smaller tree is then
trimmed, one of its ends raised to a height of three feet
by a forked stick set in the ground, and the other bevelled
off so as to slip up and down freely in the slot cut for its
reception.   This end is raised to the top of the slot and
supported there by a simple figure-four catch, leaving a
nearly square opening of about four inches below for the
admission of the sable's head.   The figure-four is then
baited and the trap is ready.   The sable rises upon his

hind legs, puts his head into the hole, and the heavy log, set free by the dropping of the figure-four, falls and crushes the animal's skull, without injuring in the slightest degree the valuable parts of his skin. One native frequently makes and sets as many as a hundred of these traps in the fall, and visits them at short intervals throughout the winter. Not content, however, with this extensive and well-organized system of trapping sables, the natives hunt them upon snow-shoes with trained dogs, drive them into holes which they surround with nets, and then, forcing them out with fire or axe, they kill them with clubs.

The number of sables caught in the Kamtchatkan peninsula annually varies from six to nine thousand, all of which are exported to Russia and distributed from there over Northern Europe. A large proportion of the whole number of Russian sables in the European market are caught by the natives of Kamtchatka and transported by *American* merchants to Moscow. W. H. Bordman, of Boston, and an American house in China—known, I believe, as Russell & Co.—practically control the fur trade of Kamtchatka and the Okhotsk sea-coast. The price paid to the Kamtchadals for an average sable skin in 1867 was nominally fifteen roubles silver, or about $11 gold; but payment was made in tea, sugar, tobacco, and sundry other articles of merchandise, at the trader's own valuation, so that the natives actually realized only a little more than half the nominal price. Nearly all the inhabitants of Central Kamtchatka are engaged directly or indirectly during the winter in the sable trade and many of them have acquired by it a comfortable independence.

Fishing and sable hunting, therefore, are the serious occupations of the Kamtchadals throughout the year; but as these are indications of the nature of the country rather than of the characteristics of its inhabitants, they give only an imperfect idea of the distinctive peculiarities of Kamtchadals and Kamtchadal life. The language, music, amusements, and superstitions of a people are much more valuable as illustrations of their real character than are their regular occupations.

The Kamtchadal language is to me one of the most curious of all the wild tongues of Asia; not on account of its construction, but simply from the strange, uncouth sounds with which it abounds, and its strangling, gurgling articulation. When rapidly spoken, it always reminded me of water running out of a narrow-mouthed jug! A Russian traveller in Kamtchatka has said that " the Kamtchadal language is spoken half in the mouth and half in the throat;" but it might be more accurately described as spoken half in the throat and half in the stomach. It has more guttural sounds than any other Asiatic language which I have ever heard, and differs considerably in this respect from the dialects of the Chookchees and Koraks. It is what comparative philologists call an agglutinative language, and seems to be made up of permanent unchangeable roots with variable prefixes. It has, so far as I could ascertain, no terminal inflections, and its gram. mar seemed to be simple and easily learned. Most of the Kamtchadals throughout the northern part of the

peninsula speak, in addition to their own language, Russian and Korak, so that, in their way, they are quite
accomplished linguists.

It has always seemed to me that the songs of a people,
and especially of a people who have composed them
themselves, and not adopted them from others, are indi-
cative to a very great degree of their character; whether,
as some author supposed, the songs have a reflex influence on the character, or whether they exist simply as its
exponents, the result is the same, viz., a greater or less
correspondence between the two. In none of the Siberian tribes is this more marked than in the Kamtchadals.
They have evidently never been a warlike, combative
people. They have no songs celebrating the heroic deeds
of their ancestors, or their exploits in the chase or in battle, as have many tribes of our North American Indians.
Their ballads are all of a melancholy, imaginative character, inspired apparently by grief, love, or domestic feeling, rather than by the ruder passions of pride, anger, and
revenge. Their music all has a wild, strange sound to a
foreign ear, but it conveys to the mind in some way a
sense of sorrow, and vague, unavailing regret for something which has forever past away, like the emotion
excited by a funeral dirge over the grave of a dear friend.
As Ossian says of the music of Carryl, "it is like the
memory of joys that are past—sweet, yet mournful to
the soul." I remember particularly a song called the
Penjinski, sung one night by the natives at Lesnoi, which
was, without exception, the sweetest, and yet the most
inexpressibly mournful combination of notes that I had

ever heard. It was a wail of a lost soul despairing, yet pleading for mercy. I tried in vain to get a translation of the words. Whether it was the relation of some bloody and disastrous encounter with their fiercer northern neighbors, or the lament over the slain body of some dear son, brother, or husband, I could not learn; but the music alone will bring the tears near one's eyes, and has an indescribable effect upon the singers, whose excitable feelings it sometimes works up almost to the pitch of frenzy. The dancing tunes of the Kamtchadals are of course entirely different in character, being generally very lively, energetic staccato passages, repeated many times in succession, without variation. Nearly all the natives accompany themselves upon a three-cornered guitar called a "Cellalika," with two strings, and some of them play quite well upon rude home-made violins. All are passionately fond of music of any kind.

The only other amusements in which they indulge are dancing, playing foot-ball on the snow in winter, and racing with dog-teams.

The winter travel of the Kamtchadals is accomplished entirely upon dog-sledges, and in no other pursuit of their lives do they spend more time or exhibit their native skill and ingenuity to better advantage. They may even be said to have made dogs for themselves in the first place, for the present Siberian animal is nothing more than a half-domesticated arctic wolf, and still retains all his wolfish instincts and peculiarities. There is probably no more hardy, enduring animal in the world. You may compel him to sleep out on the snow in a temperature of

70° below zero, drive him with heavy loads until his feet crack open and print the snow with blood, or starve him until he eats up his harness; but his strength and his spirit seem alike unconquerable. I have driven a team of nine dogs more than a hundred miles in a day and a night, and have frequently worked them hard for forty-eight hours without being able to give them a particle of food. In general they are fed once a day, their allowance being a single dried fish, weighing perhaps a pound and a half or two pounds. This is given to them at night, so that they begin another day's work with empty stomachs.

The sledge to which they are harnessed is about ten feet in length and two in width, made with seasoned birch timber, and combines to a surprising degree the two most desirable qualities of strength and lightness. It is simply a skeleton frame work, fastened together with lashings of dried seal-skin, and mounted on broad, curved runners. No iron whatever is used in its construction, and it does not weigh more than twenty pounds; yet it will sustain a load of four or five hundred pounds, and endure the severest shocks of rough mountain travel. The number of dogs harnessed to this sledge varies from seven to fifteen, according to the nature of the country to be traversed and the weight of the load. Under favorable circumstances eleven dogs will make from forty to fifty miles a day with a man and a load of four hundred pounds. They are harnessed to the sledge in successive couples by a long central thong of seal-skin, to which each individual dog is attached by a collar and a short trace. They are guided and controlled entirely by the voice and by a lead dog who is especially trained for the purpose. The driver carries no whip, but has instead a thick stick about four feet in length and two inches in diameter, called an "oerstel." This is armed at one end with a long iron spike, and is used to check the speed of the sledge in descending hills, and to stop the dogs when they leave the road, as they frequently do in pursuit of reindeer and foxes. The spiked end is then thrust down in front of one of the knees or uprights of the runners, and drags in that position through the snow, the upper end being firmly held by the driver. It is a powerful lever, and when skilfully used brakes up a sledge very promptly and effectively.

The art of driving a dog-team is one of the most deceptive in the world. The traveller at first sight imagines that driving a dog-sledge is just as easy as driving a street car, and at the very first favorable opportunity he tries it. After being run away with within the first ten minutes, capsized into a snow-drift, and his sledge dragged bottom upward a quarter of a mile from the road, the rash experimenter begins to suspect that the task is not quite so easy as he had supposed, and in less than one day he is generally convinced by hard experience that a dog-driver, like a poet, is born, not made.

The dress of the Kamtchadals in winter and summer is made for the most part of skins. Their winter costume consists of seal-skin boots called "torbassá," worn over heavy reindeer-skin stockings and coming to the knee; fur pants with the hair inside; a fox-skin hood with a long fringe of wolverine hair, ornamented with the animal's ears; and a heavy kookhlánka, or double fur over-shirt, covering the body to the knees. This is made of the very thickest and softest reindeer-skin of various colors, orna-mented around the bottom with silk embroidery, trimmed at the sleeves and neck with glossy beaver, and furnished with a square flap under the chin, to be held up over the nose, and a hood behind the neck, to be drawn over the head in bad weather. In such a costume as this the Kamtchadals defy for weeks at a time the severest cold, and sleep out on the snow safely and comfortably in temperatures of twenty, thirty, and even forty degrees be-low zero, Fahr.

Most of our time during our long detention at Lesnoi was occupied in the preparation of such costumes for our own use, in making covered dog-sledges to protect our-selves from winter storms, sewing bear-skins into capacious sleeping bags, and getting ready generally for a hard winter's campaign.

CHAPTER XVII.

ABOUT the 20th of October a Russian physician arrived from Tigil, and proceeded to reduce the little strength which the Major had by steaming, bleeding, and blistering him into a mere shadow of his former robust proportions. The fever, however, abated under this energetic treatment, and he began gradually to amend. Some time during the same week, Dodd and Meroneff returned from Tigil with a new supply of tea, sugar, rum, tobacco, and hard bread, and we began collecting dogs from the neighboring settlements of Kin-Kill and Polan for another trip across the Samanka Mountains. Snow had fallen everywhere to a depth of two feet, the weather had turned clear and cold, and there was nothing except the Major's illness to detain us longer at Lesnoi. On the 28th he declared himself able to travel, and we packed up for a start. On November 1st we put on our heavy fur-clothes, which turned us into wild animals of most ferocious appearance, bade good-by to all the hospitable people of Lesnoi, and set out with a train of sixteen sledges, eighteen men, two hundred dogs, and forty days' provisions, for the territory of the Wandering Koraks. We determined to reach Geezhega this time, or, as the newspapers say, perish in the attempt.

Late in the afternoon of November 3d, just as the long

northern twilight was fading into the peculiar steely blue of an arctic night, our dogs toiled slowly up the last summit of the Samanka Mountains, and we looked down from a height of more than two thousand feet upon the dreary expanse of snow which stretched away from the base of the mountains at our feet to the far horizon. It was the land of the Wandering Koraks. A cold breeze from the sea swept across the mountain-top, soughing mournfully through the pines as it passed, and intensifying the loneliness and silence of the white wintry landscape. The faint pale light of the vanishing sun still lingered upon the higher peaks; but the gloomy ravines below us, shaggy with forests of larch and dense thickets of trailing pine, were already gathering the shadows and indistinctness of night. At the foot of the mountains stood the first encampment of Koraks. As we rested our dogs a few moments upon the summit, before commencing our descent, we tried to discern through the gathering gloom the black tents which we imagined stood somewhere beneath our feet; but nothing save the dark patches of trailing pine broke the dead white of the level steppe. The encampment was hidden by a projecting shoulder of the mountain.

The rising moon was just throwing into dark, bold relief the shaggy outlines of the peaks on our right, as we roused up our dogs and plunged into the throat of a dark ravine which led downward to the steppe. The deceptive shadows of night, and the masses of rock which choked up the narrow defile, made the descent extremely dangerous; and it required all the skill of our practised

drivers to avoid accident.   Clouds of snow flew from the
spiked poles with which they vainly tried to arrest our
downward rush ; cries and warning shouts from those in
advance, multiplied by the mountain echoes, excited our
dogs to still greater speed, until we seemed, as the rocks
and trees flew past, to be in the jaws of a falling avalanche, which was carrying us with breathless rapidity
down the dark cañon to certain ruin.   Gradually, however, our speed slackened, and we came out into the
moonlight on the hard, wind-packed snow of the open
steppe.   Half an hour's brisk travel brought us into the
supposed vicinity of the Korak encampment, but we saw
as yet no signs of either reindeer or tents.   The dis-
turbed, torn-up condition of the snow usually apprises the
traveller of his approach to the yourts of the Koraks, as
the reindeer belonging to the band range all over the
country within a radius of several miles, and paw up the
snow in search of the moss which constitutes their food.
Failing to find any such indications, we were discussing
the probability of our having been misdirected, when
suddenly our leading dogs pricked up their sharp ears,
snuffed eagerly at the wind, and with short, excited yelps,
made off at a dashing gallop toward a low hill which lay
almost at right angles with our previous course.   The
drivers endeavored in vain to check the speed of the
excited dogs; their wolfish instincts were aroused, and
all discipline was forgotten as the fresh scent came down
upon the wind from the herd of reindeer beyond.   A
moment brought us to the brow of the hill, and before
us, in the clear moonlight, stood the conical tents of the

Koraks, surrounded by at least four thousand reindeer, whose branching antlers looked like a perfect forest of dry limbs. The dogs all gave voice simultaneously, like a pack of fox-hounds in view of the game, and dashed tumultuously down the hill, regardless of the shouts of their masters, and the menacing cries of three or four dark forms which rose suddenly up from the snow between them and the frightened deer. Above the tumult I could hear Dodd's voice, hurling imprecations in Russian at his yelping dogs, which, in spite of his most strenuous efforts, were dragging him and his capsized sledge across the steppe. The vast body of deer wavered a moment and then broke into a wild stampede, with drivers, Korak sentinels, and two hundred dogs in full pursuit.

Not desirous of becoming involved in the mêlée, I sprang from my sledge and watched the confused crowd as it swept with shout, bark, and halloo, across the plain The whole encampment, which had seemed in its quiet loneliness to be deserted, was now startled into instant activity. Dark forms issued suddenly from the tents, and grasping the long spears which stood upright in the snow by the door-way, joined in the chase, shouting and hurling lassos of walrus hide at the dogs, with the hope of stopping their pursuit. The clattering of thousands of antlers dashed together in the confusion of flight, the hurried beat of countless hoofs upon the hard snow, the deep, hoarse barks of the startled deer, and the unintelligible cries of the Koraks, as they tried to rally their panic-stricken herd, created a Pandemonium of discordant sounds which could be heard far and wide through the still, frosty atmosphere of night. It resembled a midnight attack of Camanches upon a hostile camp, rather than the peaceful arrival of three or four American travellers; and I listened with astonishment to the wild uproar of alarm which we had unintentionally aroused.

The tumult grew fainter and fainter as it swept away into the distance, and the dogs, exhausting the unnatural strength which the excitement had temporarily given them, yielded reluctantly to the control of their drivers and turned toward the tents. Dodd's dogs, panting with the violence of their exertions, limped sullenly back, casting longing glances occasionally in the direction of the deer, as if they more than half repented the weakness which had led them to abandon the chase.

"Why didn't you stop them?" I inquired of Dodd, laughingly. "A driver of your experience ought to have better control of his team than that."

"Stop them!" he exclaimed with an aggrieved air. "I'd like to see *you* stop them, with a raw-hide lasso round your neck, and a big Korak hauling like a steam windlass on the other end of it! It's all very well to cry 'stop 'em;' but when the barbarians haul you off the rear end of your sledge as if you were a wild animal, what course would your sublime wisdom suggest? I believe I've got the mark of a lasso round my neck now," and he felt cautiously about his ears for the impression of a seal-skin thong.

As soon as the deer had been gathered together again and a guard placed over them, the Koraks crowded curiously around the visitors who had entered so unceremoniously their quiet camp, and inquired through Meroneff, our interpreter, who we were and what we wanted. A wild, picturesque group they made, as the moonlight streamed white and clear into their swarthy faces, and glittered upon the metallic ornaments about their persons and the polished blades of their long spears. Their high cheek-bones, bold, alert eyes, and straight, coal-black hair, suggested an intimate relationship with our own Indians; but the resemblance went no further. Most of their faces wore an expression of bold, frank honesty, which is not a characteristic of our western aborigines, and which we instinctively accepted as a sufficient guarantee of their friendliness and good faith. Contrary to our preconceived idea of northern savages, they were athletic, able-bodied men, fully up to the average height of Americans. Heavy "kookhlánkas," or hunting-shirts of spotted deer-skin, confined about the waist with a belt, and fringed round the bottom with the long black hair of the wolverine, covered their bodies from the neck to the knee, ornamented here and there with strings of small colored beads, tassels of scarlet leather, and bits of polished metal. Fur pantaloons, long boots of seal-skin coming up to the thigh, and wolf-skin hoods, with the ears of the animal standing erect on each side of the head, completed the costume which, notwithstanding its *bizarre* effect, had yet a certain picturesque adaptation to the equally strange features of the moonlight scene. Leaving our Cossack Meroneff, seconded by the Major, to explain our business and wants, Dodd and I strolled away to make a critical inspection of the encampment. It consisted of

four large conical tents, built apparently of a framework of
poles and covered with loose reindeer skins, confined in their
places by long thongs of seal or walrus hide, which were
stretched tightly over them from the apex of the cone to
the ground.   They seemed at first sight to be illy calculated to withstand the storms which in winter sweep down
across this steppe from the Arctic Ocean; but subsequent
experience proved that the severest gales cannot tear
them from their fastenings.   Neatly constructed sledges
of various shapes and sizes were scattered here and there
upon the snow, and two or three hundred pack-saddles
for the reindeer were piled up in a symmetrical wall near
the largest tent.   Finishing our examination, and feeling
somewhat bored by the society of fifteen or twenty
Koraks who had constituted themselves a sort of super-
visory committee to watch our motions, we returned to
the spot where the representatives of civilization and barbarism were conducting their negotiations.   They had
apparently come to an amicable understanding; for, upon
our approach, a tall native with shaven head stepped out
from the throng, and leading the way to the largest tent,
lifted a curtain of skin and revealed a dark hole about
two feet and a half in diameter, which he motioned to us
to enter.

Now, if there was any branch of Vushine's Siberian education upon which he especially prided himself, it was his
proficiency in crawling into small holes.   Persevering
practice had given him a flexibility of back and a peculiar
sinuosity of movement which we might admire but could
not imitate; and although the distinction was not perhaps

an altogether desirable one, he was invariably selected to explore all the dark holes and underground passages (miscalled doors) which came in our way. This seemed to be one of the most peculiar of the many different styles of entrance which we had observed; but Vushine, assuming as an axiom, that no part of his body could be greater than the (w)hole, dropped into a horizontal position, and requesting Dodd to give his feet an initial shove, crawled cautiously in. A few seconds of breathless silence succeeded his disappearance, when supposing that all must be right, I put my head into the hole and crawled warily after him. The darkness was profound; but, guided by Vushine's breathing, I was making very fair progress, when suddenly a savage snarl and a startling yell came out of the gloom in front, followed instantly by the most substantial part of Vushine's body, which struck me with the force of a battering ram on the top of the head, and caused me, with the liveliest apprehensions of ambuscade and massacre, to back precipitately out. Vushine, with the awkward retrograde movements of a disabled crab, speedily followed.

"What in the name of Chort is the matter?" demanded Dodd in Russian, as he extricated Vushine's head from the folds of the skin curtain in which it had become enveloped. "You back out as if Shaitan and all his imps were after you!"—"You don't suppose," responded Vushine, with excited gestures, "that I'm going to stay in that hole and be eaten up by Korak dogs? If I was foolish enough to go in, I've got discretion enough to know when to come out. I don't believe the hole leads anywhere, anyhow," he added apologetically; "and it's all full of dogs." With a quick perception of Vushine's difficulties and a grin of amusement at his discomfiture, our Korak guide entered the hole, drove out the dogs, and lifting up an inner curtain, allowed the red light of the fire to stream through. Crawling on hands and knees a distance of twelve or fifteen feet through the low door-way, we entered the large open circle in the interior of the tent. A crackling fire of resinous pine boughs burned brightly upon the ground in the centre, illuminating redly the framework of black, glossy poles, and flickering fitfully over the dingy skins of the roof and the swarthy tattooed faces of the women who squatted around. A large cop-per kettle, filled with some mixture of questionable odor and appearance, hung over the blaze, and furnished occu-pation to a couple of skinny, bare-armed women, who with the same sticks were alternately stirring its contents, pok-ing up the fire, and knocking over the head two or three ill-conditioned but inquisitive dogs. The smoke, which rose lazily from the fire, hung in a blue, clearly-defined cloud about five feet from the ground, dividing the atmos-phere of the tent into a lower stratum of comparatively clear air, and an upper cloud region where smoke, vapors, and ill odors contended for supremacy.

The location of the little pure air which the yourt afforded made the boyish feat of standing upon one's head a very desirable accomplishment; and as the pungent smoke filled my eyes to the exclusion of everything else except tears, I suggested to Dodd that he reverse the respective positions of his head and feet, and try it—he would escape the smoke and sparks from the fire, and at the same time obtain a new and curious optical effect. With the sneer of contempt which always met even my most valuable suggestions, he replied that I might try my own experiments, and throwing himself down at full length on the ground, he engaged in the interesting diversion of making faces at a Korak baby. Vushine's time, as soon as his eyes recovered a little from the effects of the smoke, was about equally divided between preparations for our evening meal, and revengeful blows at the stray dogs which ventured in his vicinity; while the Major, who was probably the most usefully employed member of the party, negotiated for the exclusive possession of a " polog." The temperature of a Korak tent in winter seldom ranges above 20° or 25° Fahr., and as constant exposure to such a degree of cold would be at least very disagreeable, the Koraks construct around the inner circumference of the tent small, nearly air-tight apartments called " pologs," which are separated one from another by skin curtains, and combine the advantages of exclusiveness with the desirable luxury of greater warmth. These " pologs" are about four feet in height, and six or eight feet in width and length. They are made of the heaviest furs sewn carefully together to exclude the air, and are warmed and lighted by a burning fragment of moss floating in a wooden bowl of seal oil. The law of compensation, however, which pervades all Nature, makes itself felt even in the pologs of a Korak yourt, and for the greater degree of warmth is exacted the penalty of a closer, smokier atmosphere. The flaming wick of the lamp, which floats like a tiny burning ship in a miniature lake of rancid grease, absorbs the vital air of the polog, and returns it in the shape of carbonic acid gas, oily smoke, and sickening odors. In defiance, however, of all the known laws of hygiene, this vitiated atmosphere seems to be healthy ; or, to state the case negatively, there is no evidence to prove its unhealthiness. The Korak women, who spend almost the whole of their time in these pologs, live generally to an advanced age, and except a noticeable tendency to angular outlines and skinniness, there is nothing to distinguish them physically from the old women of other countries. It was not without what I supposed to be a well-founded apprehension of suffocation, that I slept for the first time in a Korak yourt ; but my uneasiness proved to be entirely groundless, and gradually wore away.

With a view to escape from the crowd of Koraks who squatted around us on the earthen floor, and whose watchful curiosity soon became irksome, Dodd and I lifted up the fur curtain of the polog which the Major's diplomacy had secured, and crawled in to await the advent of supper. The inquisitive Koraks, unable to find room in the narrow polog for the whole of their bodies, lay down to the number of nine on the outside, and poking their ugly, half-shaven heads under the curtain, resumed their silent supervision. The appearance in a row of nine disembodied heads, whose staring eyes rolled with synchronous motion from side to side as we moved, was so ludicrous that we involuntarily burst into laughter. A responsive smile instantly appeared upon each of the nine swarthy faces, whose simultaneous concurrence in the expression of every emotion suggested the idea of some huge monster with nine heads and but one consciousness. Acting upon Dodd's suggestion that we try and smoke them out, I took my brier-wood pipe from my pocket and proceeded to light it with one of those peculiar snapping lucifers which were among our most cherished relics of civilization. As the match, with a miniature fusillade of sharp reports, burst suddenly into flame, the nine startled heads instantly disappeared, and from beyond the curtain we could hear a chorus of long-drawn " tye-e-e's " from the astonished natives, followed by a perfect Babel of animated comments upon this diabolical method of producing fire. Fearful, however, of losing some other equally striking manifestation of the white men's supernatural power, the heads soon returned, re-enforced by several others which the report of the wonderful occurrence had attracted. The fabled watchfulness of the hundred-eyed Argus was nothing compared with the scrutiny to which we were now subjected. Every wreath of curling smoke which rose from our lips was watched by the staring eyes as intently as if it were some deadly vapor from the bottomless pit, which would shortly burst into report and flame. A loud and vigorous sneeze from Dodd was the signal for a second panic-stricken withdrawal of the row of heads, and another comparison of respective experiences outside the curtain. It was laughable enough ; but, tired of being stared at and anxious for something to eat, we crawled out of our polog and watched with unas sumed interest the preparation of supper.

Out of a little pine box which contained our telegraphic instruments, Vushine had improvised a rude, leg-less mess-table, which he was engaged in covering with cakes of hard bread, slices of raw bacon, and tumblers of steaming tea. These were the luxuries of civilization, and beside them on the ground, in a long wooden trough and a huge bowl of the same material, were the corre-sponding delicacies of barbarism. As to their nature and composition we could, of course, give only a wild conjec-ture ; but the appetites of weary travellers are not very discriminating, and we seated ourselves, like cross-legged Turks, on the ground, between the trough and the instru-ment-box, determined to prove our appreciation of Korak hospitality by eating everything which offered itself. The bowl with its strange-looking contents arrested, of course, the attention of the observant Dodd, and, poking it inquiringly with a long-handled spoon, he turned to Vushine, who, as *chef-de-cuisine*, was supposed to know all about it, and demanded :

" What's this you've got ? "

" That ? " answered Vushine, promptly, " that's 'Kasha' " (hasty pudding made of rice).

" Kasha ! " exclaimed Dodd, contemptuously. " It looks more like the stuff that the children of Israel made bricks of. They don't seem to have wanted for straw, either," he added, as he fished up several stems of dried grass. " What is it, anyhow ? "

" That," said Vushine again, with a comical assump-tion of learning, " is the celebrated 'Jamuk chi a la Poosterelsk,' the national dish of the Koraks, made from the original recipe of His High Excellency Oollcot

Ootkoo Minyegeetkin, Grand Hereditary Tyon and Veve-
sokee Prevoskhodeetbestro——"

" Hold on !" exclaimed Dodd, with a deprecating ges-
ture, " that's enough, I'll eat it ; " and taking out a half-
spoonful of the dark viscid mass, he put it to his lips.

" Well," said we expectantly, after a moment's pause,
" what does it taste like ? "

"Like the mud pies of infancy !" he replied senten-
tiously. "A little salt, pepper, and butter, and a good
deal of meat and flour, with a few well-selected vegetables, would probably improve it ; but it isn't particularly
bad as it is."

Upon the strength of this rather equivocal recommen-
dation I tasted it. Aside from a peculiar earthy flavor, it
had nothing about it which was either pleasant or disagreeable. Its qualities were all negative except its grassi-
ness, which alone gave character and consistency to the
mass.

This mixture, known among the Koraks as " manyalla,"
is eaten by all the Siberian tribes as a substitute for bread,
and is the nearest approximation which native ingenuity
can make to the staff of life. It is valued, we were told,
more for its medicinal virtues than for any intrinsic excel-
lence of taste, and our limited experience fully prepared
us to believe the statement. Its original elements are
clotted blood, tallow, and half-digested moss taken from
the stomach of the reindeer, where it is supposed to have
undergone some essential change which fits it for second-
hand consumption. These curious and heterogeneous
ingredients are boiled up together with a few handfuls of

dried grass to give the mixture consistency, and the dark
mass is then moulded into small loaves and frozen for
future use.   Our host was evidently desirous of treating
us with every civility, and, as a mark of especial consideration, bit off several choice morsels from the large cube
of venison in his grimy hand, and taking them from his
mouth, offered them to me.   I waived graciously the im-
plied compliment, and indicated Dodd as the proper
recipient of such attentions ; but the latter revenged himself by requesting an old woman to bring me some raw
tallow, which he soberly assured her constituted my only
food when at home.   My indignant denials in English
were not, of course, understood ; and the woman, delighted
to find an American whose tastes corresponded so closely
with her own, brought the tallow.   I was a helpless victim, and I could only add this last offence to the long
list of grievances which stood to Dodd's credit, and which
I hoped some time to settle in full.

Supper, in the social economy of the Koraks, is emphatically the meal of the day.   Around the kettle of "manyalla," or the trough of reindeer meat, gather the men of
the band, who during the hours of daylight have been
absent, and who, between mouthfuls of meat or moss, discuss the simple subjects of thought which their isolated
life affords.   We availed ourselves of this opportunity to
learn something of the tribes who inhabited the country
to the northward, the reception with which we would probably meet, and the mode of travel which we should be
compelled to adopt.

CHAPTER XVIII.

THE Wandering Koraks of Kamtchatka, who are divided into about forty different bands, roam over the great steppes in the northern part of the peninsula, between the 58th and the 63d parallels of latitude. Their southern limit is the settlement of Tigil, on the west coast, where they come annually to trade, and they are rarely found north of the village of Penzhina, two hundred miles from the head of the Okhotsk Sea. Within these limits they wander almost constantly with their great herds of reindeer, and so unsettled and restless are they in their habits, that they seldom camp longer than a week in any one place. This, however, is not attributable altogether to restlessness or love of change. A herd of four or five thousand reindeer will in a very few days paw up the snow and eat all the moss within a radius of a mile from the encampment, and then, of course, the band must move to fresh ground. Their nomadic life, therefore, is not entirely a choice, but partly a necessity, growing out of their dependence upon the reindeer. They *must* wander or their deer will starve, and then their own starvation follows as a natural consequence. Their unsettled mode of life probably grew, in the first place, out of the domestication of the reindeer, and the necessity which it involved of consulting first the reindeer's wants ; but the

restless, vagabondish habits thus produced have now be·
come a part of the Korak's very nature, so that he could
hardly live in any other way, even had he an opportunity
of so doing. This wandering, isolated, independent existence has given to the Koraks all those characteristic
traits of boldness, impatience of restraint, and perfect
self-reliance, which distinguish them from the Kamtchadals and the other settled inhabitants of Siberia. Give
them a small herd of reindeer, and a moss steppe to
wander over, and they ask nothing more from all the
world. They are wholly independent of civilization and
government, and will neither submit to their laws nor recognize their distinctions. Every man is a law unto himself as long as he owns a dozen reindeer ; and he can
isolate himself, if he so chooses, from all human kind, and
ignore all other interests but his own and his reindeer's.
For the sake of convenience and society they associate
themselves in bands of six or eight families each ; but
these bands are held together only by mutual consent,
and recognize no governing head. They have a leader
called a Tyón, who is generally the largest deer-owner of
the band, and he decides all such questions as the location of camps and time of removal from place to place ;
but he has no other power, and must refer all graver
questions of individual rights and general obligations to
the members of the band collectively. They have no
particular reverence for anything or anybody except the
evil spirits who bring calamities upon them, and the
"Shamáns" or priests, who act as infernal mediators
between these devils and their victims. Earthly rank

they treat with contempt, and the Czar of all the Russias, if he entered a Korak tent, would stand upon the same level with its owner. We had an amusing instance of this soon after we met the first Koraks. The Major had become impressed in some way with the idea that in order to get what he wanted from these natives he must impress them with a proper sense of his power, rank, wealth, and general importance in the world, and make them feel a certain degree of reverence and respect for his orders and wishes. He accordingly called one of the oldest and most influential members of the band to him one day, and proceeded to tell him, through an interpreter, how rich he was; what immense resources, in the way of rewards and punishments, he possessed; what high rank he held; how important a place he filled in Russia, and how becoming it was that an individual of such exalted attributes should be treated by poor wandering heathen with filial reverence and veneration. The old Korak, squatting upon his heels on the ground, listened quietly to the enumeration of all our leader's admirable qualities and perfections without moving a muscle of his face; but finally, when the interpreter had finished, he rose slowly, walked up to the Major with imperturbable gravity, and with the most benignant and patronizing condescension, patted him softly on the head! The Major turned red and broke out into a laugh; but he never tried again to overawe a Korak.

Notwithstanding this democratic independence of the Koraks, they are almost invariably hospitable, obliging, and kind-hearted; and we were assured at the first en-

campment where we stopped, that we would have no difficulty in getting the different bands to carry us on deer-
sledges from one encampment to another until we should
reach the head of Penzhinsk Gulf.　After a long conversation with the Koraks who crowded around us as we sat
by the fire, we finally became tired and sleepy, and with
favorable impressions upon the whole of this new and
strange people, we crawled into our little polog to sleep.
A voice in another part of the yourt was singing a low,
melancholy air in a minor key as I closed my eyes, and
the sad, oft-repeated refrain, so different from ordinary
music, invested with peculiar loneliness and strangeness
my first night in a Korak tent.

To be awakened in the morning by a paroxysm of
coughing, caused by the thick, acrid smoke of a low-spirited
fire—to crawl out of a skin bed-room six feet square into
the yet denser and smokier atmosphere of the tent—to eat
a breakfast of dried fish, frozen tallow, and venison out of
a dirty wooden trough, with an ill-conditioned dog standing
at each elbow and disputing one's right to every mouthful,
is to enjoy an experience which only Korak life can afford,
and which only Korak insensibility can long endure.　A
very sanguine temperament may find in its novelty some
compensation for its discomfort, but the novelty rarely
outlasts the second day, while the discomfort seems to increase in a direct ratio with the length of the experience.
Philosophers may assert that a rightly constituted mind
will rise superior to all outward circumstances; but two
weeks in a Korak tent would do more to disabuse their
minds of such an erroneous impression than any amount

of logical argument. I do not profess myself to be pre-ternaturally cheerful, and the dismal aspect of things when I crawled out of my fur sleeping-bag, on the morning after our arrival at the first encampment, made me feel anything but amiable. The first beams of daylight were just struggling in misty blue lines through the smoky atmosphere of the tent. The recently kindled fire would not burn but would smoke; the air was cold and cheerless; two babies were crying in a neighboring polog; the breakfast was not ready, everybody was cross, and rather than break the harmonious impression of general misery, I became cross also. Three or four cups of hot tea, however, which were soon forthcoming, exerted their usual inspiriting influence, and we began gradually to take a more cheerful view of the situation. Summoning the "Tyón," and quickening his dull apprehension with a preliminary pipe of strong Circassian tobacco, we succeeded in making arrangements for our transportation to the next Korak encampment in the north, a distance of about forty miles. Orders were at once given for the capture of twenty reindeer and the preparation of sledges. Snatching hurriedly a few bites of hard bread and bacon by way of breakfast, I donned fur hood and mittens, and crawled out through the low doorway to see how twenty trained deer were to be separated from a herd of four thousand wild ones.

Surrounding the tent in every direction were the deer belonging to the band, some pawing up the snow with their sharp hoofs in search of moss, others clashing their antlers together and barking hoarsely in fight, or chasing one another in a mad gallop over the steppe. Near the

tent a dozen men with lassos arranged themselves in two
parallel lines, while twenty more, with a thong of seal-skin
two or three hundred yards in length, encircled a portion
of the great herd, and with shouts and waving lassos began
driving it through the narrow gantlet. The deer strove
with frightened bounds to escape from the gradually con-
tracting circle, but the seal-skin cord, held at short distances by shouting natives, invariably turned them back,
and they streamed in a struggling, leaping throng through
the narrow opening between the lines of lassoers. Ever
and anon a long cord uncoiled itself in air, and a sliding
noose fell over the antlers of some unlucky deer whose
slit ears marked him as trained, but whose tremendous
leaps and frantic efforts to escape suggested very grave
doubts as to the extent of the training. To prevent the
interference and knocking together of the deer's antlers
when they should be harnessed in couples, one horn was
relentlessly chopped off close to the head by a native
armed with a heavy sword-like knife, leaving a red ghastly
stump from which the blood trickled in little streams over
the animal's ears. They were then harnessed to sledges
in couples, by a collar and trace passing between the fore-
legs; lines were affixed to small sharp studs in the head-
stall, which pricked the right or left side of the head when
the corresponding rein was jerked, and the equipage was
ready.

Bidding good-by to the Lesnoi Kamtchadals, who returned from here, we muffled ourselves from the biting air
in our heaviest furs, took seats on our respective sledges,
and at a laconic "tōk" (go) from the "Tyón" we were

off; the little cluster of tents looking like a group of conical islands behind us as we swept out upon the limitless
ocean of the snowy steppe. Noticing that I shivered a
little in the keen air, my driver pointed away to the northward, and exclaimed with a pantomimic shrug, "Tam
shipka Kholodno"—there it's awful cold. We needed not
to be informed of the fact; the rapidly sinking thermometer indicated our approach to the regions of perpetual
frost, and I looked forward with no little apprehension to
the prospect of sleeping out-doors in the arctic temperatures of which I had read, but which I had never yet experienced.

This was my first trial of reindeer travel, and I was
a little disappointed to find that it did not quite realize the
expectations which had been excited in my boyish days
by the pictures of galloping Lapland deer in the old
geographies. The reindeer were there, but they were not
the ideal reindeer of early fancy, and I felt a vague sense
of personal injury and unjustifiable deception at the substitution of these awkward, ungainly beasts for the spirited
and fleet-footed animals of my boyish imagination. Their
trot was awkward and heavy, they carried their heads
low, and their panting breaths and gaping mouths were
constantly suggestive of complete exhaustion, and excited
pity for their apparently laborious exertions, rather than
admiration for the speed which they really did exhibit.
My ideal reindeer would never have demeaned himself
by running with his mouth wide open. When I learned,
as I afterward did, that they were compelled to breathe
through their mouths, on account of the rapid accumula-

tion of frost in their nostrils, it relieved my apprehensions
of their breaking down, but did not alter my firm conviction that my ideal reindeer was infinitely superior in
an æsthetic point of view to the real animal. I could
not but admit, however, the inestimable value of the
reindeer to his wandering owners. Besides carrying
them from place to place, he furnishes them with clothes,
food, and covering for their tents ; his antlers are made
into rude implements of all sorts ; his sinews are dried and
pounded into thread, his bones are soaked in seal oil and
burned for fuel, his entrails are cleaned, filled with tallow,
and eaten ; his blood, mixed with the contents of his
stomach, is made into "manyalla ;" his marrow and
tongue are considered the greatest of delicacies ; the stiff,
bristly skin of his legs is used to cover snow-shoes ; and
finally his whole body, sacrificed to the Korak gods,
brings down upon his owners all the spiritual and temporal
blessings which they need. It would be hard to find
another animal which fills so important a place in the
life of any body of men, as the reindeer does in the life
and domestic economy of the Siberian Koraks. I cannot now think of one which furnishes even the four prime
requisites of food, clothing, shelter, and transportation.
It is a singular fact, however, that the Siberian natives—
the only people, so far as I know, who have ever domesticated the reindeer, except the Laps—do not use in any
way the animal's milk. Why so important and desirable
an article of food should be neglected, when every other
part of the deer's body is turned to some useful account,
I cannot imagine. It is certain, however, that no one of

the four great wandering tribes of Northeastern Siberia, Koraks, Chookchees, Tungoos, and Samóotkees, uses in any way the reindeer's milk.

By two o'clock in the afternoon it began to grow dark; but we estimated that we had accomplished at least half of our day's journey, and halted for a few moments to allow our deer to eat. The last half of the distance seemed interminable. The moon rose round and bright as the shield of Achilles, and lighted up the vast, lonely " toondra" with noonday brilliancy; but its silence and desolation, the absence of any dark object upon which the fatigued eye could rest, and the apparently boundless extent of this Dead Sea of snow, oppressed us with new and strange sensations of awe. A dense mist or steam, which is an unfailing indication of intense cold, rose from the bodies of the reindeer and hung over the road long after we had passed. Beards became tangled masses of frozen iron wire; eyelids grew heavy with white rims of frost and froze together when we winked; noses assumed a white, waxen appearance with every incautious exposure, and only by frequently running beside our sledges could we keep any "feeling" in our feet. Impelled by hunger and cold, we repeated twenty times the despairing question, " How much farther is it?" and twenty times we received the stereotyped but indefinite answer of " chaimuk," near, or occasionally the encouraging assurance that we would arrive in a minute. Now we knew very well that we *should not* arrive in a minute, nor probably in forty minutes; but it afforded temporary relief to be *told* that we would. My frequent

inquiries finally spurred my driver into an attempt to ex·
press the distance arithmetically, and with evident pride
in his ability to speak Russian, he assured me that it was
only "dva verst," or two versts more.   I brightened up
at once with anticipations of a warm fire and an infinite number of cups of hot tea, and succeeded, by the
imagination of prospective comfort, in forgetting the present sense of suffering.   At the expiration, however, of
three-quarters of an hour, seeing no indication of the
promised encampment, I asked once more if it were
much farther away.   One Korak looked around over
the steppe with a well-assumed air of seeking some
landmark, and then turning to me with a confident nod,
repeated the word "verst" and held up *four fingers!*
I sank back upon my sledge in despair.   If we had been
three-quarters of an hour in losing two versts, how long
would we be in losing versts enough to get back to the
place from which we started.   It was a discouraging
problem, and after several unsuccessful attempts to solve
it by the double rule of three backwards, I gave it up.
For the benefit of the future traveller, I give, however, a
few native expressions for distances, with their numerical
equivalents :   "Chaimuk"—near, twenty versts ; " Bol·
shai nyett"—there is no more, fifteen versts ; "Sey chass
preadem"—we will arrive this minute, means any time
in the course of the day or night ; and "diloco"—far, is a
week's journey.   By bearing in mind these simple values,
the traveller will avoid much bitter disappointment, and
may get through without entirely losing faith in human
veracity.

About six o'clock in the evening, tired, hungry, and half-frozen, we caught sight of the sparks and fire-lit smoke which arose from the tents of the second encampment, and amid a general barking of dogs and hallooing of men we stopped among them. Jumping hurriedly from my sledge, with no thought but that of getting to a fire, I crawled into the first hole which presented itself, with a firm belief, founded on the previous night's experience, that it must be a door. After groping about some time in the dark, crawling over two dead reindeer and a heap of dried fish, I was obliged to shout for assistance. Great was the astonishment of the proprietor, who came to the rescue with a torch, to find a white man and a stranger crawling around aimlessly in his fish store-house. He relieved his feelings with a ty-e-e-e of amazement, and led the way, or rather crawled away, to the interior of the tent, where I found the Major endeavoring with a dull Korak knife to cut his frozen beard loose from his fur hood and open communication with his mouth through a sheet of ice and hair. The tea-kettle was soon simmering and spouting over a brisk fire, beards were thawed out, noses examined for signs of frost-bites, and in half an hour we were seated comfortably on the ground around a candle-box, drinking tea and discussing the events of the day.

Just as Vushine was filling up our cups for the third time, the skin curtain of the low doorway at our side was lifted up, and the most extraordinary figure which I ever beheld in Kamtchatka crawled silently in, straightened up to its full height of six feet, and stood majestically before us. It was an ugly, dark-featured man about thirty years of age.

He was clothed in a scarlet dress-coat with blue facings and brass buttons, with long festoons of gold cord hung across the breast, pants of black, greasy deer-skin, and fur boots. His hair was closely shaven from the crown of his head, leaving a long fringe of lank, uneven locks hanging about his ears and forehead. Long strings of small colored beads depended from his ears, and over one of them he had plastered for future use a huge quid of masticated to-bacco. About his waist was tied a ragged seal-skin thong, which supported a magnificent silver-hilted sword and embossed scabbard. His smoky, unmistakably Korak face, shaven head, scarlet coat, greasy skin pants, gold cord, seal-skin belt, silver-hilted sword, and fur boots, made up such a remarkable combination of glaring contrasts that we could do nothing for a moment but stare at him in utter amazement. He reminded me of " Talipot, the Immortal Potentate of Manacabo, Messenger of the Morning, Enlightener of the Sun, Possessor of the Whole Earth, and Mighty Monarch of the Brass-handled Sword."

"Who are you?" suddenly demanded the Major, in Russian. A low bow was the only response. "Where in the name of Chort did you come from?" Another bow. "Where did you get that coat? Can't you say something? Ay! Meroneff! Come and talk to this —— fellow, I can't make him say anything." Dodd suggested that he might be a messenger from the Expedition of Sir John Franklin, with late advices from the Pole and the Northwest passage; and the silent owner of the sword bowed affirmatively, as if this were the true solution of the mystery. "Are you a pickled cabbage?" suddenly inquired Dodd in Russian.

The Unknown intimated by a very emphatic bow that he was. "*He* don't understand anything!" said Dodd in dis· gust; "where's Meroneff?" Meroneff soon made his appearance, and began questioning the mysterious visitor in a scarlet coat as to his residence, name, and previous history. For the first time he now found a voice. "What does he say?" asked the Major, "what's his name?"

"He says his name is Khanálpoogineek."

"Where did he get that coat and sword?"

"He says 'the Great White Chief' gave it to him for a dead reindeer." This was not very satisfactory, and Meroneff was instructed to get some more intelligible information. Who the "Great White Chief" might be, and why he should give a scarlet coat and a silver-hilted sword for a dead reindeer, were questions beyond our ability to solve. Finally, Meroneff's puzzled face cleared up, and he told us that the coat and sword had been presented to the Unknown by the Emperor, as a reward for reindeer given to the starving Russians of Kamtchatka during a famine. The Korak was asked if he had received no paper with these gifts, and he immediately left the tent, and returned in a moment with a sheet of paper tied up carefully with reindeer's sinews between a couple of thin boards. This paper explained everything. The coat and sword had been given to the present owner's father, during the reign of Alexander I., by the Russian Governor of Kamtchatka, as a reward for succor afforded the Russians in a famine. From the father they had descended to the son, and the latter, proud of his inherited distinction, had presented himself to us as soon as he heard of our arrival. He wanted nothing in particular except to show himself, and after examining his sword, which was really a magnificent weapon, we gave him a few bunches of tobacco and dismissed him. We had hardly expected to find in the interior of Kamtchatka any relics of Alexander I., dating back to the time of Napoleon.

CHAPTER XIX.

On the following morning at daybreak we continued our journey, and rode until four hours after dark, over a boundless level steppe, without a single guiding landmark to point the way. I was surprised to see how accurately our drivers could determine the points of the compass and shape their course by simply looking at the snow. The heavy north-east winds which prevail in this locality throughout the winter sweep the snow into long wave-like ridges called "sastroogee," which are always perpendicular to the course of the wind, and which almost invariably run in a north-west and south-east direction. They are sometimes hidden for a few days by freshly-fallen snow; but an experienced Korak can always tell by removing the upper layer which way is north, and he travels to his destination by night or day in a nearly straight line.

We reached the third encampment about six o'clock, and upon entering the largest tent were surprised to find it crowded with natives, as if in expectation of some ceremony or entertainment. Inquiry through our interpreter elicited the interesting fact that the ceremony of marriage was about to be performed for, or rather by, two members of the band; and instead of taking up our quarters, as we at first intended, in another less crowded tent, we deter-

mined to remain and see in what manner this rite would
be solemnized by a wholly uncivilized and barbarous
people.

The marriage ceremony of the Koraks is especially remarkable for its entire originality, and for the indifference
which it manifests to the sensibilities of the bridegroom.
In no other country does there exist such a curious mixture of sense and absurdity as that which is dignified in the
social life of the Koraks with the name of marriage; and
among no other people, let us charitably hope, is the unfortunate bridegroom subjected to such humiliating indig-
nities.   The contemplation of marriage is, or ought to be,
a very serious thing to every young man; but to a Korak
of average sensibility it must be absolutely appalling.
No other proof of bravery need ever be exhibited than a
certificate of marriage (if the Koraks have such docu-
ments), and the bravery rises into positive heroism when a
man marries two or three times.   I once knew a Korak
in Kamtchatka who had four wives, and I felt as much respect for his heroic bravery as if he had charged with the
Six Hundred at Balaklava.

The ceremony, I believe, has never been described; and
inadequate as a description may be to convey an idea of
the reality, it will perhaps enable American lovers to
realize what a calamity they escaped when they were born
in America and not in Kamtchatka.   The young Korak's
troubles begin when he first falls in love; this, like
Achilles' wrath, is "the direful spring of woes unnum-
bered."   If his intentions are serious, he calls upon the
damsel's father and makes formal proposals for her hand,

ascertains the amount of her dower in reindeer, and learns her estimated value. He is probably told that he must work for his wife two or three years—a rather severe trial of any young man's affection. He then seeks an interview with the young lady herself, and performs the agreeable or disagreeable duty which corresponds in Korak to the civilized custom of "popping the question." We had hoped to get some valuable hints from the Koraks as to the best method which their experience suggested for the successful accomplishment of this delicate task ; but we could learn nothing which would be applicable to the more artificial relations of civilized society. If the young man's sentiments are reciprocated, and he obtains a positive promise of marriage, he goes cheerfully to work, like Ferdinand in "The Tempest" for Miranda's father, and spends two or three years in cutting and drawing wood, watching reindeer, making sledges, and contributing generally to the interests of his prospective father-in-law. At the end of this probationary period comes the grand " experimentum crucis," which is to decide his fate and prove the success or the uselessness of his long labor.

At this interesting crisis we had surprised our Korak friends in the third encampment. The tent which we had entered was an unusually large one, containing twenty-six " pologs," arranged in a continuous circle around its inner circumference. The open space in the centre around the fire was crowded with the dusky faces and half-shaven heads of the Korak spectators, whose attention seemed about equally divided between sundry kettles and troughs of " manyalla," boiled venison, marrow, frozen tallow, and similar delicacies, and the discussion of some controverted point of marriage etiquette. Owing to my ignorance of the language, I was not able to enter thoroughly into the merits of the disputed question ; but it seemed to be ably argued on both sides. Our sudden entrance seemed to create a temporary diversion from the legitimate business of the evening. The tattooed women and shaven-headed men stared in open-mouthed astonishment at the pale-faced guests who had come unbidden to the marriage-feast, having on no wedding garments. Our faces were undeniably dirty, our blue hunting-shirts and buck-skin pants bore the marks of two months' rough travel, in numerous rips, tears, and tatters, which were only partially masked by a thick covering of reindeer hair from our fur "kookhlánkas." Our general appearance, in fact, suggested a more intimate acquaintance with dirty "yourts," mountain thickets, and Siberian storms, than with the civilizing influences of soap, water, razors, and needles. We bore the curious scrutiny of the assemblage, however, with the indifference of men who were used to it, and sipped our hot tea while waiting for the ceremony to begin. I looked curiously around to see if I could distinguish the happy candidates for matrimonial honors ; but they were evidently concealed in one of the closed pologs. The eating and drinking seemed by this time to be about finished, and an air of expectation and suspense pervaded the entire crowd. Suddenly we were startled by the loud and regular beating of a native "barabán" or bass drum, which fairly filled the tent with a volume of sound. At the same instant the tent opened to permit the passage

of a tall, stern-looking Korak, with an armful of willow
sprouts and alder branches, which he proceeded to dis-
tribute in all the pologs of the tent. "What do you
suppose that's for?" asked Dodd in an under-tone. "I
don't know," was the reply; "keep quiet and you'll see."
The regular throbs of the drum continued throughout the
distribution of the willow sticks, and at its close the
drummer began to sing a low, musical recitative, which
increased gradually in volume and energy until it swelled
into a wild, barbarous chant, timed by the regular beats
of the heavy drum. A slight commotion followed, the
front curtains of all the pologs were thrown up, the
women stationed themselves in detachments of two or
three at the entrance of each polog, and took up the
willow branches which had been provided. In a moment
a venerable native, whom we presumed to be the father of
one of the parties, emerged from one of the pologs near
the door, leading a good-looking young Korak and the
dark-faced bride. Upon their appearance the excitement
increased to the pitch of frenzy, the music redoubled
its rapidity, the men in the centre of the tent joined in
the uncouth chant, and uttered at short intervals peculiar
shrill cries of wild excitement. At a given signal from the
native who had led out the couple, the bride darted suddenly into the first polog, and began a rapid flight around
the tent, raising the curtains between the pologs successively, and passing under. The bridegroom instantly
followed in hot pursuit; but the women who were
stationed in each compartment threw every possible
impediment in his way, tripping up his unwary feet, hold-

ing down the curtains to prevent his passage, and apply-
ing the willow and alder switches unmercifully to a very
susceptible part of his body as he stooped to raise them.
The air was filled with drum-beats, shouts of encouragement and derision, and the sound of the heavy blows which
were administered to the unlucky bridegroom by each
successive detachment of women as he ran the gantlet.
It became evident at once that despite his most violent
efforts he would fail to overtake the flying Atalanta before
she completed the circuit of the tent. Even the golden
apples of Hesperides would have availed him little against
such disheartening odds; but with undismayed perseverance he pressed on, stumbling headlong over the outstretched feet of his female persecutors, and getting
constantly entangled in the ample folds of the reindeer-
skin curtains, which were thrown with the skill of a
matador over his head and eyes. In a moment the bride
had entered the last closed polog near the door, while the
unfortunate bridegroom was still struggling with his
accumulating misfortunes about half way around the tent.
I expected to see him relax his efforts and give up the
contest when the bride disappeared, and was preparing to protest strongly in his behalf against the
unfairness of the trial; but, to my surprise, he still struggled on, and with a final plunge burst through the curtains
of the last polog and rejoined his bride. The music suddenly ceased, and the throng began to stream out of the
tent. The ceremony was evidently over. Turning to
Meroneff, who with a delighted grin had watched its progress, we inquired what it all meant. "Were they

married ? "—" Da's," was the affirmative reply. " But," we objected, " he didn't catch her."—" She waited for him, your honor, in the last polog, and if he caught her there it was enough."—" Suppose he had *not* caught her there, then what ? "—" Then," answered the Cossack, with an expressive shrug of commiseration, " the ' Caidnak' (poor fellow) would have had to work two more years." This was pleasant—for the bridegroom ! To work two years for a wife, undergo a severe course of willow sprouts at the close of his apprenticeship, and then have no security against a possible breach of promise on the part of the bride. His faith in her constancy must be un-limited. The intention of the whole ceremony was evidently to give the woman an opportunity to marry the man or not, as she chose, since it was obviously impossi-ble for him to catch her under such circumstances, unless she voluntarily waited for him in one of the pologs. The plan showed a more chivalrous regard and deference for the wishes and preferences of the gentler sex than is common in an unreconstructed state of society ; but it seemed to me, as an unprejudiced observer, that the same result might have been obtained without so much abuse of the unfortunate bridegroom ! Some regard ought to have been paid to his feelings, if he *was* a man. I could not ascertain the significance of the chastisement which was inflicted by the women upon the bridegroom with the willow switches. Dodd suggested that it might be em-blematical of married life—a sort of foreshadowing of future domestic experience ; but in view of the masculine Korak character, this hardly seemed to me probable.

No woman in her senses would try the experiment a second time upon one of the stern, resolute men who witnessed that ceremony, and who seemed to regard it *then* as perfectly proper. Circumstances would undoubtedly alter cases.

Mr. A. S. Bickmore, in the *American Journal of Science* for May, 1868, notices this curious custom of the Koraks, and says that the chastisement is intended to test the young man's " ability to bear up against the ills of life ; " but I would respectfully submit that the ills of life do not generally come in that shape, and that switching a man over the back with willow sprouts is a very singular way of preparing him for future misfortunes of any kind.

Whatever may be the motive, it is certainly an infringement upon the generally recognized prerogatives of the sterner sex, and should be discountenanced by all Koraks who favor masculine supremacy. Before they know it, they will have a woman's suffrage association on their hands, and female lecturers will be going about from band to band advocating the substitution of hickory clubs and slung-shots for the harmless willow switches, and protesting against the tyranny which will not permit them to indulge in this interesting diversion at least three times a week.

After the conclusion of the ceremony we removed to an adjacent tent, and were surprised, as we came out into the open air, to see three or four Koraks shouting and reeling about in an advanced stage of intoxication—celebrating, I suppose, the happy event which had just transpired. I knew that there was not a drop of alcoholic liquor in all Northern Kamtchatka, nor, so far as I knew, anything from which it could be made, and it was a mystery to me how they had succeeded in becoming so suddenly, thoroughly, hopelessly, undeniably drunk. Even Ross Browne's beloved Washoe, with its "howling wilderness" saloons, could not have turned out more creditable specimens of intoxicated humanity than those before us. The exciting agent, whatever it might be, was certainly as quick in its operation, and as effective in its results, as any "tangle-foot" or "bottled lightning" known to modern civilization. Upon inquiry we learned to our astonishment that they had been eating a species of the plant vulgarly known as toadstool. There is a peculiar fungus of this class in Siberia, known to the natives as "muk-a-moor," and as it possesses active intoxicating properties, it is used as a stimulant by nearly all the Siberian tribes. Taken in large quantities it is a violent narcotic poison ; but in small doses it produces all the effects of alcoholic liquor. Its habitual use, however, completely shatters the nervous system, and its sale by Russian traders to the natives has consequently been made a penal offence by Russian law. In spite of all prohibitions, the trade is still secretly carried on, and I have seen twenty dollars worth of furs bought with a single fungus. The Koraks would gather it for themselves, but it requires the shelter of timber for its growth, and is not to be found on the barren steppes over which they wander; so that they are obliged for the most part to buy it, at enormous prices, from the Russian traders. It may sound strangely to American ears, but the invitation which a convivial Korak extends to his passing friend is not, "Come in and have a drink," but, "Won't you come in and take a toadstool?" Not a very alluring proposal perhaps to a civilized toper, but one which has a magical effect upon a dissipated Korak. As the supply of these toadstools is by no means equal to the demand, Korak ingenuity has been greatly exercised in the endeavor to economize the precious stimulant, and make it go as far as possible. Sometimes, in the course of human events, it becomes imperatively necessary that a whole band shall get drunk together, and they have only one toadstool to do it with. For a description of the manner in which this band gets drunk collectively and individually upon one fungus, and keeps drunk for a week, the curious reader is referred to Goldsmith's "Citizen of the World," Letter 32. It is but just to say, however, that this horrible practice is almost entirely confined to the settled Koraks of Penzhinsk Gulf—the lowest, most degraded portion of the whole tribe. It may prevail to a limited extent among the wandering natives, but I never heard of more than one such instance outside of the Penzhinsk Gulf settlements.

Our travel for the next few days after leaving the third encampment was fatiguing and monotonous. The unvarying routine of our daily life in smoky Korak tents, and the uniform flatness and barrenness of the country over which we journeyed, became inexpressibly tiresome, and we looked forward in longing anticipation to the Russian settlement of Geezhega, at the head of Geezheginsk Gulf, which was the Mecca of our long pilgrimage.

To spend more than a week at one time with the Wandering Koraks without becoming lonesome or homesick, required an almost inexhaustible fertility of mental resource. One is thrown for entertainment entirely upon himself. No daily paper, with its fresh material for thought and discussion, comes to enliven the long blank evenings by the tent fire; no wars or rumors of wars, no *coup d'état* of state diplomacy, no excitement of political canvass ever agitates the stagnant intellectual atmosphere of Korak existence. Removed to an infinite distance, both physically and intellectually, from all of the interests, ambitions, and excitements which make up our world, the Korak simply exists, like a human oyster, in the quiet waters of his monotonous life. An occasional birth or marriage, the sacrifice of a dog, or, on rare occasions, of a man to the Korak Ahriman, and the infrequent visits of a Russian trader, are the most prominent events in his history, from the cradle to the grave. I found it almost impossible sometimes to realize, as I sat by the fire in a Korak tent, that I was still in the modern world of railroads, telegraphs, and daily newspapers. I seemed to have been carried back by some enchantment through the long cycles of time, and made a dweller in the tents of Shem and Japheth. Not a suggestion was there in all our surroundings of the vaunted enlightenment and civilization of the nineteenth century, and as we gradually accustomed ourselves to the new and strange conditions of primitive barbarism, our recollections of a civilized life faded into the unreal imagery of a vivid dream.

CHAPTER XX.

OUR long intercourse with the Wandering Koraks gave us an opportunity of observing many of their peculiarities, which would very likely escape the notice of a transient visitor; and as our journey until we reached the head of Penzhinsk Gulf was barren of incident, I will close this chapter with all the information which I could gather relative to the language, religion, superstitions, customs, and mode of life of the Kamtchatkan Koraks.

There can be no doubt whatever that the Koraks and the powerful Siberian tribe known as Chookchees (or Tchucktchis, according to Vrangell) descended originally from the same stock, and migrated together from their ancient locations to the places where they now live. Even after several centuries of separation, they resemble each other so closely that they can hardly be distinguished, and their languages differ less one from the other than the Portuguese differs from the Spanish. Our Korak interpreters found very little difficulty in conversing with Chookchees; and a comparison of vocabularies which we afterward made showed only a slight dialectical variation, which could be easily accounted for by a few centuries of separation. None of the Siberian languages with which I am acquainted are written, and, lacking a fixed standard of reference, they change with great rapidity. This is

shown by a comparison of a modern Chookchee vocabulary with the one compiled by M. de Lesseps in 1788.
Many words have altered so materially as to be hardly
recognizable.   Others, on the contrary, such as " tin tin,"
ice, " oottoot," wood, " weeñgay," no, " āy," yes, and
most of the numerals up to ten, have undergone no change
whatever.   Both Koraks and Chookchees count by fives
instead of tens, a peculiarity which is also noticeable in the
language of the Co-Yukons in Alaska.   The Korak numerals are :—

Innín,	One.
Née-ak°h,	Two.
Nee-ók°h,	Three.
Nee-ák°h,	Four.
Míl-li-gen,	Five.
In-nín mil-li-gen,	Five-one.
Neé-ak°h "	Five-two.
Nee-ókh "	Five-three.
Nee-ákh "	Five-four.
Meen-ye-geet-k°hin,	Ten.

After ten they count ten-one, ten-two, etc., up to fifteen,
and then ten-five-one ; but their numerals become so hopelessly complicated when they get above twenty, that it
would be easier to carry a pocketful of stones and count
with them, than to pronounce the corresponding words.

Fifty-six, for instance, is " Nee-akh-khleep-kin-meen-ye-
geet-khin-par-ol-in-nin-mil-li-gen," and it is only fifty-six
after it is all pronounced!   It ought to be at least two
hundred and sixty-three millions nine hundred and fourteen thousand seven hundred and one—and then it would

be long. But the Koraks rarely have occasion to use high numbers ; and when they do, they have an abundance of time. It would be a hard day's work for a boy to explain in Korak one of the miscellaneous problems in Ray's Higher Arithmetic. To say $324 \times 5260 = 1,704,240$ would certainly entitle him to a recess of an hour and a reward of merit. We were never able to trace any resemblance whatever between the Koraki-Chookchee language and the languages spoken by the natives on the eastern side of Behring's Straits. If there be any resemblance, it must be in grammar rather than in vocabulary.

The religion of all the natives of Northeastern Siberia, wandering and settled, including six or seven widely different tribes, is that corrupted form of Buddhism known as "Shamanism." It is a religion which varies considerably in different places and among different people ; but with the Koraks and Chookchees it may be briefly defined as the worship of the evil spirits who are supposed to be embodied in all the mysterious powers and manifestations of Nature, such as epidemic and contagious diseases, severe storms, famines, eclipses, and brilliant Auroras. It takes its name from the "Shamáns" or priests, who act as interpreters of the evil spirits' wishes and as mediators between them and man. All unnatural phenomena, and especially those of a disastrous and terrible nature, are attributed to the direct action of these evil spirits, and are considered as plain manifestations of their displeasure. It is claimed by many that the whole system of "Shamanism" is a gigantic imposture practised by a few cunning priests upon the easy credulity of superstitious natives.

This I am sure is a prejudiced view. No one who has ever lived with the Siberian natives, studied their character, subjected himself to the same influences that surround them, and put himself as far as possible in their places, will ever doubt the sincerity of either priests or followers, or wonder that the worship of evil spirits should be their only religion. It is the only religion possible for such men in such circumstances. A recent writer * of great fairness and impartiality has described so admirably the character of the Siberian Koraks, and the origin and nature of their religious belief, that I cannot do better than quote his words :—

" Terror is everywhere the beginning of religion. The phenomena which impress themselves most forcibly on the mind of the savage are not those which enter manifestly into the sequence of natural laws, and which are productive of most beneficial effects ; but those which are disastrous and apparently abnormal. Gratitude is less vivid than fear, and the smallest infraction of a natural law produces a deeper impression than the most sublime of its ordinary operations. When, therefore, the most startling and terrible aspects of Nature are presented to his mind—when the more deadly forms of disease or natural convulsion desolate his land, the savage derives from them an intensely realized perception of diabolical presence. In the darkness of the night ; amid the yawning chasms and the wild echoes of the mountain gorge ; under the blaze of the comet or the solemn gloom of the eclipse ;

* W. E. H. Lecky. *Hist. of Rationalism in Europe.*

when famine has blasted the land; when the earthquake and the pestilence have slaughtered their thousands; in every form of disease which refracts and distorts the reason, in all that is strange, portentous, and deadly, he feels and cowers before the supernatural. Completely exposed to all the influences of Nature, and completely ignorant of the chain of sequence that unites its various parts, he lives in continual dread of what he deems the direct and isolated acts of evil spirits. Feeling them continually near him, he will naturally endeavor to enter into communion with them. He will strive to propitiate them with gifts. If some great calamity has fallen upon him, or if some vengeful passion has mastered his reason, he will attempt to invest himself with their authority, and his excited imagination will soon persuade him that he has succeeded in his desire."

These pregnant words are the key to the religion of the Siberian natives, and afford the only intelligible explanation of the origin of "Shamáns." If any proof were needed that this system of religion is the natural outgrowth of human nature in certain conditions of barbarism, it would be furnished by the universal prevalence of Shamanism in Northeastern Siberia among so many diverse tribes of different character and different origin. The tribe of Tungoos, for instance, is certainly of Chinese descent, and the tribe of Yakoots is certainly Turkish. Both came from different regions, bringing different beliefs, superstitions, and modes of thought; but, when both were removed from all disturbing agencies and subjected to the same external influences, both developed precisely the same system of religious belief. If a band of ignorant, barbarous Mahometans were transported to Northeastern Siberia, and compelled to live alone in tents, century after century, amid the wild, gloomy scenery of the Stanavoi Mountains, to suffer terrific storms whose causes they could not explain, to lose their reindeer suddenly by an epidemic disease which defied human remedies, to be frightened by magnificent Auroras that set the whole universe in a blaze, and decimated by pestilences whose nature they could not understand and whose disastrous effects they were powerless to avert—they would almost inevitably lose by degrees their faith in Allah and Mahomet, and become precisely such Shamanists as the Siberian Koraks and Chookchees are to-day. Even a whole century of partial civilization and Christian training cannot wholly counteract the irresistible Shamanistic influence which is exerted upon the mind by the wilder, more terrible manifestations of Nature in these lonely and inhospitable regions. The Kamtchadals who accompanied me to the Samanka Mountains were the sons of Christian parents, and had been brought up from infancy in the Greek Church; they were firm believers in the Divine atonement and in Divine Providence, and prayed always night and morning for safety and preservation; yet, when overtaken by a storm in that gloomy range of mountains, the sense of the supernatural overcame their religious convictions, God seemed far away while evil spirits were near and active, and they sacrificed a dog, like very pagans, to propitiate the diabolical wrath of which the storm was an evidence. I could cite many similar instances, where the strongest and apparently most sincere

convictions of the reality of Divine government and superintendence have been overcome by the influence upon the
imagination of some startling and unusual phenomenon of
Nature.   Man's actions are governed not so much by
what he intellectually believes as by what he vividly re-
alizes ; and it is this vivid realization of diabolical presence
which has given rise to the religion of Shamanism.

The duties of the Shamáns or priests among the Koraks
are, to make incantations over the sick, to hold communication with the evil spirits, and to interpret their wishes
and decrees to man.   Whenever any calamity, such as
disease, storm, or famine comes upon a band, it is of
course attributed to some spirit's displeasure, and the Shamán is consulted as to the best method of appeasing his
wrath.   The priest to whom application is made assembles
the people in one of the largest tents of the encampment,
puts on a long robe marked with fantastic figures of birds
and beasts and curious hieroglyphic emblems, unbinds his
long black hair, and taking up a large native drum, begins
to sing in a subdued voice to the accompaniment of slow,
steady drum-beats.   As the song progresses it increases
in energy and rapidity, the priest's eyes seem to become
fixed, he contorts his body as if in spasms, and increases
the vehemence of his wild chant until the drum-beats
make one continuous roll.   Then, springing to his feet and
jerking his head convulsively until his long hair fairly
snaps, he begins a frantic dance about the tent, and finally
sinks apparently exhausted into his seat.   In a few moments he delivers to the awe-stricken natives the message
which he has received from the evil spirits, and which

consists generally of an order to sacrifice a certain number of dogs or reindeer, or perhaps a man, to the offended
deities.

In these wild incantations the priests sometimes prac-
tise all sorts of frauds upon their credulous followers, by
pretending to swallow live coals and to pierce their bodies
with knives; but, in a majority of instances, the Shamán
seems to actually believe that he is under the control and
guidance of diabolical intelligence. The natives themselves, however, seem to doubt occasionally the priest's
pretended inspiration, and whip him severely to test the
sincerity of his professions and the genuineness of his
revelations. If his fortitude sustains him under the in-
fliction without any exhibition of human weakness or
suffering, his authority as a minister of the evil spirits is
vindicated, and his commands obeyed. Aside from the
sacrifices which are ordered by the Shamáns, the Koraks
offer general oblations at least twice a year, to insure
a good catch of fish and seal and a prosperous season.
We frequently saw twenty or thirty dogs suspended by
the hind legs on long poles over a single encampment.
Quantities of green grass are collected during the summer
and twisted into wreaths, to be hung around the necks of
the slaughtered animals; and offerings of tobacco are
always thrown to the evil spirits when the Koraks cross
the summit of a mountain. The bodies of the dead,
among all the wandering tribes, are burned, together with
all their effects, in the hope of a final resurrection of both
spirit and matter; and the sick, as soon as their recovery
becomes hopeless, are either stoned to death or speared.

We found it to be true, as we had been told by the Russians and the Kamtchadals, that the Koraks murdered all
their old people as soon as sickness or the infirmities of
age unfitted them for the hardships of a nomadic life.
Long experience has given them a terrible familiarity
with the best and quickest methods of taking life; and
they often explained to us with the most sickening
minuteness, as we sat at night in their smoky pologs, the
different ways in which a man could be killed, and pointed
out the vital parts of the body where a spear or knife
thrust would prove most instantly fatal. I thought of
De Quincey's celebrated Essay upon "Murder Considered
as one of the Fine Arts," and of the field which a Korak
encampment would afford to his "Society of Connoisseurs
in Murder." All Koraks are taught to look upon such
a death as the natural end of their existence, and they
meet it generally with perfect composure. Instances are
rare where a man desires to outlive the period of his
physical activity and usefulness. They are put to death
in the presence of the whole band, with elaborate but unintelligible ceremonies; their bodies are then burned, and
the ashes suffered to be scattered and blown away by the
wind.

These customs of murdering the old and sick, and
burning the bodies of the dead, grow naturally out of the
wandering life which the Koraks have adopted, and are
only illustrations of the powerful influence which physical
laws exert everywhere upon the actions and moral feelings of men. They both follow logically and almost
inevitably from the very nature of the country and cli-

mate. The barrenness of the soil in Northeastern Siberia, and the severity of the long winter, led man to domesticate the reindeer as the only means of obtaining a subsistence ; the domestication of the reindeer necessitated a wandering life ; a wandering life made sickness and infirmity unusually burdensome to both sufferers and supporters ; and this finally led to the murder of the old and sick, as a measure both of policy and mercy. The same causes gave rise to the custom of burning the dead. Their nomadic life made it impossible for them to have any one place of common sepulture, and only with the greatest difficulty could they dig graves at all in the perpetually frozen ground. Bodies could not be left to be torn by wolves, and burning them was the only practicable alternative. Neither of these customs presupposes any original and innate savageness or barbarity on the part of the Koraks themselves. They are the natural development of certain circumstances, and only prove that the strongest emotions of human nature, such as filial reverence, fraternal affection, selfish love of life, and respect for the remains of friends, all are powerless to oppose the operation of great natural laws. The Russian Church is endeavoring by missionary enterprise to convert all the Siberian tribes to Christianity ; and although they have met with a certain degree of apparent success among the settled tribes of Yookágaree, Chooáncee, and Kamtchadálle, the wandering natives still cling to Shamanism, and there are more than 70,000 followers of that religion in the scanty population of Northeastern Siberia. Any permanent and genuine conversion of the Wandering Koraks and Chook-

chees must be preceded by some educational enlightenment and an entire change in their mode of life.

Among the many superstitions of the Wandering Koraks and Chookchees, one of the most noticeable is their
reluctance to part with a living reindeer.   You may purchase as many dead deer as you choose, up to five hundred, for about seventy cents apiece ; but a living deer
they will not give to you for love nor money.   You may
offer them what they consider a fortune in tobacco, copper kettles, beads, and scarlet cloth, for a single live reindeer, but they will persistently refuse to sell him ; yet, if
you will allow them to kill the very same animal, you can
have his carcass for one small string of common glass
beads.   It is useless to argue with them about this absurd
superstition.   You can get no reason for it or explanation
of it, except that " to sell a live reindeer would be ' atkin '—bad."   As it was very necessary in the construction
of our proposed telegraph line to have trained reindeer
of our own, we offered every conceivable inducement to
the Koraks to part with one single deer ; but all our
efforts were in vain.   They could sell us a hundred dead
deer for a hundred pounds of tobacco ; but five hundred
pounds would not tempt them to part with a single animal as long as the breath of life was in his body.   During
the two years and a half which we spent in Siberia, no
one of our parties, so far as I know, ever succeeded in
buying from the Koraks or Chookchees a single living
reindeer.   All the deer which we eventually owned—
some eight hundred—we obtained from the Wandering
Tungoos.

The Koraks are probably the weathiest deer-owners in Siberia, and consequently in the world. Many of the herds which we saw in Northern Kamtchatka numbered from eight to twelve thousand ; and we were told that a certain rich Korak, who lived in the middle of the great "Toondra," had three immense herds in different places, numbering in the aggregate thirty thousand head. The care of these great herds is almost the only occupation of the Koraks' lives. They are obliged to travel constantly from place to place to find them food, and to watch them night and day to protect them from wolves. Every day, eight or ten Koraks, armed with spears and knives, leave the encampment just before dark, walk a mile or two to the place where the deer happen to be pastured, build themselves little huts of trailing pine branches, about three feet in height and two in diameter, and squat in them throughout the long, cold hours of an arctic night, watching for wolves. The worse the weather is, the greater the necessity for vigilance. Sometimes, in the middle of a dark winter's night, when a terrible northeast storm is howling across the steppe in clouds of flying snow, a band of wolves will make a fierce, sudden attack upon a herd of deer, and scatter it to the four winds. This it is the business of the Korak sentinels to prevent. Alone and almost unsheltered on a great ocean of snow, each man squats down in his frail bee-hive of a hut, and spends the long winter nights in watching the magnificent Auroras, which seem to fill the blue vault of heaven with blood and dye the earth in crimson, listening to the pulsating of the blood in his ears and the faint distant

howls of his enemies the wolves.   Patiently he endures
cold which freezes mercury into solid lumps, and storms
which sweep away his frail shelter like chaff in a mist of
flying snow.   Nothing discourages him ; nothing frightens
him into seeking the shelter of the tents.   I have seen
him watching deer at night, with nose and cheeks frozen
so that they had mortified and turned black ; and have
come upon him early cold winter mornings, squatting
under three or four bushes, with his face buried in his fur
coat, as if he were dead.   I could never pass one of those
little bush-huts on a great desolate " toondra" without
thinking of the man who had once squatted in it alone,
and trying to imagine what had been his thoughts while
watching through long dreary nights for the first faint
flush of dawn.   Had he never wondered, as the fiery arms
of the Aurora waved over his head, what caused these
mysterious streamers?   Had the solemn far-away stars
which circled ceaselessly above the snowy plain never
suggested to him the possibility of other brighter, happier
worlds than this ?   Had not some

> "—— revealings faint and far,
>   Stealing down from moon and star,
>   Kindled in that human clod
>   Thought of Destiny and God?"

Alas for poor unaided human nature !   Supernatural
influences he could and did feel ; but the drum and wild
shrieks of the Shamán showed how utterly he failed to understand their nature and teachings.

The natural disposition of the Wandering Koraks is thoroughly good. They treat their women and children with great kindness; and during all my intercourse with them, extending over two years, I never saw a woman or a child struck. Their honesty is remarkable. Frequently they would harness up a team of reindeer after we had left their tents in the morning, and overtake us at a distance of five or ten miles, with a knife, a pipe, or some such trifle which we had overlooked and forgotten in the hurry of departure. Our sledges, loaded with tobacco, beads, and trading goods of all kinds, were left unguarded outside their tents; but never, so far as we knew, was a single article stolen. We were treated by many bands with as much kindness and generous hospitality as I ever experienced in a civilized country and among Christian people; and if I had no money or friends, I would appeal to a band of Wandering Koraks for help with much more confidence than I would ask the same favor of many an American family. Cruel and barbarous they may be, according to our ideas of cruelty and barbarity; but they have never been known to commit an act of treachery, and I would trust my life as unreservedly in their hands as I would in the hands of any other uncivilized people whom I have ever known.

Night after night, as we journeyed to the northward, the polar star approached nearer and nearer to the zenith, until finally, at the sixty-second parallel of latitude, we caught sight of the white peaks of the Stanavoi Mountains, at the head of Penzhinsk Gulf, which marked the northern boundary of Kamtchatka. Under the shelter of their snowy slopes we camped for the last time in the smoky tents of the Kamtchatkan Koraks, ate for the last time from their wooden troughs, and bade good-by with little regret to the desolate steppes of the peninsula and to tent-life with its wandering people.

CHAPTER XXI.

On the morning of November 23d, in a clear, bracing atmosphere of twenty-five degrees below zero, we arrived at the mouth of the large river called the Penzhina, which empties into Penzhinsk Gulf, at the head of the Okhotsk Sea. A dense cloud of frozen mist, which hung over the middle of the gulf, showed the presence there of open water; but the mouth of the river was completely choked up with great hummocks, rugged green slabs, and confused masses of ice, hurled in by a southwest storm, and frozen together in the wildest shapes of angular disorder. Through the gray mist we could see dimly, on a high bluff opposite, the strange outlines of the X-shaped yourts of the Kamenoi Koraks.

Leaving our drivers to get the reindeer and sledges across as best they could, the Major, Dodd, and I started on foot, picking our way between huge irregular blocks of clear green ice, climbing on hands and knees over enormous bergs, falling into wide, deep crevices, and stumbling painfully across the *chevaux-de-frise* of sharp splintered fragments into which the ice had been broken by a heavy sea. We had almost reached the other side, when Dodd suddenly cried out, " *Oh*, Kennan! Your nose is all white; rub it with snow—quick!" I have not

the slightest doubt that the rest of my face also turned
white at this alarming announcement; for the loss of my
nose at the very outset of my Arctic career would be a
very serious misfortune.   I caught up a handful of snow,
however, mixed with sharp splinters of ice, and rubbed
the insensible member until there was not a particle of
skin left on the end of it, and then continued the friction
with my mitten until my arm ached.   If energetic treatment would save it, I was determined not to lose it that
time. Feeling at last a painful thrill of returning circulation,
I relaxed my efforts, and climbed up the steep bluff behind
Dodd and the Major, to the Korak village of Kamenoi.

The settlement resembled as much as anything a collection of Titanic wooden hour-glasses, which had been
half shaken down and reduced to a state of rickety
dilapidation by an earthquake.   The houses—if houses
they could be called—were about twenty feet in height,
rudely constructed of drift-wood which had been thrown
up by the sea, and could be compared in shape to nothing
but hour-glasses.   They had no doors or windows of any
kind, and could only be entered by climbing up a pole on
the outside, and sliding down another pole through the
chimney—a mode of entrance whose practicability depended entirely upon the activity and intensity of the
fire which burned underneath.   The smoke and sparks,
although sufficiently disagreeable, were trifles of comparative insignificance.   I remember being told, in early
infancy, that Santa Claus always came into a house
through the chimney; and although I accepted the statement with the unreasoning faith of childhood, I could

never understand how that singular feat of climbing down
a chimney could be safely accomplished. To satisfy myself, I felt a strong inclination, every Christmas, to try
the experiment, and was only prevented from doing so
by the consideration of stove-pipes. I might succeed, I
thought, in getting down the chimney; but coming out
into a room through an eight-inch stove-pipe and a narrow stove-door was utterly out of the question. My first
entrance into a Korak yourt, however, at Kamenoi,
solved all my childish difficulties, and proved the possibility of entering a house in the eccentric way which
Santa Claus is supposed to adopt. A large crowd of
savage-looking fur-clad natives had gathered around us
when we entered the village, and now stared at us with
stupid curiosity as we made our first attempt at climbing
a pole to get into a house. Out of deference for the
Major's rank and superior attainments, we permitted him
to go first. He succeeded very well in getting up the
first pole, and lowered himself with sublime faith into the
dark narrow chimney-hole, out of which were pouring
clouds of smoke; but at this critical moment, when his
head was still dimly visible in the smoke, and his body
out of sight in the chimney, he suddenly came to grief.
The holes in the log down which he was climbing were
too small to admit even his toes, covered as they were
with heavy fur boots; and there he hung in the chimney,
afraid to drop and unable to climb out—a melancholy
picture of distress. Tears ran out of his closed eyes as
the smoke enveloped his head, and he only coughed and
strangled whenever he tried to shout for help. At last a

native on the inside, startled at the appearance of his struggling body, came to his assistance, and succeeded in lowering him safely to the ground. Profiting by his experience, Dodd and I paid no attention to the holes, but putting our arms around the smooth log, slid swiftly down until we struck bottom. As I opened my tearful eyes, I was saluted by a chorus of drawling "Zda-rō'-ō-o-va's" from half a dozen skinny, greasy old women, who sat cross-legged on a raised platform around the fire, sewing fur clothes.

The interior of a Korak yourt—that is, of one of the wooden yourts of the *settled* Koraks—presents a strange and not very inviting appearance to one who has never become accustomed by long habit to its dirt, smoke, and frigid atmosphere. It receives its only light, and that of a cheerless, gloomy character, through the round hole, about twenty feet above the floor, which serves as window, door, and chimney, and which is reached by a round log with holes in it, that stands perpendicularly in the centre. The beams, rafters, and logs which compose the yourt are all of a glossy blackness, from the smoke in which they are constantly enveloped. A wooden platform, raised about a foot from the earth, extends out from the walls on three sides to a width of six feet, leaving an open spot eight or ten feet in diameter in the centre for the fire and a huge copper kettle of melting snow. On the platform are pitched three or four square skin pologs, which serve as sleeping apartments for the inmates and as refuges from the smoke, which sometimes becomes almost unendurable. A little circle of flat stones on the ground, in the centre of the yourt, forms the fire-place, over which is usually simmering a kettle of fish or rein-deer-meat, which, with dried salmon, seal's blubber, and rancid oil, makes up the Korak bill of fare. Everything which you see or touch bears the distinguishing marks of Korak origin—grease and smoke. Whenever any one enters the yourt, you are apprised of the fact by a total eclipse of the chimney-hole and a sudden darkness, and as you look up through a mist of reindeer hairs, scraped off from the coming man's fur coat, you see a thin pair of legs descending the pole in a cloud of smoke. The legs of your acquaintances you soon learn to recognize by some peculiarity of shape and covering; and their faces, considered as means of personal identification, assume a secondary importance. If you see Ivan's legs coming down the chimney, you feel a moral certainty that Ivan's head is somewhere above in the smoke; and Nicolai's boots, appearing in bold relief against the sky through the entrance hole, afford as satisfactory proof of Nicolai's identity as his head would, provided that part of his body came in first. Legs, therefore, are the most expressive features of a Korak's countenance, when con-sidered from an interior standpoint. When snow drifts up against the yourt, so as to give the dogs access to the chimney, they take a perfect delight in lying around the hole, peering down into the yourt, and snuffing the odors of boiling fish which rise from the huge kettle underneath. Not unfrequently they get into a grand comprehensive free fight for the best place of observation; and just as you are about to take your dinner of boiled salmon off the fire, down comes a struggling, yelping dog into the kettle, while his triumphant antagonist looks down through the chimney-hole with all the complacency of gratified vengeance upon his unfortunate victim. A Korak takes the half-scalded dog by the back of the neck, carries him up the chimney, pitches him over the edge of the yourt into a snow-drift, and returns with unruffled serenity to eat the fish-soup which has thus been irregularly flavored with dog and thickened with hairs. Hairs, and especially reindeer's hairs, are among the indispensable ingredients of everything cooked in a Korak yourt, and we soon came to regard them with perfect indifference. No matter what precautions we might take, they were sure to find their way into our tea and soup, and stick persistently to our fried meat. Some one was constantly going out or coming in over the fire, and the reindeer-skin coats scraping back and forth through the chimney-hole shed a perfect cloud of short gray hairs, which sifted down over and into everything of an eatable nature underneath. Our first meal in a Korak yourt, therefore, at Kamenoi, was not at all satisfactory.

We had not been twenty minutes in the settlement before the yourt which we occupied was completely crowded with stolid, brutal-looking men, dressed in spotted deer-skin clothes, wearing strings of colored beads in their ears, and carrying heavy knives two feet in length in sheaths tied around their legs. They were evidently a different class of natives from any we had yet seen, and their savage animal faces did not inspire us with much confidence. A good-looking Russian, however, soon made his appearance, and

coming up to us with uncovered head, bowed and introduced himself as a Cossack from Geezhega, sent to meet
us by the Russian Governor at that place. The courier
who had preceded us from Lesnoi had reached Geezhega
ten days before us, and the Governor had despatched a Cossack at once to meet us at Kamenoi, and conduct us through
the settled Korak villages around the head of Penzhinsk
Gulf. The Cossack soon cleared the yourt of natives,
and the Major proceeded to question him about the character of the country north and west of Geezhega, the distance from Kamenoi to the Russian outpost of Anadyrsk,
the facilities for winter travel, and the time necessary for
the journey. Fearful for the safety of the party of men
which he presumed to have been landed by the engineer-
in-chief at the mouth of the Anadyr River, Major Abaza
had intended to go directly from Kamenoi to Anadyrsk
himself in search of them, and to send Dodd and me
westward along the coast of the Okhotsk Sea to meet
Mahood and Bush. The Cossack, however, told us that
a party of men from the Anadyr River had arrived at
Geezhega on dog-sledges just previous to his departure,
and that they had brought no news of any Americans in
the vicinity of Anadyrsk or on the river. Col. Bulkley,
the chief-engineer of the enterprise, had promised us,
when we sailed from San Francisco, that he would land a
party of men with a whaleboat at or near the mouth of
the Anadyr River, early enough in the season so that they
could ascend the river to the settlement of Anadyrsk and
open communication with us by the first winter road.
This he had evidently failed to do ; for, if a party had been

so landed, the Anadyrsk people would certainly have heard something about it.   The unfavorable nature of the country around Behring's Straits, or the lateness of the season when the company's vessels reached that point, had probably compelled the abandonment of this part of the original plan.   Major Abaza had always disapproved the idea of leaving a party near Behring's Straits ; but he could not help feeling a little disappointment when he found that no such party had been landed, and that he was left with only four men to explore the eighteen hundred miles of country between the straits and the Amoor River. The Cossack said that no difficulty would be experienced in getting dog-sledges and men at Geezhega to explore any part of the country west or north of that place, and that the Russian Governor would give us every possible assistance.

Under these circumstances there was nothing to be done but to push on to Geezhega, which could be reached, the Cossack said, in two or three days.   The Kamenoi Koraks were ordered to provide a dozen dog-sledges at once, to carry us on to the next settlement of Shestakóva ; and the whole village was soon engaged, under the Cossack's superintendence, in transferring our baggage and provisions from the deer-sledges of the Wandering Koraks to the long, narrow dog-sledges of their settled relations. Our old drivers were then paid off in tobacco, beads, and showy calico prints, and after a good deal of quarreling and disputing about loads between the Koraks and our new Cossack Kerrillof, everything was reported ready. Although it was now almost noon, the air was still keen as a knife; and, muffling up our faces and heads in great tippets, we took seats on our respective sledges, and the fierce Kamenoi dogs went careering out of the village and down the bluff in a perfect cloud of snow, raised by the spiked " oerstels " of their drivers.

The Major, Dodd, and I were travelling in covered sledges, known to the Siberians as " pavoskas," and the reckless driving of the Kamenoi Koraks made us wish, in less than an hour, that we had taken some other means of conveyance, from which we could escape more readily in case of accident or overturn. As it was, we were so boxed up that we could hardly move without assistance. Our pavoskas resembled very much long narrow coffins, covered with seal-skin and mounted on runners, and roofed over at the head by a stiff hood just large enough to sit up in. A heavy curtain was fastened to the edge of this top or hood, and in bad weather it could be pulled down and buttoned so as to exclude the air and flying snow. When we were seated in these sledges our legs were thrust down into the long coffin-shaped boxes upon which the drivers sat, and our heads and shoulders sheltered by the seal-skin hoods. Imagine an eight-foot coffin mounted on runners, and a man sitting up in it with a bushel basket over his head, and you will have a very correct idea of a Siberian pavoska. Our legs were immovably fixed in boxes, and our bodies so wedged in with pillows and heavy furs that we could neither get out nor turn over. In this helpless condition we were completely at our drivers' mercy; if they chose to let us slide over the edge of a precipice in the mountains, all we could do

was to shut our eyes and trust in Providence. Seven
times in less than three hours my Kamenoi driver, with
the assistance of fourteen crazy dogs and a spiked stick,
turned my pavoska exactly bottom side up, dragged it in
that position until the hood was full of snow, and then
left me standing on my head, with my legs in a box and
my face in a snow-drift, while he took a smoke and calmly
meditated upon the difficulties of mountain travel and the
versatility of dog-sledges! It was enough to make Job
curse his grandmother! I threatened him with a revolver,
and swore indignantly by all the evil spirits in the Korak
theogony, that if he upset me in that way again I would
kill him without benefit of clergy, and carry mourning
and lamentation to the houses of all his relatives. But it
was of no use. He didn't know enough to be afraid of a
pistol, and couldn't understand my murderous threats.
He only just squatted down upon his heels on the snow,
puffed his cheeks out with smoke, and stared at me in
stupid amazement, as if I had been some singular species
of wild animal, which exhibited a strange propensity to
jabber and gesticulate in the most ridiculous manner
without any apparent cause. Then, whenever he wanted
to ice his sledge runners, which was as often as three
times an hour, he coolly capsized the pavoska, prpoped it
up with his spiked stick, and I stood on my head while
he rubbed the runners down with water and a piece of
deer-skin. This finally drove me to desperation, and I
succeeded, after a prolonged struggle, in getting out of
my coffin-shaped box, and seated myself with indignant
feelings and murderous inclinations by the side of my im-

perturbable driver. Here my unprotected nose began to
freeze again, and my time, until we reached Shestakova,
was about equally divided between rubbing that trouble
some feature with one hand, holding on with the other,
and picking myself up out of snow-drifts with both.

The only satisfaction which I had was in seeing the
state of aggravation to which the Major was reduced by
the stupidity and ugliness of his driver. Whenever he
wanted to go on, the driver insisted upon stopping to take
a smoke; when he wanted to smoke, the driver capsized
him skilfully into a snow-drift; when he wanted to walk
down a particularly steep hill, the driver shouted to his
dogs and carried him to the bottom like an avalanche, at
the imminent peril of his life ; when he desired to sleep,
the driver intimated by impudent gestures that he had
better get out and walk up the side of a mountain ; until,
finally, the Major called Kerrillof and made him tell the
Korak distinctly and emphatically, that if he did not obey
orders and show a better disposition, he would be lashed
on his sledge, carried to Geezhega, and turned over to
the Russian Governor for punishment. He paid some
attention to this ; but all our drivers exhibited an insolent
rudeness which we had never before met with in Siberia,
and which was very provoking. The Major declared that
when our line should be in process of construction and
he should have force enough to do it, he would teach
the Kamenoi Koraks a lesson that they would not soon
forget.

We travelled all the afternoon over a broken country,
perfectly destitute of vegetation, which lay between a range

of bare white mountains and the sea, and just before dark
reached the settlement of Shestakova, which was situated
on the coast, at the mouth of a small wooded stream.
Stopping here only a few moments to rest our dogs, we
pushed on to another Korak village called Meekina, ten miles
farther west, where we finally stopped for the night.

Meekina was only a copy of Kamenoi on a smaller
scale. It had the same hour-glass houses, the same conical "bologans" elevated on stilts, and the same large
skeletons of seal-skin "baideras" or ocean canoes were
ranged in a row on the beach. We climbed up the best-
looking yourt in the village—over which hung a dead dis-
embowelled dog, with a wreath of green grass around his
neck—and slid down the chimney into a miserable room
filled to suffocation with blue smoke, lighted only by a
small fire on the earthen floor, and redolent of decayed
fish and rancid oil.   Vushine soon had a tea-kettle over the
fire, and in twenty minutes we were seated like cross-legged Turks on the raised platform at one end of the yourt,
munching hard bread and drinking tea, while about twenty
ugly, savage-looking men squatted in a circle around us
and watched our motions.   The settled Koraks of Penzhinsk Gulf are unquestionably the worst, ugliest, most
brutal and degraded natives in all Northeastern Siberia.
They do not number more than three or four hundred,
and live in five different settlements along the sea-coast;
but they made us more trouble than all the other inhabitants of Siberia and Kamtchatka together.   They led,
originally, a wandering life like the other Koraks; but, losing
their deer by some misfortune or disease, they built them-

selves houses of drift-wood on the sea-coast, settled down, and now gain a scanty subsistence by fishing, catching seals, and hunting for carcasses of whales which have been killed by American whaling vessels, stripped of blubber, and then cast ashore by the sea. They are cruel and brutal in disposition, insolent to everybody, revengeful, dishonest, and untruthful. Everything which the Wandering Koraks are, they are not. The reasons for the great difference between the settled and the Wandering Koraks are various. In the first place, the former live in fixed villages, which are visited very frequently by the Russian traders; and through these traders and Russian peasants they have received many of the worst vices of civilization without any of its virtues. To this must be added the demoralizing influence of American whalers, who have given the settled Koraks rum and cursed them with horrible diseases, which are only aggravated by their diet and mode of life. They have learned from the Russians to lie, cheat, and steal; and from whalers to drink rum and be licentious. Besides all these vices, they eat the intoxicating Siberian toadstool in inordinate quantities, and this habit alone will in time debase and brutalize any body of men to the last degree. From nearly all these demoralizing influences the Wandering Koraks are removed by the very nature of their life. They spend more of their time in the open air, they have healthier and better-balanced physical constitutions, they rarely see Russian traders or drink Russian vodka, and they are generally temperate, chaste, and manly in all their habits. As a natural consequence they are better men, morally, physically, and intel-

lectually, than the settled natives ever will or can be. I
have very sincere and hearty admiration for many Wandering
Koraks whom I met occasionally on the great Siberian
"toondras," but their settled relatives are the worst specimens of men that I ever saw in all Northern Asia, from
Behring's Straits to the Ural Mountains.

CHAPTER XXII.

WE left Meekina early, November 23d, and started out upon another great snowy plain, where there was no vegetation whatever except a little wiry grass and a few meagre patches of trailing pine.

Ever since leaving Lesnoi I had been studying attentively the art or science, whichever it be, of dog-driving, with the fixed but unexpressed resolution that at some future time, when everything should be propitious, I would assume the control of my own team, and astonish Dodd and the natives with a display of my skill as a "kiour."

I had found by some experience that these unlettered Koraks estimated a man, not so much by what he knew which they did not, as by what he knew concerning their own special and peculiar pursuits; and I determined to demonstrate, even to their darkened understandings, that the knowledge of civilization was universal in its application, and that the white man, notwithstanding his disadvantage in color, could drive dogs better by intuition than they could by the aggregated wisdom of centuries; that in fact he could, if necessary, " evolve the principles of dog-driving out of the depths of his moral consciousness." I must confess, however, that I was not a thorough convert to my own ideas; and I therefore did not disdain to avail myself of the results of native experience, as far as they coincided with my own convictions, as to the nature of the true and beautiful in dog-driving. I had watched every motion of my Korak driver; had learned theoretically the manner of thrusting the spiked stick between the uprights of the runners into the snow, to act as a brake; had committed to memory and practised assiduously the guttural monosyllables which meant, in dog-language, "right" and "left," as well as many others which meant something else, but which I had heard addressed to dogs; and I laid the flattering unction to my soul that I could drive as well as a Korak, if not better. To my inexperienced eye it was as easy as losing money in California mining stocks. On this day, therefore, as the road was good and the weather propitious, I determined to put my ideas, original as well as acquired, to the test of practice. I accordingly motioned my Korak driver to take a back seat and deliver up to me the insignia of office. I observed in the expression of his lips, as he handed me the spiked stick, a sort of latent smile of ridicule, which indicated a very low estimate of my dog-driving abilities; but I treated it as knowledge should always treat the sneers of ignorance—with silent contempt; and seating myself firmly astride the sledge back of the arch, I shouted to the dogs, "Noo! Pashol!" My voice failed to produce the startling effect which I had anticipated. The leader —a grim, bluff Nestor of a dog—glanced carelessly over his shoulder and very perceptibly slackened his pace. This sudden and marked contempt for my authority on the part of the dogs did more than all the sneers of the Koraks to shake my confidence in my own skill. But my

resources were not yet exhausted, and I hurled monosyl-
lable, dissyllable, and polysyllable at their devoted heads,
shouted " Akh ! Te shelma ! Proclataya takaya ! Smatree !
Ya tibi dam !" but all in vain ; the dogs were evidently
insensible to rhetorical fireworks of this description, and
manifested their indifference by a still slower gait. As I
poured out upon them the last vial of my verbal wrath,
Dodd, who understood the language which I was so recklessly using, drove slowly up, and remarked carelessly,
" You swear pretty well for a beginner." Had the ground
opened beneath me I should have been less astonished.
" Swear ! I swear ! You don't mean to say that I've been
swearing ?"—" Certainly you have, like a pirate." I dropped my spiked stick in dismay. Were these the principles
of dog-driving which I had evolved out of the depths of
my *moral* consciousness ? They seemed rather to have
come from the depths of my *im*moral *un*consciousness.
" Why, you reckless reprobate," I exclaimed impressively,
" didn't you teach me those very words yourself ? "—" Certainly I did," was the unabashed reply ; " but you didn't
ask me what they meant ; you asked how to pronounce
them correctly, and I told you. I didn't know but that
you were making researches in comparative philology—
trying to prove the unity of the human race by identity
of oaths, or by a comparison of profanity to demonstrate
that the Digger Indians are legitimately descended from
the Chinese. You know that your head (which is a pretty
good one in other respects) always *was* full of such non-
sense."—" Dodd," I observed, with a solemnity which I
intended should awaken repentance in his hardened sen-

sibilities, "I have been betrayed unwittingly into the commission of sin ; and as a little more or less won't materially alter my guilt, I've as good a notion as ever I had to give you the benefit of some of your profane instruction." D. laughed derisively and drove on. This little episode considerably dampened my enthusiasm, and made me very cautious in my use of foreign language. I feared the existence of terrific imprecations in the most common dog-phrases, and suspected lurking profanity even in the monosyllabic "Khta" and "Hoogh," which I had been taught to believe meant "right" and "left." The dogs, quick to observe any lack of attention on the part of their driver, now took encouragement from my silence and exhibited a doggish propensity to stop and rest, which was in direct contravention of all discipline, and which they would not have dared to do with an experienced driver. Determined to vindicate my authority by more forcible measures, I launched my spiked stick like a harpoon at the leader, intending to have it fall so that I could pick it up as the sledge passed. The dog however dodged it cleverly, and it rolled away ten feet from the road. Just at that moment three or four wild reindeer bounded out from behind a little rise of ground three or four hundred yards away, and galloped across the steppe toward a deep precipitous ravine, through which ran a branch of the Meekina River. The dogs, true to their wolfish instincts, started with fierce, excited howls in pursuit. I made a frantic grasp at my spiked stick as we rushed past, but failed to reach it, and away we went over the toondra toward the ravine, the sledge half the time on one runner,

and rebounding from the hard sastroogee or snow-drifts
with a force which suggested speedy dislocation of one's
joints. The Korak, with more common sense than I had
given him credit for, had rolled off the sledge several seconds before, and a backward glance showed a miscellaneous
bundle of arms and legs revolving rapidly over the snow
in my wake. I had no time, however, with ruin staring
me in the face, to commiserate his misfortune. My energies were all devoted to checking the terrific speed with
which we were approaching the ravine. Without the
spiked stick we were perfectly helpless, and in a moment
we were on the brink. I shut my eyes, clung tightly to
the arch, and took the plunge. About half-way down the
descent became suddenly steeper, and the lead-dog swerv-
ed to one side, bringing the sledge around like the lash
of a whip, overturning it, and shooting me like a huge
living meteor through the air into a deep soft drift of snow
at the bottom. I must have fallen at least eighteen feet,
for I buried myself entirely, with the exception of my
lower extremities, which, projecting above the snow, kicked
a faint signal for rescue. Encumbered with heavy furs, I
extricated myself with difficulty ; and as I at last emerged
with three pints of snow down my neck, I saw the round,
leering face of my late driver grinning at me through the
bushes on the edge of the bluff. "Ooma," he hailed.
Well," replied the snowy figure standing waist-high in
the drift. "Amerikanski nyett dobra kiour, eh ?" (American no good driver). "Nyett sofsem dobra" was the melancholy reply as I waded out. The sledge, I found, had
become entangled in the bushes near me, and the dogs

were all howling in chorus, nearly wild with the restraint.
I was so far satisfied with my experiment that I did not
desire to repeat it at present, and made no objections to
the Korak's assuming again his old position.   I was fully
convinced, by the logic of circumstances, that the science
of dog-driving demanded more careful and earnest consideration than I had yet given to it; and I resolved to
study carefully its elementary principles, as expounded by
its Korak professors, before attempting again to put my
own ideas upon the subject into practice.

As we came out of the ravine upon the open steppe I
saw the rest of our party a mile away, moving rapidly
toward the Korak village of Kooeel.   We passed Kooeel
late in the afternoon, and camped for the night in a forest
of birch, poplar, and aspen trees, on the banks of the
Paren River.

We were now only about seventy miles from Geezhega.
On the following night we reached a small log yourt on a
branch of the Geezhega River, which had been built there
by the government to shelter travellers, and Friday morning, November 25th, about eleven o'clock, we caught
sight of the red church steeple which marked the location
of the Russian settlement of Geezhega.   No one who
has not travelled for three long months through a wilderness like Kamtchatka, camped out in storms among desolate mountains, slept for three weeks in the smoky tents,
and yet smokier and dirtier yourts of the Koraks, and
lived altogether like a perfect savage and barbarian—no
one who has not experienced this can possibly understand with what joyful hearts we welcomed that red

church steeple, and the civilization of which it was the sign. For almost a month we had slept every night on the ground or the snow; had never seen a chair, a table, a bed, or a mirror; had never been undressed night or day; and had washed our faces only three or four times in an equal number of weeks! We were grimy and smoky from climbing up and down Korak chimneys; our hair was long and matted around our ears; the skin had peeled from our noses and cheek-bones where they had been frozen; our cloth coats and pantaloons were gray with reindeer hairs from our fur "kookhlánkas;" and we presented, generally, as wild and neglected an appearance as men could present, and still retain any lingering traces of better days. We had no time or inclination, however, to "fix up;" our dogs dashed at a mad gallop into the village with a great outcry, which awakened a responsive chorus of howls from two or three hundred other canine throats; our drivers shouted "khta! khta! hoog! hoog!" and raised clouds of snow with their spiked sticks as we rushed through the streets, and the whole population came running to their doors to ascertain the cause of the infernal tumult. One after another our fifteen sledges went careering through the village, and finally drew up before a large, comfortable house, with double glass windows, where arrangements had been made, Kerrillof said, for our reception. Hardly had we entered a large, neatly swept and scrubbed room, and thrown off our heavy frosty furs, than the door again opened, and in rushed a little impetuous, quick-motioned man, with a heavy auburn moustache, and light hair cut short all over his head, dressed in neat broadcloth coat and pantaloons and a spotless linen shirt, with seal rings on his fingers, a plain gold chain at his vest button, and a cane. We recognized him at once as the "Ispravnik," or Russian Governor. Dodd and I made a sudden attempt to escape from the room, but we were too late, and saluting our visitor with "zdrastvuitia," we sat down awkwardly enough on our chairs, rolled our smoky hands up in our scarlet and yellow cotton handkerchiefs, and, with a vivid consciousness of our dirty faces and generally disreputable appearance, tried to look self-possessed, and to assume the dignity which befitted officers of the great Russo-American Telegraph Expedition! It was a pitiable failure. We could not succeed in looking like anything but Wandering Koraks in reduced circumstances. The Ispravnik, however, did not seem to notice anything unusual in our appearance, but rattled away with an incessant fire of quick, nervous questions, such as " When did you leave Petropavlovski ? Are you just from America ? I sent a Cossack. Did you meet him ? How did you cross the toondras ; with the Koraks ? Akh! those proclatye Koraks! Any news from St. Petersburg ? You must come over and dine with me. How long will you stay in town ? You can take a bath right after dinner. Ay! l6odee! (very loud and peremptory.) Go and tell my Ivan to heat up the bath quick! Akh! Chort yeekh vazmee!" and the restless little man finally stopped from sheer exhaustion, and began pacing nervously across the room, while the Major related our adventures, gave him the latest news from Russia, explained our plans, the object of our expedition, told him of the murder of Lincoln, the end of the Rebellion, the latest news from the French invasion of Mexico, the gossip of the Imperial Court, and no end of other news which had been old with us for six months, but of which the poor exiled Ispravnik had never heard a word. He had had no communication with Russia in almost eleven months. After insisting again upon our coming over to his house immediately to dine, he bustled out of the room, and gave us an opportunity to wash and dress.

Two hours afterward, in all the splendor of blue coats, brass buttons, and shoulder-straps, with shaven faces, starched shirts, and polished leather boots, the " First Siberian Exploring Party" marched over to the Ispravnik's to dine. The Russian peasants whom we met instinctively took off their frosty fur hoods and gazed wonderingly at us as we passed, as if we had mysteriously dropped down from some celestial sphere. No one would have recognized in us the dirty, smoky, ragged vagabonds who had entered the village two hours before. The grubs had developed into blue and golden butterflies! We found the Ispravnik waiting for us in a pleasant, spacious room furnished with all the luxuries of a civilized home. The walls were papered and ornamented with costly pictures and engravings, the windows were hung with curtains, the floor was covered with a soft, brightly-colored carpet, a large walnut writing-desk occupied one corner of the room, a rosewood melodeon the other, and in the centre stood the dining-table, covered with a fresh cloth, polished china, and glittering silver. We were fairly dazzled at the sight of so much unusual and unexpected magnificence. After the inevitable "fifteen drops" of brandy, and the lunch of smoked fish, rye bread, and caviar, which always precede a Russian dinner, we took seats at the table and spent an hour and a half in getting through the numerous courses of cabbage soup, salmon pie, venison cutlets, game, small meat pies, pudding and pastry, which were successively set before us, and in discussing the news of all the world, from the log villages of Kamtchatka to the imperial palaces of Moscow and St. Petersburg. Our hospitable host then ordered champagne, and over tall, slender glasses of cool beaded Cliquot we meditated upon the vicissitudes of Siberian life. Yesterday we sat on the ground in a Korak tent and ate reindeer-meat out of a wooden trough with our fingers, and to-day we dined with the Russian Governor, in a luxurious house, upon venison cutlets, plum pudding, and champagne. With the exception of a noticeable but restrained inclination on the part of Dodd and myself to curl up our legs and sit on the floor, there was nothing I believe in our behavior to betray the barbarous freedom of the life which we had so recently lived, and the demoralizing character of the influences to which we had been subjected. We handled our knives and forks, and leisurely sipped our champagne with a grace which would have excited the envy of Lord Chesterfield himself. But it was hard work. No sooner did we return to our quarters than we threw off our uniform coats, spread our bearskins on the floor, and sat down upon them with crossed legs, to enjoy a comfortable smoke in the good old free-and-easy style.

If our faces had only been just a little dirty we should have been perfectly happy!

The next ten days of our life at Geezhega were passed in comparative idleness. We walked out a little when the weather was not too cold, received formal calls from the Russian merchants of the place, visited the Ispravnik and drank his delicious "flower-tea" and smoked his paperoses in the evening, and indemnified ourselves for three months of rough life by enjoying to the utmost such mild pleasures as the little village afforded. This pleasant, aimless existence, however, was soon terminated by an order from the Major to prepare for the winter's campaign, and hold ourselves in readiness to start for the Arctic Circle or the west coast of the Okhotsk Sea at a moment's notice. He had determined to explore a route for our proposed line from Behring's Straits to the Amoor River before spring should open, and there was no time to be lost. The information which we could gather at Geezhega with regard to the interior of the country was scanty, indefinite, and unsatisfactory. According to native accounts, there were only two settlements between the Okhotsk Sea and Behring's Straits, and the nearest of these—Penzhina—was four hundred versts distant. The intervening country consisted of great moss "toondras," impassable in summer, and perfectly destitute of timber; and that portion of it which lay north-east of the last settlement was utterly uninhabitable on account of the absence of wood. A Russian officer by the name of Phillippeus had attempted to explore it in the winter of 1860, but had returned unsuccessful, in a starving and exhausted condition. In the whole distance of eight hundred versts between Geezhega and the mouth of the Anadyr River there were said to be only four or five places where timber could be found large enough for telegraph poles, and over most of the route there was no wood except occasional patches of trailing pine. A journey from Geezhega to the last settlement of Anadyrsk, on the Arctic Circle, would occupy from twenty to thirty days, according to weather, and beyond that point there was no possibility of going under any circumstances. The region west of Geezhega, along the coast of the Okhotsk Sea, was reported to be better, but very rugged and mountainous, and heavily timbered with pine and larch. The village of Okhotsk, eight hundred versts distant, could be reached on dog-sledges in about a month. This, in brief, was all the information we could get, and it did not inspire us with very much confidence in the ultimate success of our enterprise. I realized for the first time the magnitude of the task which the Russo-American Telegraph Company had undertaken. We were "in for it," however, now, and our first duty was obviously to go through the country, ascertain its extent and nature, and find out what facilities, if any, it afforded for the construction of our line.

The Russian settlements of Okhotsk and Geezhega divided the country between Behring's Straits and the Amoor River into three nearly equal sections, of which two were mountainous and wooded, and one comparatively level and almost barren. The first of these sections, between the Amoor and Okhotsk, had been as-

signed to Mahood and Bush, and we presumed that they
were already engaged in its exploration.   The other two
sections, comprising all the region between Okhotsk and
Behring's Straits, were to be divided between the Major,
Dodd, and myself.   In view of the supposed desolation
of the unexplored territory immediately west of Behring's
Straits, it was thought best to leave it unsurveyed until
spring, and perhaps until another season.   The promised
co-operation of the Anadyr River party had failed us, and
without more men, the Major did not consider it expe-
dient to undertake the exploration of a region which presented so many and so great obstacles to mid-winter
travel.   The distance which remained to be traversed,
therefore, was only about fourteen hundred versts from
Okhotsk to the Russian outpost of Anadyrsk, just south
of the Arctic Circle.   After some deliberation the Major
concluded to send Dodd and me with a party of natives
to Anadyrsk, and to start himself on dog-sledges for the
settlement of Okhotsk, where he expected to meet
Mahood and Bush.   In this way it was hoped that we
should be able in the course of five months to make a rough
but tolerably accurate survey of nearly the whole route of
the line.   The provisions which we had brought from Petropavlovski had all been used up, with the exception of
some tea, sugar, and a few cans of preserved beef; but
we obtained at Geezhega two or three poods of black
rye bread, four or five frozen reindeer, some salt, and an
abundant supply of "yookala" or dried fish.   These,
with some tea and sugar, and a few cakes of frozen milk,
made up our store of provisions.   We provided ourselves

also with six or eight poods of Circassian leaf tobacco, to be used instead of money; divided equally our little store of beads, pipes, knives, and trading goods, purchased new suits of furs throughout, and made every preparation for three or four months of camp-life in an Arctic climate. The Russian Governor ordered six of his Cossacks to transport Dodd and I on dog-sledges as far as the Korak village of Shestakova, and sent word to Penzhina by the returning Anadyrsk people to have three or four men and dog-teams at the former place by Dec. 20th, ready to carry us on to Penzhina and Anadyrsk. We engaged an old and experienced Cossack named Gregorie Zinevief as guide and Chookchee interpreter, hired a young Russian called Yagor as cook and aide-de-camp (in the literal sense), packed our stores on our sledges and secured them with lashings of seal-skin thongs, and by December 13th were ready to take the field. That evening the Major delivered to us our instructions. They were simply, to follow the regular sledge road to Anadyrsk via Shestakova and Penzhina, to ascertain what facilities it offered in the way of timber and soil for the construction of a telegraph line, to set the natives at work cutting poles at Penzhina and Anadyrsk, and to make side explorations where possible in search of timbered rivers connecting Penzhinsk Gulf with Behring's Sea. Late in the spring we were to return to Geezhega with all the information which we could gather relative to the country between that point and the Arctic Circle. The Major himself would remain at Geezhega until about December 17th, and then leave on dog-sledges with Vushine and a small party of Cossacks for the settlement of Okhotsk. If he made a junction with Mahood and Bush at that place he would return at once, and meet us again at Geezhega by the 1st of April, 1866.

CHAPTER XXIII.

ARCTIC TRAVELLING IN WINTER.

THE morning of December 13th dawned clear, cold and still, with a temperature of thirty-one degrees below zero; but as the sun did not rise until half-past ten, it was nearly noon before we could get our drivers together, and our dogs harnessed for a start. Our little party of ten men presented quite a novel and picturesque appearance in their gayly embroidered fur coats, red sashes, and yellow fox-skin hoods, as they assembled in a body before our house to bid good-by to the Ispravnik and the Major. Eight heavily loaded sledges were ranged in a line in front of the door, and almost a hundred dogs were springing frantically against their harnesses, and raising deafening howls of impatience, as we came out of the house into the still, frosty atmosphere. We bade everybody good-by, received a hearty "God bless you, boys!" from the Major, and were off in a cloud of flying snow, which stung our faces like burning sparks of fire. Old Paderin, the chief of the Geezhega Cossacks, with white frosty hair and beard, stood out in front of his little red log house as we passed, and waved us a last good-by with his fur hood as we swept out upon the great level steppe behind the town.

It was just mid-day ; but the sun, although at its great-est altitude, glowed like a red ball of fire low down in the southern horizon, and a peculiar gloomy twilight hung over the white wintry landscape. I could not overcome the impression that the sun was just rising and that it would soon be broad day. A white ptarmigan now and then flew up with a loud whir before us, uttered a harsh "querk, querk, querk" of affright, and sailing a few rods away, settled upon the snow and became suddenly invis-ible. A few magpies sat motionless in the thickets of trailing pine as we passed, but their feathers were ruffled up around their heads, and they seemed chilled and stu-pefied by the intense cold. The distant blue belt of tim-ber along the Geezhega river wavered and trembled in its outlines as if seen through currents of heated air, and the white ghost-like mountains thirty miles away to the southward were thrown up and distorted by refraction into a thousand airy, fantastic shapes which melted imper-ceptibly one into another, like a series of dissolving views. Every feature of the scenery was strange, weird, Arctic. The red sun rolled slowly along the southern horizon, un-til it seemed to rest on a white snowy peak far away in the southwest, and then, while we were yet expecting day it suddenly disappeared and the gloomy twilight deepened gradually into night. Only three hours had elapsed since sunrise, and yet stars of the first magnitude could already be plainly distinguished.

We stopped for the night at the house of a Russian peasant who lived on the bank of the Geezhega River, about fifteen versts east of the settlement. While we were drinking tea a special messenger arrived from the village, bringing two frozen blueberry pies as a parting token of regard from the Major, and a last souvenir of civilization. Pretending to fear that something might happen to these delicacies if we should attempt to carry them with us, Dodd, as a precautionary measure, ate one of them up to the last blueberry; and rather than have him sacrifice himself to a mistaken idea of duty by trying to eat the other, I attended to its preservation myself and put it forever beyond the reach of accidental contingencies.

On the following day we reached the little log yourt on the Malmofka, where we had spent one night on our way to Geezhega; and as the cold was still intense we were glad to avail ourselves again of its shelter, and huddle around the warm fire which Yagor kindled on a sort of clay altar in the middle of the room. There was not space enough on the rough plank floor to accommodate all our party, and our men built a huge fire of tamarack logs outside, hung over their tea-kettles, thawed out their frosty beards, ate dry fish, sang jolly Russian songs, and made themselves so boisterously happy, that we were tempted to give up the luxury of a roof for the sake of sharing in their out-door amusements and merriment. Our thermometers, however, marked 35° below zero, and we did not venture out of doors except when an unusually loud burst of laughter announced some stupendous Siberian joke which we thought would be worth hearing. The atmosphere outside seemed to be just cool enough to exert an inspiriting influence upon our lively Cossacks, but it was altogether too bracing for unaccustomed American constitutions. With a good fire, however, and plenty of hot tea, we succeeded in making ourselves very comfortable inside the yourt, and passed away the long evening in smoking Circassian tobacco and pine bark, singing American songs, telling stories, and quizzing our good-natured but unsophisticated Cossack Meroneff.

It was quite late when we finally crawled into our fur bags to sleep ; but long afterward we could hear the songs, jokes, and laughter of our drivers as they sat around the camp-fire, and told funny stories of Siberian travel.

We were up on the following morning long before daylight ; and, after a hasty breakfast of black bread, dried fish, and tea, we harnessed our dogs, wet down our sledge-runners with water from the tea-kettle to cover them with a coating of ice, packed up our camp equipage, and, leaving the shelter of the tamarack forest around the yourt, drove out upon the great snowy Sahara which lies between the Malmofka River and Penzhinsk Gulf. It was a land of desolation. A great level steppe, as boundless to the weary eye as the ocean itself, stretched away in every direction to the far horizon, without a single tree or bush to relieve its white, snowy surface. Nowhere did we see any sign of animal or vegetable life, any suggestion of summer or flowers or warm sunshine, to brighten the dreary waste of storm-drifted snow.

White, cold, and silent, it lay before us like a vast frozen ocean, lighted up faintly by the slender crescent of the waning moon in the east, and the weird blue streamers of the Aurora, which went racing swiftly back and forth along the northern horizon. Even when the sun rose, huge and fiery, in a haze of frozen moisture at the south, it did not seem to infuse any warmth or life into the bleak wintry landscape. It only drowned, in a dull red glare, the blue, tremulous streamers of the Aurora, and the white radiance of the moon and stars tinged the snow with a faint color like a stormy sunset, and lighted up a splendid mirage in the northwest which startled us with its solemn mockery of familiar scenes. The wand of the Northern Enchanter touched the barren snowy steppe, and it suddenly became a blue tropical lake, upon whose distant shore rose the walls, domes, and slender minarets of a vast oriental city. Masses of luxuriant foliage seemed to overhang the clear blue water, and to be reflected in its depths, while the white walls above just caught the first flush of the rising sun. Never was the illusion of summer in winter, of life in death, more palpable or more perfect. One almost instinctively glanced around to assure himself, by the sight of familiar objects, that it was not a dream; but as his eye turned again to the northwest across the dim blue lake, the vast tremulous outlines of the mirage still confronted him in their unearthly beauty, and the " cloud-capped towers and gorgeous palaces" seemed, by their mysterious solemnity, to rebuke the doubt which would ascribe them to a dream. The bright apparition faded, glowed, and faded again into indistinctness, and from its ruins rose two colossal pillars sculptured from rose quartz, which gradually united their capitals and formed a Titanic arch like the grand portal of heaven. This, in turn, melted into an extensive fortress, with massive bastions and buttresses, flanking towers, and deep embrasures, and salient and re-entering angles, whose shadows and perspective were as natural as reality itself. Nor was it only at a distance that these deceptive mirages seemed to be formed. A crow, standing upon the snow at a distance of perhaps two hundred yards, was exaggerated and distorted beyond recognition ; and once, having lingered a little behind the rest of the party, I was startled at seeing a long line of shadowy dog- ⬦ sledges moving swiftly through the air a short distance ahead, at a height of eight or ten feet from the ground. The mock sledges were inverted in position, and the mock dogs trotted along with their feet in the air ; but their outlines were almost as clear as those of the real sledges and real dogs underneath. This curious phenomenon lasted only a moment, but it was succeeded by others equally strange, until at last we lost faith in our eyesight entirely, and would not believe in the existence of anything unless we could touch it with our hands. Every bare hillock or dark object on the snow was a nucleus around which were formed the most deceptive images, and two or three times we started out with our rifles in pursuit of wolves or black foxes, which proved, upon closer inspection, to be nothing but crows. I had never before known the light and atmosphere to be so favorable to refraction, and had never been so deceived in the size, shape, and distance of objects on the snow.

The thermometer at noon marked —35°, and at sunset it was —38°, and sinking. We had seen no wood since leaving the yourt on the Malmoťka River, and, not daring to camp without a fire, we travelled for five hours

after dark, guided only by the stars and a bluish Aurora
which was playing away in the north. Under the influence of the intense cold, frost formed in great quantities
upon everything which was touched by our breaths.
Beards became stiff tangled masses of frozen iron wire,
eyelids grew heavy with long white rims of frost, and
froze together when we winked, and our dogs, enveloped
in dense clouds of steam, looked like snowy polar wolves.
Only by running constantly beside our sledges could we
keep any sensation of life in our feet. About eight o'clock
a few scattered trees loomed up darkly against the eastern
sky, and a joyful shout from our leading drivers announced
the discovery of wood. We had reached a small stream
called the Ooseénova, seventy-five versts east of Geezhega,
in the very middle of the great steppe. It was like coming to an island after having been long at sea. Our dogs
stopped and curled themselves up into little round balls
on the snow, as if conscious that the long day's journey
was ended, while our drivers proceeded to make rapidly
and systematically a Siberian half-faced camp. Three
sledges were drawn up together, so as to make a little
semi-enclosure about ten feet square ; the snow was all
shovelled out of the interior, and banked up around the
three closed sides, like a snow fort, and a huge fire of
trailing pine branches was built at the open end. The
bottom of this little snow-cellar was then strewn to a
depth of three or four inches with twigs of willow and
alder, shaggy bear-skins were spread down to make a warm,
soft carpet, and our fur sleeping-bags arranged for the
night. Upon a small table extemporized out of a candle

box, which stood in the centre, Yagor soon placed two cups of steaming hot tea and a couple of dried fish. Then stretching ourselves out in luxurious style upon our bear-skin carpet, with our feet to the fire and our backs against pillows, we smoked, drank tea, and told stories in perfect comfort. After supper the drivers piled dry branches of trailing pine upon the fire until it sent up a column of hot ruddy flame ten feet in height, and then gathering in a picturesque group around the blaze, they sang for hours the wild melancholy songs of the Kam- tchadals, and told never-ending stories of hardship and adventure on the great steppes and along the coast of the "icy sea." At last the great constellation of Orion marked bed-time. Amid a tumult of snarling and fight- ing the dogs were fed their daily allowance of one dried fish each, fur stockings, moist with perspiration, were taken off and dried by the fire, and putting on our heaviest fur "kookhlánkas," we crawled feet first into our bear-skin bags, pulled them up over our heads, and slept.

A camp in the middle of a clear, dark winter's night presents a strange, wild appearance. I was awakened, soon after midnight, by cold feet, and, raising myself upon one elbow, I pushed my head out of my frosty fur bag to see by the stars what time it was. The fire had died away to a red heap of smouldering embers. There was just light enough to distinguish the dark outlines of the loaded sledges, the fur-clad forms of our men, lying here and there in groups about the fire, and the frosty dogs, curled up into a hundred little hairy balls upon the snow. Away beyond the limits of the camp stretched the deso-

late steppe in a series of long snowy undulations, which
blended gradually into one great white frozen ocean, and
were lost in the distance and darkness of night.   High
over head, in a sky which was almost black, sparkled the
bright constellations of Orion and the Pleiades—the
celestial clocks which marked the long, weary hours between sunrise and sunset.   The blue mysterious streamers of the Aurora trembled in the north, now shooting up
in clear bright lines to the zenith, then waving back and
forth in great majestic curves over the silent camp, as if
warning back the adventurous traveller from the unknown
regions around the pole.   The silence was profound,
oppressive.   Nothing but the pulsating of the blood in
my ears, and the heavy breathing of the sleeping men at
my feet, broke the universal lull.   Suddenly there rose
upon the still night-air a long, faint, wailing cry like that
of a human being in the last extremity of suffering.   Gradually it swelled and deepened until it seemed to fill the
whole atmosphere with its volume of mournful sound,
dying away at last into a low, despairing moan.   It was
the signal-howl of a Siberian dog; but so wild and unearthly did it seem in the stillness of the Arctic midnight,
that it sent the startled blood bounding through my veins
to my very finger-ends.   In a moment the mournful cry
was taken up by another dog, upon a higher key—two or
three more joined in, then ten, twenty, forty, sixty, eighty,
until the whole pack of a hundred dogs howled one infernal chorus together, making the air fairly tremble with
sound, as if from the heavy bass of a great organ.   For
fully a minute heaven and earth seemed to be filled with

yelling, shrieking fiends. Then one by one they began gradually to drop off, the unearthly tumult grew momentarily fainter and fainter, until at last it ended as it began, in one long, inexpressibly melancholy wail, and all was still. One or two of our men moved restlessly in their sleep, as if the mournful howls had blended unpleasantly with their dreams ; but no one awoke, and a death-like silence again pervaded heaven and earth. Suddenly the Aurora shone out with increased brilliancy, and its waving swords swept back and forth in great semicircles across the dark starry sky, and lighted up the snowy steppe with transitory flashes of colored radiance, as if the gates of heaven were opening and closing upon the dazzling brightness of the celestial city. Presently it faded away again to a faint diffused glow in the north, and one pale-green streamer, slender and bright as the spear of Ithuriel, pushed slowly up toward the zenith until it touched with its translucent point the jewelled belt of Orion; then it, too, faded and vanished, and nothing but a bank of pale white mist on the northern horizon showed the location of the celestial armory whence the Arctic spirits drew the gleaming swords and lances which they shook and brandished nightly over the lonely Siberian steppes. Crawling back into my bag as the Aurora disappeared, I fell asleep, and did not wake until near morning. With the first streak of dawn the camp began to show signs of animation. The dogs crawled out of the deep holes which their warm bodies had melted in the snow; the Cossacks poked their heads out of their frosty fur coats, and whipped off with little sticks the mass of frost which had accumulated around their breathing-holes. A fire was built, tea boiled, and we crawled out of our sleeping-bags to shiver around the fire and eat a hasty breakfast of rye-bread, dried fish, and tea. In twenty minutes the dogs were harnessed, sledges packed, and runners covered with ice, and one after another we drove away at a brisk trot from the smoking fire, and began another day's journey across the barren steppe.

In this monotonous routine of riding, camping, and sleeping on the snow, day after day slowly passed until, on December 20th, we arrived at the settled Korak village of Shestakova, near the head of Penzhinsk Gulf. From this point our Geezhega Cossacks were to return, and here we were to wait until the expected sledges from Penzhina should arrive. We lowered our bedding, pillows, camp equipage, and provisions, down through the chimney-hole of the largest yourt in the small village, arranged them as tastefully as possible on the wide wooden platform which extended out from the wall on one side, and made ourselves as comfortable as darkness, smoke, cold, and dirt would permit.

CHAPTER XXIV.

OUR short stay at Shestakova, while waiting for the Penzhina sledges, was dismal and lonesome beyond expression. It began to storm furiously about noon on the 20th, and the violent wind swept up such tremendous clouds of snow from the great steppe north of the village, that the whole earth was darkened as if by an eclipse, and the atmosphere, to a height of a hundred feet from the ground, was literally packed with a driving mist of white snow-flakes. I ventured to the top of the chimney-hole once, but I was nearly blown over the edge of the yourt, and, blinded and choked by snow, I hastily retreated down the chimney, congratulating myself that I was not obliged to lie out all day on some desolate plain, exposed to the fury of such a storm. To keep out the snow, we were obliged to extinguish the fire and shut up the chimney hole with a sort of wooden trap-door, so that we were left to total darkness and a freezing atmosphere. We lighted candles and stuck them against the black smoky logs above our heads with melted grease, so that we could see to read; but the cold was so intense that we were finally compelled to give up the idea of literary amusement, and putting on fur coats and hoods. we crawled into our bags to try and sleep away the day Shut up in a dark half-underground dungeon, with a temperature ten degrees below the freezing-point, we had no other resource.

It is a mystery to me how human beings with any feeling at all can be satisfied to live in such abominable, detestable houses as those of the settled Koraks. They have not one solitary redeeming feature. They are entered through the chimney, lighted by the chimney, and ventilated by the chimney; the sunshine falls into them only once a year—in June; they are cold in winter, close and uncomfortable in summer, and smoky all the time. They are pervaded by a smell of rancid oil and decaying fish; their logs are black as jet and greasy with smoke, and their earthen floors are an indescribable mixture of reindeer's hairs and filth dried and trodden hard. They have no furniture except wooden bowls of seal oil, in which burn fragments of moss, and black wooden troughs which are alternately used as dishes and as seats. Sad is the lot of children born in such a place. Until they are old enough to climb up the chimney-pole they never see the outside world.

The weather on the day after our arrival at Shestakova was much better, and our Cossack Meroneff, who was on his way back to Tigil, bade us good-by, and started with two or three natives for Kamenoi. Dodd and I managed to pass away the day by drinking tea eight or ten times simply as an amusement, reading an odd volume of Cooper's novels which we had picked up at Geezhega, and strolling along the high bluffs over the gulf with our rifles in search of foxes. Soon after dark, just as we were drinking tea in final desperation for the seventh time, our dogs who were tied around the yourt set up a general howl, and Yagor came sliding down the chimney in the most reckless and disorderly manner, with the news that a Russian Cossack had just arrived from Petropavlovski, bringing letters from the Major. Dodd sprang up in great excitement, kicked over the tea-kettle, dropped his cup and saucer, and made a frantic rush for the chimney-pole; but before he could reach it we saw somebody's legs coming down into the yourt, and in a moment a tall figure in a spotted reindeer-skin coat appeared, crossed himself carefully two or three times, as if in gratitude for his safe arrival, and then turned to us with the Russian salutation "zdrastvuitia."—"At Kooda?"—where from, demanded Dodd, quickly. "From Petropavlovski with letters for the Myóor," was the reply; "three telegraph ships have been there, and I am sent with important letters from the American Nechalnik; I have been thirty-nine days and nights on the road from Petropavlovski." This was important news. Col. Bulkley had evidently touched at the southern end of Kamtchatka on his return from Behring's Sea, and the letters brought by the courier would undoubtedly explain why he had not landed the party at the mouth of the Anadyr River, as he had intended. I felt a strong temptation to open the letters; but not thinking that they could have any bearing upon my movements, I finally concluded to send them on without a moment's delay to Geezhega, in the faint hope that the Major had not yet left there for Okhotsk. In twenty minutes the Cossack was gone, and we were left to form all sorts of wild conjectures as to the contents of the letters, and the movements of the parties which Col. Bulkley had carried up to Behring's Straits. I regretted a hundred times that I had not opened the letters, and found out to a certainty that the Anadyr River party had not been landed. But it was too late now, and we could only hope that the courier would overtake the Major before he had started from Geezhega, and that the latter would send somebody to us at Anadyrsk with the news.

There were no signs yet of the Penzhina sledges, and we spent another night and another long dreary day in the smoky yourt ar Shestakova, waiting for transportation. Late in the evening of Dec. 22d, Yagor, who acted in the capacity of sentinel, came down the chimney with another sensation. He had heard the howling of dogs in the direction of Penzhina. We went up on the roof of the yourt and listened for several minutes, but hearing nothing but the wind, we concluded that Yagor had either been mistaken, or that a pack of wolves had howled in the valley east of the settlement. Yagor however was right; he had heard dogs on the Penzhina road, and in less than ten minutes the long-expected sledges drew up, amid general shouting and barking, before our yourt. In the course of conversation with the new arrivals, I thought I understood one of the Penzhina men to say something about a party who had mysteriously appeared near the mouth of the Anadyr River, and who were building a house there as if with the intention of spending the winter. I did not yet understand Russian very well, but I guessed at once that the long-talked of Anadyr River party had been landed, and springing up in considerable excitement, I called Dodd to interpret. It seemed from all the information which the Penzhina men could give us that a small party of Americans had mysteriously appeared, early in the winter, near the mouth of the Anadyr, and had commenced to build a house of drift-wood and a few boards which had been landed from the vessel in which they came. What their intentions were, who they were, or how long they intended to stay, no one knew, as the report came through bands of Wandering Chookchees, who had never seen the Americans themselves, but who had heard of them from others. The news had been passed along from one encampment of Chookchees to another until it had finally reached Penzhina, and had thus been brought on to us at Shestakova, more than five hundred miles from the place where the Americans were said to be. We could hardly believe that Col. Bulkley had landed an exploring party in the desolate region south of Behring's Straits, at the very beginning of an Arctic winter; but what could Americans be doing there, if they did not belong to our expedition? It was not a place which civilized men would be likely to select for a winter residence, unless they had in view some very important object. The nearest settlement—Anadyrsk—was almost two hundred and fifty miles distant; the country along the lower Anadyr was said to be wholly destitute of wood, and inhabited only by roving bands of Chookchees, and a party landed there without an interpreter would have no means of communicating even with these wild, lawless natives, or of obtaining any means whatever of transportation. If there were any

Americans there, they were certainly in a very unpleasant situation.

Dodd and I talked the matter over until nearly midnight, and finally concluded that upon our arrival at Anadyrsk we would make up a strong party of experienced natives, take thirty days' provisions, and push through to the Pacific Coast on dog-sledges in search of these mysterious Americans. It would be an adventure just novel and hazardous enough to be interesting, and if we succeeded in reaching the mouth of the Anadyr in winter, we would do something never before accomplished and never but once attempted. With this conclusion we crawled into our fur bags and dreamed that we were starting for the open Polar Sea in search of Sir John Franklin.

On the morning of Dec. 23d, as soon as it was light enough to see, we loaded our tobacco, provisions, tea, sugar, and trading goods upon the Penzhina sledges, and started up the shallow bushy valley of the Shestakova Creek toward a mountainous ridge, a spur of the great Stanavoi range, in which the stream had its source. We crossed the mountain early in the afternoon, at a height of about a thousand feet, and slid swiftly down its northern slope into a narrow valley, which opened upon the great steppes which bordered the river Aklán. The weather was clear and not very cold, but the snow in the valley was deep and soft, and our progress was provokingly slow. We had hoped to reach the Aklán by night, but the day was so short and the road so bad that we travelled five hours after dark, and then had to stop ten versts south of the river. We were rewarded, however, by seeing two very fine mock moons, and by finding a magnificent patch of trailing pine, which furnished us with dry wood enough for a glorious camp-fire. The curious tree or bush known to the Russians as " Kedrevnik," and rendered in the English translation of Vrangel's Travels as "trailing cedar," is one of the most singular productions of Siberia. I hardly know whether to call it a tree, a bush, or a vine, for it partakes more or less of the characteristics of all three, and yet does not look much like any of them. It resembles as much as anything a dwarf pine tree, with a remarkably gnarled, crooked, and contorted trunk, growing horizontally like a neglected vine along the ground, and sending up perpendicular branches through the snow. It has the needles and cones of the common white pine, but it never stands erect like a tree, and grows in great patches from a few yards to several acres in extent. A man might walk over a dense growth of it in winter and yet see nothing but a few bunches of sharp green needles, sticking up here and there through the snow. It is found on the most desolate steppes and upon the rockiest mountain sides from the Okhotsk Sea to the Arctic Ocean, and seems to grow most luxuriantly where the soil is most barren and the storms most severe. On great ocean-like plains, destitute of all other vegetation, this trailing pine lurks beneath the snow, and covers the ground in places with a perfect net-work of gnarled, twisted, and interlocking trunks. For some reason it always seems to die when it has attained a certain age, and wherever you find its green spiny foliage

you will also find dry white trunks as inflammable as tin-
der.　It furnishes almost the only fire-wood of the Wandering Koraks and Chookchees, and without it many
parts of Northeastern Siberia would be absolutely uninhabitable by man.　Scores of nights during our explorations in Siberia, we should have been compelled to camp
without fire, water, or warm food, had not Nature provided everywhere an abundance of trailing pine, and
stored it away under the snow for the use of travellers.

We left our camp in the valley early on the following
morning, pushed on across the large and heavily timbered
river called the Aklán, and entered upon the great steppe
which stretches away from its northern bank toward
Anadyrsk.　For two days we travelled over this barren
snowy plain, seeing no vegetation but stunted trees and
patches of trailing pine along the banks of occasional
streams, and no life except one or two solitary ravens
and a red fox.　The bleak and dreary landscape
could have been described in two words—snow and sky.
I had come to Siberia with full confidence in the ultimate
success of the Russo-American Telegraph line, but as I
penetrated deeper and deeper into the country and saw
its utter desolation I grew less and less sanguine.　Since
leaving Geezhega we had travelled nearly three hundred
versts, had found only four places where we could obtain
poles, and had passed only three settlements.　Unless
we could find a better route than the one over which we
had been, I feared that the Siberian telegraph line would
be a failure.

Up to this time we had been favored with unusually

fine weather ; but it was a season of the year when storms were of frequent occurrence, and I was not surprised to be awakened Christmas night by the roaring of the wind and the hissing sound of the snow as it swept through our un-protected camp and buried up our dogs and sledges. We were having a slight touch of a Siberian "poorga." A fringe of trees along the little stream on which we were camped sheltered us in a measure from the storm, but out on the steppe it was evidently blowing a gale. We rose as usual at daylight and made an attempt to travel; but no sooner did we leave the cover of the trees than our dogs became almost unmanageable, and, blinded and half suffocated with flying snow, we were driven back again into the timber. It was impossible to see thirty feet, and the wind blew with such fury that our dogs would not face it. We massed our sledges together as a sort of breastwork against the drifting snow, spread our fur bags down behind them, crawled in and covered up our heads with deer-skins and blankets, and prepared for a long dismal siege. There is nothing so thoroughly, hopelessly dreary and uncomfortable, as camping out upon a Siberian steppe in a storm. The wind blows with such violence that a tent cannot possibly be made to stand ; the fire is half extinguished by drifting snow, and fills the eyes with smoke and cinders when it burns at all ; conversation is impossible on account of the roaring of the wind and the beating of the snow in one's face ; bear-skins, pillows, and furs become stiff and icy with half-melted sleet, sledges are buried up, and there remains nothing for the unhappy traveller to do but crawl into his sleeping-bag, cover up his head, and shiver away the long, dismal hours.

We lay out on the snow in this storm for two days, spending nearly all the time in our fur bags and suffering severely from the cold during the long, dark nights. On the 28th, about four o'clock in the morning, the storm began to abate, and by six we had dug out our sledges and were under way. There was a low spur of the Stanavoi Mountains about ten versts north of our camp, and our men said that if we could get across that before daylight we would probably have no more bad weather until we reached Penzhina. Our dog-food was entirely exhausted, and we must make the settlement within the next twenty-four hours if possible.

The snow had been blown hard by the wind, our dogs were fresh from two days' rest, and before daylight we had crossed the ridge and stopped in a little valley on the northern slope of the mountain to drink tea. When compelled to travel all night, the Siberian natives always make a practice of stopping just before sunrise and allowing their dogs to get to sleep. They argue that if a dog goes to sleep while it is yet dark, and wakes up in an hour and finds the sun shining, he will suppose that he has had a full night's rest and will travel all day without thinking of being tired. An hour's stop, however, at any other time will be of no use whatever. As soon as we thought we had deluded our dogs into the belief that they had slept all night, we roused them up and started down the valley toward a tributary of the Penzhina River, known as the Ooskanova. The weather was clear and not very cold, and we all enjoyed the pleasant change and the brief two hours of sunshine which were vouchsafed us before the sun sank behind the white peaks of Stanavoi. Just at dark we crossed the river Kondra, fifteen miles from Penzhina, and in two hours more we were hopelessly lost on another great level steppe, and broken up into two or three separate and bewildered parties. I had fallen asleep soon after passing the Kondra, and had not the slightest idea how we were progressing or whither we were going, until Dodd shook me by the shoulder and said, "Kennan, we're lost." Rather a startling announcement to wake a man with, but as Dodd did not seem to be much concerned about it, I assured him that I didn't care, and lying back on my pillow went to sleep again, fully satisfied that my driver would find Penzhina some time in the course of the night.

Guided by the stars, Dodd, Gregorie, and I, with one other sledge which remained with us, turned away to the eastward, and about nine o'clock came upon the Penzhina River somewhere below the settlement. We started up it on the ice, and had gone but a short distance when we saw two or three sledges coming down the river. Surprised to find men travelling away from the village at that hour of the night, we hailed them with a " Halloo ! "

" Halloo ! "

" Vwe kooda yáydetia ? "—Where are you going ?

"We're going to Penzhina ; who are you ?"

"We're Geezheginski, also going to Penzhina ; what you coming down the river for ?"

"We're trying to find the village, devil take it; we've been travelling all night and can't find anything!"

Upon this Dodd burst into a loud laugh, and as the mysterious sledges drew nearer we recognized in their drivers three of our own men who had separated from us soon after dark, and who were now trying to reach Penzhina by going down the river toward the Okhotsk Sea. We could hardly convince them that the village did not lie in that direction. They finally turned back with us, however, and some time after midnight we drove into Penzhina, roused the sleeping inhabitants with a series of unearthly yells, startled fifty or sixty dogs into a howling protest against such untimely disturbance, and threw the whole settlement into a general uproar.

In ten minutes we were seated on bear-skins before a warm fire in a cozy Russian house, drinking cup after cup of fragrant tea, and talking over our night's adventures.

CHAPTER XXV.

The village of Penzhina is a little collection of log-houses, flat-topped yourts, and four-legged bologans, situated on the north bank of the river which bears its name, about half-way between the Okhotsk Sea and Anadyrsk. It is inhabited principally by "mescháns," or free Russian peasants, but contains also in its scanty population a few "Chooances" or aboriginal Siberian natives, who were subjugated by the Russian Cossacks in the eighteenth century, and who now speak the language of their conquerors and gain a scanty subsistence by fishing and trading in furs. The town is sheltered on the north by a very steep bluff about a hundred feet in height, which, like all hills in the vicinity of Russian settlements, bears upon its summit a curiously-shaped Greek cross with three arms. The river opposite the settlement is about a hundred yards in width, and its banks are heavily timbered with birch, larch, poplar, willow, and aspen. Owing to warm springs in its bed, it never entirely freezes over at this point, and in a temperature of 40° below zero gives off dense clouds of steam which hide the village from sight as effectually as a London fog.

We remained at Penzhina three days, gathering information about the surrounding country and engaging men to cut poles for our line. We found the people to be

cheerful, good-natured, and hospitable, and disposed to
do all which lay in their power to further our plans ; but,
of course, they had never heard of a telegraph, and could
not imagine what we were going to do with the poles
which we were so anxious to have cut. Some said that
we intended to build a wooden road from Geezhega to
Anadyrsk, so that it would be possible to travel back and
forth in the summer ; others contended with some show
of probability that two men, even if they *were* Americans,
could not construct a wooden road, six hundred versts
long, and that our real object was to build some sort of a
huge house. When questioned as to the use of this immense edifice, however, the advocates of the house theory
were covered with confusion, and could only insist upon
the physical impossibility of a road, and call upon their
opponents to accept the house or suggest something better. We succeeded in engaging sixteen able-bodied men,
however, to cut poles for a reasonable compensation,
gave them the required dimensions—twenty-one feet long
and five inches in diameter at the top—and instructed
them to cut as many as possible, and pile them up along
the banks of the river.

I may as well mention here, that when I returned from
Anadyrsk in March I went to look at the poles, 500 in
number, which the Penzhina men had cut. I found, to
my great astonishment, that there was hardly one of them
less than twelve inches in diameter at the top, and that
the majority were so heavy and unwieldy that a dozen
men could not move them. I told the natives that they
would not do, and asked why they had not cut smaller

ones, as I had directed. They replied that they supposed I wanted to build some kind of a road on the tops of these poles, and they knew that poles only five inches in diameter would not be strong enough to hold it up! They had accordingly cut trees large enough to be used as pillars for a state-house. They still lie there, buried in Arctic snows; and I have no doubt that many years hence, when Macaulay's New Zealander shall have finished sketching the ruins of St. Paul's and shall have gone to Siberia to complete his education, he will be entertained by his native drivers with stories of how two crazy Americans once tried to build an elevated railroad from the Okhotsk Sea to Behring's Straits. I only hope that the New Zealander will write a book, and confer upon the two crazy Americans the honor and the immortality which their labors deserved, but which the elevated railroad failed to give.

We left Penzhina on the 31st day of December for Anadyrsk. After travelling all day, as usual, over a barren steppe, we camped for the night near the foot of a white isolated peak called Nalgim, in a terrible temperature of 53° below zero. It was New Year's Eve; and as I sat by the fire in my heaviest furs, covered from head to foot with frost, I thought of the great change which a single year had made in my surroundings. New Year's Eve, 1864, I had spent in Central America; riding on a mule from Lake Nicaragua to the Pacific Coast, through a magnificent tropical forest. New Year's Eve, 1865, found me squatting on a great snowy plain near the Arctic circle, trying, in a temperature of 53° below zero, to eat up my soup before it froze solidly to the plate. Hardly could there have been a greater contrast.

Our camp near Mount Nalgim abounded in trailing pine, and we made a fire which sent up a column of ruddy flame ten feet in height; but it did not seem to have much influence upon the atmosphere. Our eyelids froze together while we were drinking tea; our soup, taken hot from the kettle, froze in our tin plates before we could possibly finish eating it; and the breasts of our fur-coats were covered with a white rime, while we sat only a few feet from a huge blazing camp-fire. Tin plates, knives, and spoons burned the bare hand when touched, almost exactly as if they were red hot; and water, spilled on a little piece of board only fourteen inches from the fire, froze solid in less than two minutes. The warm bodies of our dogs gave off clouds of steam; and even the bare hand, wiped perfectly dry, exhaled a thin vapor when exposed to the air. We had never before experienced so low a temperature; but we suffered very little except from cold feet, and Dodd declared, that with a good fire and plenty of fat food he would not be afraid to try fifteen degrees lower. The greatest cause of suffering in Siberia is wind. Twenty degrees below zero, with a fresh breeze, is almost unendurable; and a gale of wind, with a temperature of $-40°$, would kill every living thing exposed to its influence. Intense cold of itself is not particularly dangerous to life. A man who will eat a hearty supper of dried fish and tallow, dress himself in a Siberian costume, and crawl into a heavy fur bag, may spend a night out-doors in a temperature of $-70°$ without any very serious danger ; but if he is tired out with long travel, if his clothes are wet with perspiration, or if he has not enough to eat, he may freeze to death with the thermometer at zero. The most important rules for an Arctic traveller are : To eat plenty of fat food ; to avoid over-exertion and night journeys ; and never to get into a profuse perspiration by violent exercise for the sake of temporary warmth. I have seen Wandering Chookchees, in a region destitute of wood and in a dangerous tempera- ture, travel all day with aching feet rather than exhaust their strength by trying to warm them in running. They would never exercise except when it was absolutely neces- sary to keep from freezing. As a natural consequence, they were almost as fresh at night as they had been in the morning, and if they failed to find wood for a fire, or were compelled by some unforeseen exigency to travel through- out the twenty-four hours, they had the strength to do it. An inexperienced traveller, under the same circumstances, would have exhausted all his energy during the day in try- ing to keep perfectly warm ; and at night, wet with per- spiration and tired out by too much violent exercise, he would almost inevitably have frozen to death.

For two hours after supper, Dodd and I sat by the fire, trying experiments to see what the intense cold would do. About eight o'clock the heavens became suddenly over- cast with clouds, and in less than an hour the thermo- meter had risen nearly thirty degrees. Congratulating ourselves upon this fortunate change in the weather, we crawled into our fur bags and slept away as much as we could of the long Arctic night.

Our life for the next few days was the same monotonous routine of riding, camping and sleeping with which we
were already so familiar. The country over which we
passed was generally bleak, desolate, and uninteresting ;
the weather was cold enough for discomfort, but not
enough so to make out-door life dangerous or exciting ;
the days were only two or three hours in length and the
nights were interminable. Going into camp early in the
afternoon, when the sun disappeared, we had before us
about twenty hours of darkness, in which we must either
amuse ourselves in some way, or sleep. Twenty hours'
sleep for any one but a Rip Van Winkle was rather an
over-dose, and during at least half that time we could think
of nothing better to do than sit around the camp-fire on
bear-skins and talk. Ever since leaving Petropavlovski,
talking had been our chief amusement ; and although it
had answered very well for the first hundred nights or so,
it was now becoming a little monotonous and our mental
resources were running decidedly low. We could not
think of a single subject about which we knew anything
that had not been talked over, criticised, and discussed
to the very bone. We had related to each other in detail
the whole history of our respective lives, together with the
lives of all our ancestors as far back as we knew anything
about them. We had discussed in full every known problem of Love, War, Science, Politics, and Religion, including a great many that we knew nothing whatever about,
and had finally been reduced to such topics of conversation as the size of the army with which Xerxes invaded
Greece and the probable extent of the Noachian deluge.

As there was no possibility of arriving at any mutually satisfactory conclusion with regard to either of these important questions, the debate had been prolonged for twenty
or thirty consecutive nights and finally left open for future
consideration. In cases of desperate emergency, when all
other topics of conversation failed, we knew that we could
return to Xerxes and the Flood ; but these subjects had
been dropped by the tacit consent of both parties soon
after leaving Geezhega, and were held in reserve as a
" dernier ressort " for stormy nights in Korak yourts. One
night as we were encamped on a great steppe north of
Shestakova, the happy idea occurred to me that I might
pass away these long evenings out of doors, by delivering
a course of lectures to my native drivers upon the wonders
of modern science. It would amuse me, and at the same
time instruct them—or at least I hoped it would, and I
proceeded at once to put the plan into execution. I turned
my attention first to Astronomy. Camping out on the open
steppe, with no roof above except the starry sky, I had
every facility for the illustration of my subject, and night
after night as we travelled to the northward I might have
been seen in the centre of a group of eager natives, whose
swarthy faces were lighted up by the red blaze of the camp-
fire, and who listened with childish curiosity while I explained the phenomena of the seasons, the revolution of
the planets round the sun, and the causes of a lunar eclipse.
I was compelled, like John Phœnix, to manufacture my
own orrery, and I did it with a lump of frozen tallow to represent the earth, a chunk of black bread for the moon, and
small pieces of dried meat for the lesser planets. The re-

semblance to the heavenly bodies was not, I must confess, very striking ; but by making believe pretty hard we man aged to get along. A spectator would have been amused could he have seen with what grave solemnity I circula- ted the bread and tallow in their respective orbits, and have heard the long-drawn exclamations of astonishment from the natives as I brought the bread into eclipse be- hind the lump of tallow. My first lecture would have been a grand success if my native audience had only been able to understand the representative and symbolical character of the bread and tallow. The great trouble was that their imaginative faculties were weak. They could not be made to see that bread stood for the moon and tallow for the earth, but persisted in regarding them as so many terres- trial productions having an intrinsic value of their own. They accordingly melted up the earth to drink, devoured the moon whole, and wanted another lecture immediately. I endeavored to explain to them that these lectures were intended to be *as*tronomical, not *gas*tronomical, and that eating and drinking up the heavenly bodies in this reckless way was very improper. Astronomical science I assured them did not recognize any such eclipses as those pro- duced by swallowing the planets, and however satisfactory such a course might be to them, it was very demoralizing to my orrery. Remonstrances had very little effect, and I was compelled to provide a new sun, moon, and earth for every lecture. It soon became evident to me that these astronomical feasts were becoming altogether too popular, for my audience thought nothing of eating up a whole so- lar system every night, and planetary material was becoming scarce. I was finally compelled, therefore, to use stones and snow-balls to represent celestial bodies, instead of bread and tallow, and from that time the interest in astronomical phenomena gradually abated and the popularity of my lectures steadily declined until I was left without a single hearer.

The short winter day of three hours had long since closed and the night was far advanced when after twenty-three days of rough travel we drew near our final destination—the *ultima Thule* of Russian civilization. I was lying on my sledge nearly buried in heavy furs and half asleep, when the distant barking of dogs announced our approach to the village of Anadyrsk. I made a hurried attempt to change my thick fur "torbassa" and overstockings for American boots, but was surprised in the very act by the drawing up of my sledge before the house of the Russian priest, where we intended to stop until we could make arrangements for a house of our own.

A crowd of curious spectators had gathered about the door to see the wonderful Amerikanse about whom they had heard, and prominent in the centre of the fur-clad group stood the priest, with long flowing hair and beard, dressed in a voluminous black robe, and holding above his head a long tallow candle which flared wildly in the cold night air. As soon as I could disencumber my feet of my over-stockings I alighted from my sledge, amid profound bows and "zdrastvuitias" from the crowd, and received a hearty welcome from the patriarchal priest. Three weeks rough-ing it in the wilderness had not, I fancy, improved my personal appearance, and my costume would have excited a

sensation anywhere except in Siberia.   My face, which was
not over clean, was darkened by three weeks' growth of
beard; my hair was in confusion and hung in long ragged
locks over my forehead, and the fringe of shaggy black
bear-skin around my face gave me a peculiarly wild and
savage expression of countenance.   The American boots
which I had hastily drawn on as we entered the village
weɪe all that indicated any previous acquaintance with civilization.   Replying to the respectful salutations of the
Chooánces, Yoo-kág-hirs, and Russian Cossacks who in
yellow fur hoods and spotted deer-skin coats crowded
about the door, I followed the priest into the house.   It
was the second dwelling worthy the name of house which
I had entered in twenty-two days, and after the smoky
Korak yourts of Kooeel, Meekina, and Shestakova, it
seemed to me to be a perfect palace.   The floor was carpeted with soft, dark deer-skins in which one's feet sank
deeply at every step; a blazing fire burned in a neat fire-
place in one corner, and flooded the room with cheerful
light; the tables were covered with bright American table-
cloths; a tiny gilt taper was lighted before a massive gilt
shrine opposite the door; the windows were of glass
instead of the slabs of ice and the smoky fish-bladders to
which I had become accustomed; a few illustrated newspapers lay on a stand in one corner, and everything in the
house was arranged with a taste and view to comfort
which were as welcome to a tired traveller as they were
unexpected in this land of desolate steppes and uncivilized
people.   Dodd, who was driving his own sledge, had not
yet arrived; but from the door we could hear a voice in

the adjoining forest singing "Won't I be glad when I get
out of the wilderness, out o' the wilderness, out o' the
wilderness"—the musician being entirely unconscious that
he was near the village, or that his melodiously expressed
desire to "get out o' the wilderness" was overheard by
any one else. My Russian was not extensive or accurate
enough to enable me to converse very satisfactorily with
the priest, and I was heartily glad when Dodd *got* out of
the wilderness, and appeared to relieve my embarrassment.
He didn't look much better than I did; that was one
comfort. I drew mental comparisons as soon as he entered the room and convinced myself that one looked as
much like a Korak as the other, and that either could
claim precedence in point of civilization on account of
superior elegance of dress. We shook hands with the
priest's wife—a pale slender lady with light hair and dark
eyes—made the acquaintance of two or three pretty little
children, who fled from us in affright as soon as they were
released, and finally seated ourselves at the table to drink
tea.

Our host's cordial manner soon put us at our ease, and
in ten minutes Dodd was rattling off fluently a highly-
colored account of our adventures and sufferings, laughing, joking, and drinking vodka with the priest, as unceremoniously as if he had known him for ten years
instead of as many minutes. That was a peculiar gift of
Dodd's, which I often used to envy. In five minutes,
with the assistance of a little vodka, he would break down
the ceremonious reserve of the severest old patriarch in
the whole Greek Church, and completely carry him by

storm ; while I could only sit by and smile feebly, without being able to say a word.   Great is "the gift o' gab."

After an excellent supper of "schee" or cabbage-soup, fried cutlets, white bread and butter, we spread our bear-skins down on the floor, undressed ourselves for the second time in three weeks, and went to bed.   The sensation of sleeping without furs, and with uncovered heads, was so strange, that for a long time we lay awake, watching the red flickering fire-light on the wall, and enjoying the delicious warmth of soft, fleecy blankets, and the luxury of unconfined limbs and bare feet.

CHAPTER XXVI.

THE four little Russian and native villages just south of the Arctic circle, which are collectively known as Anadyrsk, form the last link in the great chain of settlements which extends in one almost unbroken line from the Ural Mountains to Behring's Straits. Owing to their peculiarly isolated situation, and the difficulties and hardships of travel during the only season in which they are accessible, they had never, previous to our arrival, been visited by any foreigner, with the single exception of a Swedish officer in the Russian service, who led an exploring party from Anadyrsk toward Behring's Straits, in the winter of 1859–60. Cut off, during half the year, from all the rest of the world, and visited only at long intervals by a few half-civilized traders, this little quadruple village was almost as independent and self-sustained as if it were situated in the midst of the open Polar Sea. Even its existence, to those who had no dealings with it, was a matter of question. It was founded early in the eighteenth century, by a band of roving, adventurous Cossacks, who, having conquered nearly all the rest of Siberia, pushed through the mountains from Kolyma to the Anadyr, drove out the Chookchees, who resisted their advance and established a military post on the river, a few versts above the site of the present settlement. A

desultory warfare then began between the Chookchees
and the Russian invaders, which lasted, with varying suc
cess, for many years.   During a considerable part of the
time Anadyrsk was garrisoned by a force of six hundred
men and a battery of artillery; but after the discovery
and settlement of Kamtchatka it sank into comparative
unimportance, the troops were mostly withdrawn, and it
was finally captured by the Chockchees and burned.
During the war which resulted in the destruction of
Anadyrsk, two native tribes called the Chooances and
Yookaghirs, who had taken sides with the Russians, were
almost annihilated by the Chookchees, and were nevei
able afterward to regain their distinct tribal individuality.
The few who were left lost all their reindeer and camp
equipage, and were compelled to settle down with their
Russian allies, and gain a livelihood by hunting and fishing.   They have gradually adopted Russian customs
and lost all their distinctive traits of character; and in a
few years not a single living soul will speak the languages
of those once powerful tribes.   By the Russians, Chooances, and Yookaghirs, Anadyrsk was finally rebuilt, and
became in time a trading-post of considerable importance.
Tobacco, which had been introduced by the Russians, soon
acquired great popularity with the Chookchees; and for
the sake of obtaining this highly-prized luxury they ceased
hostilities, and began making yearly visits to Anadyrsk
for the purpose of trade.   They never entirely lost, however, a certain feeling of enmity against the Russians who
had invaded their territory, and for many years would
have no dealings with them except at the end of a spear

They would hang a bundle of furs or a choice walrus tooth upon the sharp polished blade of a long Chookchee lance, and if a Russian trader chose to take it off and suspend in its place a fair equivalent in the shape of tobacco, well and good; if not, there was no trade. This plan guaranteed absolute security against fraud, for there was not a Russian in all Siberia who dared to cheat one of these fierce savages, with the blade of a long lance ten inches from his breast bone. Honesty was emphatically the best policy, and the moral suasion of a Chookchee spear developed the most disinterested benevolence in the breast of the man who stood at the sharp end. The trade which was thus established still continues to be a source of considerable profit to the inhabitants of Anadyrsk, and to the Russian merchants who come there every year from Geezhega.

The four small villages which compose the settlement and which are distinctively known as "Pokorookof," "Psolkin," "Markova," and "The Crepast," have altogether a population of perhaps two hundred souls. The central village, called Markova, is the residence of the priest and boasts a small rudely-built church, but in winter it is a dreary place. Its small log-houses have no windows but thick slabs of ice cut from the river; many of them are sunken in the ground for the sake of greater warmth, and all are more or less buried in snow. A dense forest of larch, poplar, and aspen surrounds the town, so that the traveller coming from Geezhega sometimes has to hunt for it a whole day, and if he be not familiar with the net-work of channels into which the Anadyr River is here divided, he may not find it at all. The inhabitants of all four settlements divide their time in summer be-tween fishing and hunting the wild reindeer, which make annual migrations across the river in immense herds. In winter they are generally absent with their sledges, visit-ing and trading with bands of Wandering Chookchees, going with merchandise to the great annual fair at Kolyma, and hiring their services to the Russian traders from Geezhega. The Anadyr River, in the vicinity of the village and for a distance of seventy-five miles above, is densely wooded with trees eighteen and twenty four inches in dia-meter, although the latitude of the upper portion of it is 66° N. The climate is very severe; meteorological ob-servations which we made at Markova in February, 1867, showed that on sixteen days in that month the thermo-meter went to —40°, on eight days it went below —50°, five days below —60°, and once to —68°. This was the lowest temperature we ever experienced in Siberia. The changes from intense cold to comparative warmth are some-times very rapid. On February 18th, at 9 A.M., the thermometer stood at —52°, but in twenty-seven hours it had risen seventy-three degrees and stood at +21°. On the 21st it marked +3° and on the 22d —49°, an equally rapid change in the other direction. Notwithstand-ing the climate, however, Anadyrsk is as pleasant a place to live as are nine-tenths of the Russian settlements in Northeastern Siberia, and we enjoyed the novelty of our life there in the winter of 1866 as much as we had enjoy-ed any part of our previous Siberian experience.

The day which succeeded our arrival we spent in rest-

ing and making ourselves as presentable as possible, with
the limited resources afforded by our seal-skin trunks.

Thursday, January 6th, N. S., was the Russian Christmas, and we all rose about four hours before daylight to
attend an early service in the church.   Everybody in the
house was up; a fire burned brightly in the fire-place;
gilded tapers were lighted before all the holy pictures and
shrines in our room, and the air was fragrant with incense.
Out of doors there was not yet a sign of daybreak.   The
Pleiades were low down in the west, the great constellation of Orion had begun to sink, and a faint aurora was
streaming up over the tree-tops north of the village.
From every chimney around rose columns of smoke and
sparks, which showed that the inhabitants were all astir.
We walked over to the little log-church as quickly as
possible, but the service had already commenced when
we entered, and silently took our places in the crowd of
bowing worshippers.   The sides of the room were lined
with pictures of patriarchs and Russian saints, before
which were burning long wax candles wound spirally
with strips of gilded paper.   Clouds of blue fragrant in-
cense rolled up toward the roof from swinging censers,
and the deep intonation of the gorgeously-attired priest
contrasted strangely with the high soprano chanting of
the choir.   The service of the Greek Church is more
impressive, if anything, than that of the Romish; but as
it is conducted in the old Sclavonic language, it is almost
wholly unintelligible.   The priest is occupied during most
of the time in gabbling rapid prayers which nobody can
understand; swinging a censer, bowing, crossing himself,

and kissing a huge Bible, which I should think would weigh thirty pounds. The administration of the sacrament and the ceremonies attending the transubstantiation of the bread and wine are made very effective. The most beautiful feature in the whole service of the Greco-Russian Church is the music. No one can listen to it without emotion, even in a little log-chapel far away in the interior of Siberia. Rude as it may be in execution, it breathes the very spirit of devotion; and I have often stood through a long service of two or three hours, for the sake of hearing a few chanted psalms and prayers. Even the tedious, rapid, and mixed-up jabbering of the priest is relieved at short intervals by the varied and beautifully-modulated "Gospodi pameelui" (God, have mercy!) and "Padai Gospodin" (Grant, O Lord!) of the choir. The congregation stands throughout even the longest service, and seems to be wholly absorbed in devotion. All cross themselves and bow incessantly in response to the words of the priest, and not unfrequently prostrate themselves entirely, and reverently press their foreheads and lips to the floor. To a spectator this seems very curious. One moment he is surrounded by a crowd of fur-clad natives and Cossacks, who seem to be listening quietly to the service; then suddenly the whole congregation goes down upon the floor, like a platoon of infantry under the fire of a masked battery, and he is left standing alone in the midst of nearly a hundred prostrate forms. At the conclusion of the Christmas morning service the choir burst forth into a jubilant hymn, to express the joy of the angels over the Saviour's birth; and amid the discordant jangling of

a chime of bells, which hung in a little log-tower at the
door, Dodd and I made our way out of the church, and
returned to the house to drink tea. I had just finished
my last cup and lighted a cigarette, when the door suddenly opened, half a dozen men, with grave, impassioned
countenances, marched in in single file, stopped a few
paces from the holy pictures in the corner, crossed themselves devoutly in unison, and began to sing a simple but
sweet Russian melody, beginning with the words, " Christ
is born." Not expecting to hear Christmas carols in a
little Siberian settlement on the Arctic circle, I was taken
completely by surprise, and could only stare in amazement—first at Dodd, to see what he thought about it,
and then at the singers. The latter, in their musical
ecstasy, seemed to entirely ignore our presence, and not
until they had finished did they turn to us, shake hands,
and wish us a merry Christmas. Dodd gave each of
them a few kopecks, and with repeated wishes of merry
Christmas, long life, and much happiness to our " High
Excellencies," the men withdrew to visit in turn the
other houses of the village. One band of singers came
after another, until at daylight all the younger portion of
the population had visited our house, and received our
kopecks. Some of the smaller boys, more intent upon
the acquisition of coppers than they were upon the solemnity of the ceremony, rather marred its effect by
closing up their hymn with " Christ is born ; gim'me
some money !" but most of them behaved with the utmost propriety, and left us greatly pleased with a custom
so beautiful and appropriate. At sunrise all the tapers

were extinguished, the people donned their gayest ap
parel, and the whole village gave itself up to the unre·
strained enjoyment of a grand holiday. Bells jangled
incessantly from the church tower; dog-sledges, loaded
with girls, went dashing about the streets, capsizing
into snow-drifts, and rushing furiously down hills, amid
shouts of laughter; women in gay flowery calico dresses,
with their hair tied up in crimson silk handkerchiefs,
walked from house to house, paying visits of congratula-
tion, and talking over the arrival of the distinguished
American officers; crowds of men played foot-ball on the
snow, and the whole settlement presented an animated,
lively appearance.

On the evening of the third day after Christmas, the
priest gave in our honor a grand Siberian ball, to which
all the inhabitants of the four villages were invited, and
for which the most elaborate preparations were made.
A ball at the house of a priest on Sunday night struck me
as implying a good deal of inconsistency, and I hesitated
about sanctioning so plain a violation of the fourth com-
mandment. Dodd, however, proved to me in the most
conclusive manner that, owing to difference in time, it
was Saturday in America and not Sunday at all; that our
friends at that very moment were engaged in business or
pleasure, and that our happening to be on the other side
of the world was no reason why we should not do what
our antipodal friends were doing at exactly the same
time. I was conscious that this reasoning was sophisti-
cal, but Dodd mixed me up so with his "longitude,"
"Greenwich time," "Bowditch's Navigators," "Russian

Sundays" and "American Sundays," that I was hopelessly
bewildered, and couldn't have told for my life whether it
was to-day in America or yesterday, or when a Siberian
Sunday did begin. I finally concluded that as the Russians kept Saturday night, and began another week at sunset on the Sabbath, a dance would perhaps be sufficiently
innocent for that evening. According to Siberian ideas
of propriety it was just the thing.

A partition was removed in our house, the floor made
bare, the room brilliantly illuminated with candles stuck
against the wall with melted grease, benches placed
around three sides of the house for the ladies, and about
five o'clock the pleasure seekers began to assemble.
Rather an early hour perhaps for a ball, but it seemed
a very long time after dark. The crowd which soon
gathered numbered about forty, the men being all
dressed in heavy fur kookhlánkas, fur pantaloons, and fur
boots, and the ladies in thin white muslin and flowery
calico prints. The costumes of the respective sexes did
not seem to harmonize very well, one being light and
airy enough for an African summer, and the other suitable
for a Polar expedition in search of Sir John Franklin.
However, the general effect was very picturesque. The
orchestra which was to furnish the music consisted of
two rudely made violins, two "bellalikas" or triangular
native guitars with two strings each, and a huge comb,
prepared with a piece of paper in a manner familiar to
all boys. Feeling a little curiosity to see how an affair
of this kind would be managed upon Siberian principles
of etiquette, I sat quietly in a sheltered corner and watched

the pioceedings. The ladies, as fast as they arrived,
seated themselves in a solemn row along a wooden bench
at one end of the room, and the men stood up in a dense
throng at the other. Everybody was preternaturally
sober. No one smiled, no one said anything; and the
silence was unbroken save by an occasional rasping
sound from an asthmatic fiddle in the orchestra, or a
melancholy toot, toot, as one of the musicians tuned his
comb. If this was to be the nature of the entertainment,
I could not see any impropriety in having it on Sunday.
It was as mournfully suggestive as a funeral. Little did
I know, however, the capabilities of excitement which
were concealed under the sober exteriors of those natives.
In a few moments a little stir around the door announced
refreshments, and a young Chooancee brought round and
handed to me a huge wooden bowl, holding about four
quarts of raw frozen cranberries. I thought it could not
be possible that I was expected to eat four quarts of
frozen cranberries! but I took a spoonful or two, and
looked to Dodd for instructions. He motioned to me to
pass them along, and as they tasted like acidulated hail-
stones, and gave me the toothache, I was very glad to do so.

The next course consisted of another wooden bowl,
filled with what seemed to be white pine shavings, and I
looked at it in perfect astonishment. Frozen cranberries and pine shavings were the most extraordinary refreshments which I had ever seen—even in Siberia; but
I prided myself upon my ability to eat almost anything,
and if the natives could stand cranberries and shavings I
knew I could. What seemed to be white pine shavings

I found upon trial to be thin shavings of raw frozen fish
—a great delicacy among the Siberians, and one with
which, under the name of " strooganini," I afterward
became very familiar. I succeeded in disposing of these
fishy shavings without any more serious result than an
aggravation of my toothache. They were followed by
white bread and butter, cranberry tarts, and cups of boiling hot tea, with which the supper finally ended. We
were then supposed to be prepared for the labors of the
evening ; and after a good deal of preliminary scraping
and tuning the orchestra struck up with a lively Russian dance called "kapalooshka." The heads and right
legs of the musicians all beat time emphatically to the
music, the man with the comb blew himself red in the
face, and the whole assembly began to sing. In a moment one of the men, clad in a spotted deer-skin coat and
buck-skin pantaloons, sprang into the centre of the room
and bowed low to a lady who sat upon one end of a long
crowded bench. The lady rose with a graceful courtesy
and they began a sort of half dance half pantomime about
the room, advancing and retiring in perfect time to the
music, crossing over and whirling swiftly around, the man
apparently making love to the lady, and the lady repuls-
ing all his advances, turning away and hiding her face
with her handkerchief. After a few moments of this
dumb show the lady retired and another took her place ;
the music doubled its energy and rapidity, the dancers
began the execution of a tremendous "break-down,"
and shrill exciting cries of " Heekh ! Heekh ! Heekh !
Vallai-i-i ! Ne fstavai-i-i !" resounded from all parts of the

room, together with terrific tootings from the comb and
the beating of half a hundred feet on the bare planks.
My blood began to dance in my veins with the contagious
excitement. Suddenly the man dropped down upon his
stomach on the floor at the feet of his partner, and began
jumping around like a huge broken-legged grasshopper
upon his elbows and the ends of his toes! This extraordinary feat brought down the house in the wildest enthusiasm, and the uproar of shouting and singing drowned
all the instruments except the comb, which still droned
away like a Scottish bag-pipe in its last agonies! Such
singing, such dancing, and such excitement, I had never
before witnessed. It swept away my self-possession like
the blast of a trumpet sounding a charge. At last, the
man, after dancing successively with all the ladies in the
room, stopped, apparently exhausted—and I have no
doubt that he was—and with the perspiration rolling in
streams down his face, went in search of some frozen
cranberries to refresh himself after his violent exertion.
To this dance, which is called the "Rooske," succeeded
another known as the "Cossack waltz," in which Dodd
to my great astonishment promptly joined. I knew I
could dance anything he could; so, inviting a lady in red
and blue calico to participate, I took my place on the
floor. The excitement was perfectly indescribable, when
the two Americans began revolving swiftly around the
room; the musicians became almost frantic in their en-
deavors to play faster, the man with the comb blew himself into a fit of coughing and had to sit down, and a
regular tramp, tramp, tramp, from fifty or sixty feet,

marked time to the music, together with encouraging shouts of " Vallai ! Amerikanse ! Heekh ! Heekh ! Heekh !" and the tumultuous singing of the whole crazy multitude. The pitch of excitement to which these natives work themselves up in the course of these dances is almost incredible, and it has a wonderfully inspiriting effect even upon a foreigner. Had I not been temporarily insane with unnatural enthusiasm, I should never have made myself ridiculous by attempting to dance that Cossack waltz. It is considered a great breach of etiquette in Siberia, after once getting upon the floor, to sit down until you have danced, or at least offered to dance with all the ladies in the room ; and if they are at all numerous, it is a very fatiguing sort of amusement. By the time Dodd and I finished we were ready to rush out doors, sit down on a snow-bank, and eat frozen fish and cranberry hail-stones by the quart. Our whole physical system seemed melting with fervent heat.

As an illustration of the esteem with which Americans are regarded in that benighted settlement of Anadyrsk, I will just mention that in the course of my Cossack waltz I stepped accidentally with my heavy boot upon the foot of a Russian peasant. I noticed that his face wore for a moment an expression of intense pain, and as soon as the dance was over, I went to him with Dodd as interpreter to apologize. He interrupted me with a profusion of bows, protested that it didn't hurt him *at all*, and declared with an emphasis which testified to his sincerity, that he considered it an honor to have his toe stepped on by an American ! I had never before realized what a proud and enviable distinction I enjoyed in being a native of our highly favored country ! I could stalk abroad into foreign lands with a reckless disregard for everybody's toes, and the full assurance that the more toes I stepped on the more honor I would confer upon benighted foreigners, and the more credit I would reflect upon my own bene-volent disposition ! This was clearly the place for unap-preciated Americans to come to ; and if any young man finds that his merits are not properly recognized at home, I advise him in all seriousness to go to Siberia, where the natives will consider it an honor to have him step on their toes.

Dances interspersed with curious native games and frequent refreshments of frozen cranberries prolonged the entertainment until two o'clock, when it finally broke up, having lasted nine hours. I have described somewhat in detail this dancing party because it is the principal amuse-ment of the semi-civilized inhabitants of all the Russian settlements in Siberia, and shows better than anything else the careless, happy disposition of the people.

Throughout the holidays the whole population did no-thing but pay visits, give tea parties, and amuse them-selves with dancing, sleigh-riding, and playing ball. Every evening between Christmas and New Year, bands of masqueraders dressed in fantastic costumes went around with music to all the houses in the village and treated the inmates to songs and dances. The inhabitants of these little Russian settlements in Northeastern Sibe-ria are the most careless, warm-hearted, hospitable people in the world, and their social life, rude as it is, partakes of all these characteristics. There is no ceremony or affectation, no putting on of style by any particular class. All mingle unreservedly together and treat each other with the most affectionate cordiality, the men often kissing one another when they meet and part, as if they were brothers. Their isolation from all the rest of the world seems to have bound them together with ties of mutual sympathy and dependence, and banished all feelings of envy, jealousy, and petty selfishness. During our stay with the priest we were treated with the most thoughtful consideration and kindness, and his small store of luxuries, such as flour, sugar, and butter, was spent lavishly in providing for our table. As long as it lasted he was glad to share it with us, and never hinted at compensation or seemed to think that he was doing any more than hospitality required.

With the first ten days of our stay at Anadyrsk are connected some of the pleasantest recollections of our Siberian life.

CHAPTER XXVII.

SIBERIAN ADVENTURES IN SEARCH OF OUR COMRADES.

IMMEDIATELY after our arrival at Anadyrsk we had made inquiries as to the party of Americans who were said to be living somewhere near the mouth of the Anadyr River; but we were not able to get any information in addition to that we already possessed. Wandering Chookchees had brought the news to the settlement that a small band of white men had been landed on the coast south of Behring's Straits late in the fall, from a "fire-ship" or steamer; that they had dug a kind of cellar in the ground, covered it over with bushes and boards, and gone into winter quarters. Who they were, what they had come for, and how long they intended to stay, were questions which now agitated the whole Chookchee nation, but which no one could answer. Their little subterranean hut had been entirely buried, the natives said, by the drifting snows of winter, and nothing but a curious iron tube out of which came smoke and sparks showed where the white men lived. This curious iron tube which so puzzled the Chookchees we at once supposed to be a stove-pipe, and it furnished the strongest possible confirmation of the truth of the story. No Siberian native could ever have invented the idea of a stove-pipe—somebody must have seen one; and this fact alone convinced us beyond a doubt that there were Americans living somewhere on the coast of Behring's Sea—probably an exploring party landed by Colonel Bulkley to co-operate with us.

The instructions which the Major gave me when we left Geezhega did not provide for any such contingency as the landing of this party near Behring's Straits, because at that time we had abandoned all hope of such co-operation and expected to explore the country by our own unaided exertions. The Engineer-in-chief had promised faithfully when we sailed from San Francisco, that if he should leave a party of men at the mouth of the Anadyr River at all, he would leave them there early in the season with a large whale-boat, so that they could ascend the river to a settlement before the opening of winter. When we met the Anadyrsk people, therefore, at Geezhega, late in November, and learned that nothing had been heard of any such party, we of course concluded that for some reason the plan which Col. Bulkley proposed had been given up. No one dreamed that he would leave a mere handful of men in the desolate region south of Behring's Straits at the beginning of an Arctic winter, without any means whatever of transportation, without any shelter, surrounded by fierce tribes of lawless natives, and distant more than two hundred miles from the nearest civilized human being. What was such an unfortunate party to do ? They could only live there in inactivity until they starved, were murdered, or were brought away by an expedition sent to their rescue from the interior. Such was the situation when Dodd and I arrived at Anadyrsk. Our orders were to leave the Anadyr River unexplored until another season ; but we knew

that as soon as the Major should receive the letters which
had passed through our hands at Shestakova he would
learn that a party had been landed south of Behring's
Straits, and would send us orders by special courier to go
in search of it and bring it to Anadyrsk, where it would be
of some use.   We therefore determined to anticipate these
orders and hunt up that American stove-pipe upon our
own responsiblity.

Our situation, however, was a very peculiar one.   We
had no means of finding out where we were ourselves,
or where the American party was.   We had not been
furnished with instruments for making astronomical ob-
servations, could not determine with any kind of accuracy
our latitude and longitude, and did not know whether
we were two hundred miles from the Pacific Coast or five
hundred.   According to the report of Lieut. Phillippeus,
who had partially explored the Anadyr River, it was
about a thousand versts from the settlement to Anadyr
Bay, while according to the dead reckoning which we
had kept from Geezhega it could not be over four hundred.   The real distance was to us a question of vital
importance, because we should be obliged to carry dog-
food for the whole trip, and if it was anything like a
thousand versts we should in all probability lose our dogs
by starvation before we could possibly get back.   Besides
this, when we finally reached Anadyr Bay, if we ever did,
we would have no means of finding out where the Americans were ; and unless we happened to meet a band of
Chookchees who had seen them, we might wander over
those desolate plains for a month without coming across

the stove-pipe, which was the only external sign of their subterranean habitation. It would be far worse than the proverbial search for a needle in a haystack.

When we made known to the people of Anadyrsk our intention of going to the Pacific Coast, and called for volunteers to make up a party, we met with the most discouraging opposition. The natives declared unanimously that such a journey was impossible, that it had never been accomplished, that the lower Anadyr was swept by terrible storms, and perfectly destitute of wood, that the cold there was always intense, and that we should inevitably starve to death, freeze to death, or lose all our dogs. They quoted the experience of Lieut. Phillippeus, who had narrowly escaped utter starvation in the same region in 1860, and said that while he started in the spring we proposed to go in mid-winter, when the cold was most intense and the storms most severe. Such an adventure they declared was almost certain to end in disaster. Our Cossack Gregorie, a brave and trustworthy old man, had been Lieut. Phillippeus's guide and Chookchee interpreter in 1860, and had been down the river about a hundred and fifty miles in winter, and knew something about it. We accordingly dismissed the natives and talked the matter over with him. He said that as far as he had ever been towards Anadyr Bay there was trailing pine enough along the banks of the river to supply us with fire-wood, and that the country was no worse than much of that over which we had already travelled between Geezhega and Anadyrsk. He said that he was entirely willing to undertake the trip, and would go with his own team of dogs wherever we would lead the way. The priest also, who had been down the river in summer, believed the journey to be practicable, and said he would go himself if he could do any good. Upon the strength of this encouragement we gave the natives our final decision, showed them the letter which we brought from the Russian Governor at Geezhega authorizing us to demand men and sledges for all kinds of service, and told them that if they still refused to go we would send a special messenger to Geezhega and report their disobedience. This threat and the example of our Cossack Gregorie, who was known to be an experienced guide from the Okhotsk Sea to the Arctic Ocean, finally had the desired effect. Eleven men agreed to go, and we began at once to collect dog-food and provisions for an early start. We had as yet only the vaguest, most indefinite information with regard to the situation of the American party, and we determined to wait a few days until a Cossack named Kozhevin, who had gone to visit some Wandering Chookchees, should return. The priest was sure that he would bring later and more trustworthy intelligence, because the wandering natives throughout the whole country knew of the arrival of the mysterious white men, and would probably tell Kozhevin approximately where they were. In the mean time we made some additions to our heavy suits of furs, prepared masks of squirrel-skin to be worn over the face in extremely low temperatures, and set all the women in the village at work upon a large fur tent.

On Saturday, Jan. 20th, N. S., Kozhevin returned from

his visit to the Chookchees north of Anadyrsk, bringing as
we expected later and fuller particulars with regard to the
party of exiled Americans south of Behring's Straits. It
consisted, according to the best Chookchee intelligence, of
only five men, and was located on or near the Anadyr
River, about one day's journey above its mouth. These
five men were living, as we had previously been told, in a
little subterranean hut rudely constructed of bushes and
boards, and entirely buried in drifted snow. They were
said to be well supplied with provisions, and had a great
many barrels, which the Chookchees supposed to contain
"vodka," but which we presumed to be barrels of salt-beef.
They made a fire, the natives said, in the most wonderful
manner by burning "black stones in an iron box," while
all the smoke came out mysteriously through a crooked
iron tube which turned around when the wind blew! In
this vivid but comical description we of course recognized
a coal stove and a pipe with a rotary funnel. They had
also, Kozhevin was told, an enormous tame black bear,
which they allowed to run loose around the house, and
which chased away the Chookchees in a most energetic
manner. When I heard this I could no longer restrain a
hurrah of exultation. The party was made up of our old
San Francisco comrades, and the tame black bear was Robinson's Newfoundland dog! I had petted him a hundred
times in America and had his picture among my photo-
graphs. He was the dog of the Expedition. There could
no longer be any doubt whatever that the party thus bur-
rowed under the snow on the great steppes south of Behring's Straits was the long talked of Anadyr River Explor-

ing Party, under the command of Lieut. Macrae ; and our
hearts beat fast with excitement as we thought of the surprise which we would give our old friends and comrades
by coming upon them suddenly in that desolate, God-forsaken region, almost two thousand miles away from the
point where they supposed we had landed.   Such a meeting would repay us tenfold for all the hardships of our
Siberian life.

Everything, by this time, was ready for a start.   Our
sledges were loaded five feet high with provisions and dog-
food for thirty days ; our fur tent was completed and packed away, to be used if necessary in intensely cold weather ;
bags, overstockings, masks, thick sleeping-coats, snow-
shovels, axes, rifles, and long Siberian snow-shoes were
distributed around among the different sledges, and everything which Gregorie, Dodd, and I could think of was done
to insure the success of the expedition.

On Monday morning, Jan. 22d, the whole party assembled in front of the priest's house.   For the sake of econo-
mizing transportation, and sharing the fortunes of our men,
whatever they might be, Dodd and I abandoned our pavó-
skas, and drove our own loaded sledges.   We did not mean
to have the natives say that we compelled them to go and
then avoided our share of work and hardships.   The entire
population of the village, men, women, and children, turned out to see us off, and the street before the priest's house
was blocked up with a crowd of dark-faced men in spotted
fur coats, scarlet sashes, and fierce-looking fox-skin hoods,
anxious-faced women running to and fro and bidding their
husbands and brothers good-by, eleven long, narrow

sledges piled high with dried fish and covered with yellow buckskin and lashings of seal-skin thongs, and finally a hundred and twenty-five shaggy wolfish dogs, who drowned every other sound with their combined howls of fierce impatience.

Our drivers went into the priest's house, and crossed themselves and prayed before the picture of the Saviour, as is their custom when starting on a long journey. Dodd and I bade good-by to the kind-hearted priest, and received the cordial "s' bokhem" (go with God), which is the Russian farewell; and then springing upon our sledges, and releasing our frantic dogs, we went flying out of the village in a cloud of snow which glittered like powdered jewel-dust in the red sunshine.

Beyond the two or three hundred miles of snowy desert which lay before us we could see, in imagination, a shadowy stove-pipe rising out of a bank of snow—the "San greal" of which we, as Arctic knights-errant, were in search.

CHAPTER XXVIII.

I WILL not detain the reader long with the first part of our journey from Anadyrsk to the Pacific Coast, as it was only a new and revised edition of our previous Siberian experience. Riding all day over the ice of the river, or across barren steppes, and camping out at night on the snow, in all kinds of weather, made up our life; and its dreary monotony was only relieved by anticipations of a joyful meeting with our exiled friends, and the exciting consciousness that we were penetrating a country never before visited by civilized man. Day by day the fringe of alder-bushes along the river-bank grew lower and more scanty, and the great steppes that bordered the river became whiter and more barren as the river widened toward the sea. Finally we left behind us the last vestige of vegetation, and began the tenth day of our journey along a river which had increased to a mile in width, and amidst plains perfectly desolate of all life, which stretched away in one unbroken white expanse until they blended with the distant sky. It was not without uneasiness that I thought of the possibility of being overtaken by a ten days' storm in such a region as this. We had made, as nearly as we could estimate, since leaving Anadyrsk, about two hundred versts; but whether we were any-where near the sea-coast or not we had no means of knowing. The weather for nearly a week had been generally clear, and not very cold; but on the night of February 1st the thermometer sank to −35°, and we could find only just enough small green bushes to boil our tea-kettle. We dug everywhere in the snow in search of wood, but found nothing except moss, and a few small cranberry-bushes which would not burn. Tired with the long day's travel and the fruitless digging for wood, Dodd and I returned to camp, and threw ourselves down upon our bear-skins to drink tea. Hardly had Dodd put his cup to his lips when I noticed that a curious, puzzled expression came over his face, as if he found something singular and unusual in the taste of the tea. I was just about to ask him what was the matter, when he cried out in a joyful and surprised voice, "Tide-water! The tea is salt!" Thinking that perhaps a little salt might have been dropped accidentally into the tea, I sent the men down to the river for some fresh ice, which we carefully melted. It was unquestionably salt. We had reached the tide-water of the Pacific, and the ocean itself could not be far distant. One more day must certainly bring us to the house of the American party, or to the mouth of the river. From all appearances we should find no more wood; and anxious to make the most of the clear weather, we slept only about six hours, and started on at midnight, by the light of a brilliant moon.

On the eleventh day after our departure from Anadyrsk, toward the close of the long twilight which succeeds an Arctic day, our little train of eleven sledges drew near the place where, from Chookchee accounts, we expected to

find the long-exiled party of Americans. The night was
clear, still, and intensely cold, the thermometer at sunset
marking forty-four degrees below zero, and sinking rapidly
to —50° as the rosy flush in the west grew fainter and
fainter, and darkness settled down upon the vast steppe.
Many times before, in Siberia and Kamtchatka, I had
seen nature in her sterner moods and winter garb; but
never before had the elements of cold, barrenness, and
desolation seemed to combine into a picture so dreary
as the one which was presented to us that night near
Behring's Straits. Far as eye could pierce the gathering
gloom in every direction lay the barren steppe like a
boundless ocean of snow, blown into long wave-like
ridges by previous storms. There was not a tree, nor a
bush, nor any sign of animal or vegetable life, to show
that we were not travelling on a frozen ocean. All was
silence and desolation. The country seemed abandoned
by God and man to the Arctic Spirit, whose trembling
banners of auroral light flared out fitfully in the north in
token of his conquest and dominion. About eight
o'clock the full moon rose huge and red in the east, casting a lurid glare over the vast field of snow; but as if it
too were under the control of the Arctic Spirit, it was
nothing more than the mockery of a moon, and was constantly assuming the most fantastic and varied shapes.
Now it extended itself laterally into a long ellipse, then
gathered itself up again into the semblance of a huge red
urn, lengthened out to a long perpendicular bar with
rounded ends, and finally became triangular. It can
hardly be imagined what added wildness and strangeness

this blood-red distorted moon gave to a scene already wild and strange. We seemed to have entered upon some frozen abandoned world where all the ordinary laws and phenomena of Nature were suspended, where animal and vegetable life were extinct, and from which even the favor of the Creator had been withdrawn. The intense cold, the solitude, the oppressive silence, and the red, gloomy moonlight, like the glare of a distant but mighty conflagration, all united to excite in the mind feelings of awe, which were perhaps intensified by the consciousness that never before had any human being, save a few Wandering Chookchees, ventured in winter upon these domains of the Frost King. There was none of the singing, joking, and hallooing, with which our drivers were wont to enliven a night-journey. Stolid and unimpressible though they might be, there was something in the scene which even *they* felt and were silent. Hour after hour wore slowly and wearily away until midnight. We had passed by more than twenty miles the point on the river where the party of Americans was supposed to be; but no sign had been found of the subterranean house or its projecting stove-pipe, and the great steppe still stretched away before us, white, ghastly, and illimitable as ever. For nearly twenty-four hours we had travelled without a single stop, night or day, except one at sunrise to rest our tired dogs; and the intense cold, fatigue, anxiety, and lack of warm food, began at last to tell upon our silent but suffering men. We realized for the first time the hazardous nature of the adventure in which we were engaged, and the almost absolute hope-

lessness of the search which we were making for the lost
American party. We had not one chance in a hundred
of finding at midnight on that vast waste of snow a little
buried hut, whose location we did not know within fifty
miles, and of whose very existence we were by no means
certain. Who could tell whether the Americans had not
abandoned their subterranean house two months before,
and removed with some friendly natives to a more comfortable and sheltered situation? We had heard nothing
from them later than December 1st, and it was now
February. They might in that time have gone a hundred miles down the coast looking for a settlement, or
have wandered far back into the interior with a band of
Reindeer Chookchees. It was not probable that they
would have spent four months in that dreary, desolate region without making an effort to escape. Even if they
were still in their old camp, however, how were we to
find them? We might have passed their little underground hut unobserved hours before, and might now be
going farther and farther away from it, from wood, and
from shelter. It had seemed a very easy thing before we
left Anadyrsk, to simply go down the river until we came
to a house on the bank, or saw a stove-pipe sticking out
of a snow-drift; but now, two hundred and fifty or three
hundred miles from the settlement, in a temperature of 50°
below zero, when our lives perhaps depended upon finding
that little buried hut, we realized how wild had been our anticipations, and how faint were our prospects of success.
The nearest wood was more than fifty miles behind us,
and in our chilled and exhausted condition we dared not

camp without a fire. We must go either forward or back
—find the hut within four hours or abandon the search,
and return as rapidly as possible to the nearest wood.
Our dogs were beginning already to show unmistakable
signs of exhaustion, and their feet, swollen with long travel,
had cracked open between the toes and were now spot-
ting the white snow with blood at every step. Unwilling
to give up the search while there remained any hope, we
still went on to the eastward, along the edges of high
bare bluffs skirting the river, separating our sledges as
widely as possible, and extending our line so as to cover
a greater extent of ground. A full moon, now high in
the heavens, lighted up the vast lonely plain on the north
side of the river as brilliantly as day; but its whiteness was
unbroken by any dark object, save here and there little
hillocks of moss and swampy grass from which the snow
had been swept by furious winds.

We were all suffering severely from cold, and our fur
hoods and the breasts of our fur coats were masses of
white frost which had been formed by our breaths. I had
put on two heavy reindeer-skin kookhlánkas weighing in
the aggregate about thirty pounds, belted them tightly
about the waist with a sash, drawn their thick hoods up
over my head and covered my face with a squirrel-skin
mask; but in spite of all I could only keep from freezing
by running beside my sledge. Dodd said nothing, but was
evidently disheartened and half frozen, while the natives
sat silently upon their sledges as if they expected nothing
and hoped for nothing. Only Gregorie and an old Chookchee whom we had brought with us as a guide showed any

energy or seemed to have any confidence in the ultimate
discovery of the party.   They went on in advance, digging everywhere in the snow for wood, examining carefully the banks of the river, and making occasional détours
into the snowy plain to the northward.   At last Dodd,
without saying anything to me, gave his spiked stick to
one of the natives, drew his head and arms into the body
of his fur coat, and lay down upon his sledge to sleep, regardless of my remonstrances, and paying no attention
whatever to my questions.   He was evidently becoming
stupefied by the deadly chill, which struck through the
heaviest furs, and which was constantly making insidious
advances from the extremities to the seat of life.   He probably would not live through the night unless he could be
roused, and might not live two hours.   Discouraged by
his apparently hopeless condition, and exhausted by the
constant struggle to keep warm, I finally lost all hope and
reluctantly decided to abandon the search and camp.   By
stopping where we were, breaking up one of our sledges
for fire-wood, and boiling a little tea, I thought that Dodd
might be revived; but to go on to the eastward seemed to
be needlessly risking the lives of all without any apparent
prospect of discovering the party or of finding wood.   I
had just given the order to the natives nearest me to camp,
when I thought I heard a faint halloo in the distance.   All
the blood in my veins suddenly rushed with a great throb
to the heart as I threw back my fur hood and listened.
Again, a faint, long-drawn cry came back through the
still atmosphere from the sledges in advance.   My dogs
pricked up their ears at the startling sound and dashed

eagerly forward, and in a moment I came upon several of our leading drivers gathered in a little group around what seemed to be an old overturned whale-boat, which lay half buried in snow by the river's bank. The footprint in the sand was not more suggestive to Robinson Crusoe than was this weather-beaten, abandoned whale-boat to us, for it showed that somewhere in the vicinity there was shelter and life. One of the men a few moments before had driven over some dark, hard object in the snow, which he at first supposed to be a log of driftwood ; but upon stopping to examine it, he found it to be an American whale-boat. If ever we thanked God from the bottom of our hearts, it was then. Brushing away with my mitten the long fringe of frost which hung to my eyelashes, I looked eagerly around for a house, but Gregorie had been quicker than I, and a joyful shout from a point a little farther down the river announced another discovery. I left my dogs to go where they chose, threw away my spiked stick, and started at a run in the direction of the sound. In a moment I saw Gregorie and the old Chookchee standing beside a low mound of snow, about a hundred yards back from the river-bank, examining some dark object which projected from its smooth white surface. It was the long talked of, long looked for stove-pipe ! The Anadyr River party was found.

The unexpected discovery late at night of this party of countrymen, when we had just given up all hope of shelter, and almost of life, was a God-send to our disheartened spirits, and I hardly knew in my excitement what I did. I remember now walking hastily back and

forth in front of the snow-drift, repeating softly to myself
at every step, "Thank God!" "thank God!" but at the
time I was not conscious of anything except the great
fact of our safety.   Dodd, who had been roused from his
half-frozen lethargy by the strong excitement of the discovery, now suggested that we try and find the entrance
to the house and get in as quickly as possible, as he was
nearly dead with the cold and exhaustion.   There was
no sound of life in the lonely snow-drift before us, and
the inmates, if it had any, were evidently asleep.   Seeing
no sign anywhere of a door, I walked up on the drift, and
shouted down through the stove-pipe in tremendous tones,
"Halloo the house!"—A startled voice from under my
feet demanded "Who's there?"

"Come out and see! Where's the door?"

My voice seemed to the astounded Americans inside
to come out of the stove—a phenomenon which was
utterly unparalleled in all their previous experience; but
they reasoned very correctly that any stove which could
ask in good English for the door in the middle of the
night had an indubitable right to be answered; and they
replied in a hesitating and half-frightened tone that the
door was "on the southeast corner."   This left us
about as wise as before.   In the first place we did not
know which way southeast was, and in the second a
snow-drift could not properly be described as having a
corner.   I started around the stove-pipe, however, in a
circle, with the hope of finding some sort of an entrance.
The inmates had dug a deep ditch or trench about thirty
feet in length for a doorway, and had covered it over

with sticks and reindeer-skins to keep out the drifting snow. Stepping incautiously upon this frail roof, I fell through just as one of the startled men was coming out in his shirt and drawers, holding a candle above his head, and peering through the darkness of the tunnel to see who would enter. The sudden descent through the roof of such an apparition as I knew myself to be, was not calculated to restore the steadiness of startled nerves. I had on two heavy "kookhlánkas" which swelled out my figure to gigantic proportions, two thick reindeer-skin hoods with long frosty fringes of black bear-skin were pulled up over my head, a squirrel-skin mask frozen into a sheet of ice concealed my face, and nothing but the eyes peering out through tangled masses of frosty hair, showed that the furs contained a human being. The man took two or three frightened steps backward and nearly dropped his candle. I came in such a "questionable shape" that he might well demand "whether my intents were wicked or charitable!" As I recognized his face, however, and addressed him again in English, he stopped; and tearing off my mask and fur hoods I spoke my name. Never was there such rejoicing as that which then took place in that little underground cellar, as I recognized in the exiled party two of my old comrades and friends, to whom eight months before I had bid goodby, as the "Olga" sailed out of the "Golden Gate" of San Francisco. I little thought when I shook hands with Harder and Robinson then, that I should next meet them at night, in a little snow-covered cellar, on the great lonely steppes of the lower Anadyr. As soon as we had

taken off our heavy furs and seated ourselves beside a
warm fire, we began to feel the sudden reaction which
necessarily followed twenty-four hours of such exposure,
suffering, and anxiety. Our over-strained nerves gave
way all at once, and in ten minutes I could hardly raise
a cup of coffee to my lips. Ashamed of such womanish
weakness, I tried to conceal it from the Americans, and I
presume they do not know to this day that Dodd and I
nearly fainted several times within the first twenty minutes,
from the suddenness of the change from 50° below zero
to 70° above, and the nervous exhaustion produced by
lack of sleep and anxiety. We felt an irresistible craving
for some powerful stimulant and called for brandy, but
there was no liquor of any kind to be had. This weakness, however, soon passed away, and we proceeded to
relate to each other our respective histories and adventures, while our drivers huddled together in a mass at one
end of the little hut and refreshed themselves with hot tea.

The party of Americans which we had thus found
buried in the snow, more than three hundred versts from
Anadyrsk, had been landed there by one of the Company's vessels, some time in September. Their intention had been to ascend the river in a whale-boat until
they should reach some settlement, and then try to open
communication with us; but winter set in so suddenly,
and the river froze over so unexpectedly, that this plan
could not be carried out. Having no means of transportation but their boat, they could do nothing more than
build themselves a house, and go into winter quarters,
with the faint hope that, some time before spring, Major

Abaza would send a party of men to their relief. They had built a sort of burrow underground, with bushes, drift-wood, and a few boards which had been left by the vessel, and there they had been living by lamp-light for five months, without ever seeing the face of a civilized human being. The Wandering Chookchees had soon found out their situation, and frequently visited them on reindeer sledges, and brought them fresh meat, and blubber which they used for lamp-oil; but these natives, on account of a superstition which I have previously mentioned, refused to sell them any living reindeer, so that all their efforts to procure transportation were unavailing. The party originally consisted of five men—Macrae, Arnold, Robinson, Harder, and Smith; but Macrae and Arnold, about three weeks previous to our arrival, had organized themselves into a "forlorn hope," and had gone away with a large band of Wandering Chookchees in search of some Russian settlement. Since that time nothing had been heard from them, and Robinson, Harder, and Smith had been living alone.

Such was the situation when we found the party. Of course, there was nothing to be done but carry these three men and all their stores back to Anadyrsk, where we should probably find Macrae and Arnold awaiting our arrival. The Chookchees came to Anadyrsk, I knew, every winter, for the purpose of trade, and would probably bring the two Americans with them.

After three days spent in resting, refitting, and packing up, we started back with the rescued party, and on February 6th we returned in safety to Anadyrsk.

CHAPTER XXIX.

ALL the inhabitants of the settlement were in the streets to meet us when we returned; but we were disappointed not to see among them the faces of Macrae and Arnold. Many bands of Chookchees from the lower Anadyr had arrived at the village, but nothing had been heard of the missing men. Forty-five days had now elapsed since they left their camp on the river, and, unless they had died or been murdered, they ought long since to have arrived. I would have sent a party in search of them, but I had not the slightest clue as to the direction in which they had gone, or the intentions of the party who had carried them away; and to look for a band of Wandering Chookchees on those great steppes was as hopeless as to look for a missing vessel in the middle of the Pacific Ocean, and far more dangerous. We could only wait, therefore, and hope for the best. We spent the first week after our return in resting, writing up our journals, and preparing a report of our explorations, to be forwarded by special courier to the Major. During this time great numbers of wild, wandering natives— Chookchees, Lamootkees, and a few Koraks—came into the settlement to exchange their furs and walrus teeth for tobacco, and gave us an excellent opportunity of studying their various characteristics and modes of life. The

Wandering Chookchees, who visited us in the greatest numbers, were evidently the most powerful tribe in Northeastern Siberia, and impressed us very favorably with their general appearance and behavior. Except for their dress, they could hardly have been distinguished from North American Indians—many of them being as tall, athletic, and vigorous specimens of savage manhood as I had ever seen. They did not differ in any essential particular from the Wandering Koraks, whose customs, religion, and mode of life I have already described.

The Lamootkees, however, were an entirely different race, and resembled the Chookchees only in their nomadic habits. All the natives in Northeastern Siberia, except the Kamtchadals, Chooances, and Yookaghirs, who are partially Russianized, may be referred to one or the other of three great classes. The first of these, which may be called the North American Indian class, comprises the Wandering and settled Chookchees and Koraks, and covers that part of Siberia lying between the 160th meridian of east longitude and Behring's Straits. It is the only class which has ever made a successful stand against Russian invasion, and embraces without doubt the bravest, most independent savages in all Siberia. I do not think that this class numbers altogether more than six or eight thousand souls, although the estimates of the Russians are much larger.

The second class comprises all the natives in Siberia who are evidently and unmistakably of Chinese origin, including the Tongoos, the Lamootkees, the Monzhours, and the Gilyaks of the Amoor River. It covers a greater extent of ground probably than both of the other classes together, its representatives being found as far west as the Yenesei, and as far east as Anadyrsk, in 169° E. lon. The only branches of this class which I have ever seen are the Lamootkees and the Tongoos. They are almost exactly alike, both being very slenderly built men, with straight black hair, dark olive complexions, no beards, and more or less oblique eyes. They do not resemble a Chookchee or a Korak any more than a Chinaman resembles a Camanche or a Sioux. Their dress is very peculiar. It consists of fur hoods, tight fur pantaloons, short deer-skin boots, Masonic aprons, made of soft flexible buckskin and elaborately ornamented with beads and pieces of metal, and singular looking frock-coats cut in very civilized style out of deer-skin, and ornamented with long strings of colored reindeer hair made into chenille. You can never see one without having the impression that he is dressed in some kind of a regalia or uniform. The men and women resemble each other very much in dress and appearance, and by a stranger cannot be distinguished apart. Like the Chookchees and Koraks, they are Reindeer Nomads, but differ somewhat from the former in their mode of life. Their tents are smaller and differently constructed, and instead of dragging their tent-poles from place to place as the Chookchees do, they leave them standing when they break camp, and either cut new ones or avail themselves of frames left standing by other bands. Tent-poles in this way serve as landmarks, and a day's journey is from one collection of frames to another. Few of the Tongoos or Lamootkees own many deer. Two or three hundred are considered to be a large herd, and a man who owns more than that is regarded as a sort of millionaire. Such herds as are found among the Koraks in Northern Kamtchatka, numbering from five to ten thousand, are never to be seen west of Geezhega. The Tongoos, however, use their few deer to better advantage and in a greater variety of ways than do the Koraks. The latter seldom ride their deer or train them to carry packs, while the Tongoos do both. The Tongoos are of a mild, amiable disposition, easily governed and easily influenced, and seem to have made their way over so large an extent of country more through the sufferance of other tribes than through any aggressive power or disposition of their own. Their original religion was Shamanism, but they now profess almost universally the Greco-Russian faith and receive Christian names. They acknowledge also their subjection to the authority of the Czar, and pay a regular annual tribute in furs. Nearly all the Siberian squirrel-skins which reach the European market are bought by Russian traders from Wandering Tongoos around the Okhotsk Sea. When I left the settlement of Okhotsk, in the fall of 1867, there were more than seventy thousand squirrel-skins there in the hands of one Russian merchant, and this was only a small part of the whole number caught by the Tongoos during that summer. The Lamootkees, who are first cousins to the Tongoos, are fewer in number, but live in precisely the same way. I never met more than three or four bands during two years of almost constant travel in all parts of Northeastern Siberia.

The third great class of natives is the Turkish. It comprises only the Yakoots, who are settled chiefly along the Lena River from its head-waters to the Arctic Ocean. Their origin is unknown, but their language is said to resemble the Turkish or modern Osmanli so closely that a Constantinopolitan of the lower class could converse tolerably with a Yakoot from the Lena. I regret that I was not enough interested in comparative philology while in Siberia to compile a vocabulary and grammar of the Yakoot language. I had excellent opportunities for doing so, but was not aware at that time of its close resemblance to the Turkish, and looked upon it only as an unintelligible jargon which proved nothing but the active participation of the Yakoots in the construction of the Tower of Babel. The bulk of this tribe is settled immediately around the Asiatic pole of cold, and they can unquestionably endure a lower temperature with less suffering than any other natives in Siberia. They are called by the Russian explorer Vrangell, "iron men," and well do they deserve the appellation. The thermometer at Yakootsk, where several thousands of them are settled, *averages* during the three winter months thirty-seven degrees below zero; but this intense cold does not seem to occasion them the slightest inconvenience. I have seen them in a temperature of −40°, clad only in a shirt and one sheep-skin coat, standing quietly in the street, talking and laughing as if it were a pleasant summer's day and they were enjoying the balmy air! They are the most thrifty, industrious natives in all Northern Asia. It is a proverbial saying in Siberia, that if you take a Yakoot, strip him naked, and set him down in the middle of a great desolate steppe, and then return to that spot at the expiration of a year, you will find him living in a large, comfortable house, surrounded by barns and hay-stacks, owning herds of horses and cattle, and enjoying himself like a patriarch. They have all been more or less civilized by Russian intercourse, and have adopted Russian manners and the religion of the Greek Church. Those settled along the Lena cultivate rye and hay, keep herds of Siberian horses and cattle, and live principally upon coarse black bread, milk, butter, and horse-flesh. They are notorious gluttons. All are very skilful in the use of the "topor" or short Russian axe, and with that instrument alone will go into a primeval forest, cut down trees, hew out timber and planks, and put up a comfortable house, complete even to panelled doors and window-sashes. They are the only natives in all North-eastern Siberia who are capable of doing and willing to do hard continuous work.

These three great classes, viz., American Indian natives, Chinese natives, and Turko-yakoot natives, comprise all the aboriginal inhabitants of Northeastern Siberia except the Kamtchadals, the Chooances, and the Yookaghirs. These last have been so modified by Russian influence, that it is hard to tell to which class they are most nearly allied, and the ethnologist will shortly be relieved from all further consideration of the problem by their inevitable extinction. The Chooances and Yookaghirs have already become mere fragments of tribes, and their languages will perish with the present generation.

The natives of whom we saw most at Anadyrsk were

as I have already said, the Chookchees. They frequently called upon us in large parties, and afforded us a great deal of amusement by their naïve and child-like comments upon Americans, American instruments, and the curious American things generally which we produced for their inspection. I shall never forget the utter astonishment with which a band of them once looked through my field-glass. I had been trying it one clear cold day out of doors, and quite a crowd of Chookchees and Yookaghirs had gathered around me to see what I was doing. Observing their curiosity, I gave the glass to one of them and told him to look through it at another native who happened to be standing out on the plain, at a distance of perhaps two hundred yards. The expression of blank half-incredulous surprise which gradually came over his features as he saw that native brought up, apparently within a few feet, was irresistibly comical. He did not dream for a moment that it was a mere optical illusion; he supposed that the wonderful instrument had actually transported the man physically from a distance of a hundred yards up to the place where he stood, and as he held the glass to his eyes with one hand, he stretched out the other to try and catch hold of him. Finding to his great astonishment that he could not, he removed the glass, and saw the man standing quietly as before, two hundred yards away. The idea then seemed to occur to him that if he could only get this mysterious instrument to his eyes quickly enough, he would surprise the man in the very act of coming up —catch him perhaps about half-way—and find out how it was done. He accordingly raised the glass toward his face very slowly (watching the man meanwhile intently, to see that he took no unfair advantage and did not start too soon) until it was within an inch of his eyes, and then looked through it suddenly. But it was of no use. The man was right beside him again, but how he came there he didn't know. Perhaps he could catch him if he made a sudden dash, and he tried it. This, however, was no more successful than his previous experiments, and the other natives looked at him in perfect amazement, wondering what he was trying to do with all these singular motions. He endeavored to explain to them in great excitement that the man had been brought up apparently within arm's length, and yet he could not touch him. His comrades of course denied indignantly that the man had moved at all, and they engaged in a furious dispute as to whether this innocent and unconscious man had been anywhere near them or not. The native who maintained the affirmative appealed to me ; but, convulsed with laughter, I could make no reply, and he started off at a run, to see the man and find out whether he had been brought up or not, and how it felt to be transported over two hundred yards of space in an instant of time ! We who are familiar with these discoveries of science can hardly realize how they appear to a wholly uneducated savage ; but if a superior race of beings should come from the planet Jupiter and show us a mysterious instrument which enabled a man to be in two different places at the same time, we would understand the sensations of a poor Chookchee in looking through a field-glass.

Soon after this I happened to be encamped one night

on a great plain near Anadyrsk, with a party of these same natives; and having received a note from Dodd by a special messenger, I was engaged in reading it by the camp-fire. At several humorous passages I burst out into a loud laugh; whereupon the natives punched each other with their elbows and pointed significantly at me, as much as to say, "Just look at the crazy American! What's the matter with him now?" Finally one of them, an old gray-haired man, asked me what I was laughing about. "Why," said I, "I am laughing at this," and pointed to the piece of paper. The old man thought about it for a moment, compared notes with the others, and they all thought about it; but no one seemed to succeed in getting any light as to the cause of my incomprehensible laughter. In a few moments the old man picked up a half-burned stick which was lying by the fire and said, "Now suppose I should look at this stick for a minute and then laugh; what would you think?"—"Why," said I candidly, "I should think you were a fool."—"Well," he rejoined with grave satisfaction, "that's just exactly what I think of you!" He seemed to be very much pleased to find that our several opinions of such insane conduct so exactly coincided. Looking at a stick and laughing, and looking at a piece of paper and laughing, seemed to him equally absurd. The languages of the Chookchees and Koraks have never been reduced to writing; nor, so far as I know, do either of those tribes ever attempt to express ideas by signs or pictures. Written thought is to many of them an impossible conception. It can be imagined, perhaps, with what wonder and baffled curiosity they pore over the illustrated newspapers which are occasionally given to them by the sailors of whaling vessels which visit the coast. Some of the pictures they recognize as representations of things with which they are acquainted; but by far the greater number are as incomprehensible as the hieroglyphics of the Aztecs. I remember that a Korak once brought to me an old tattered fashion-plate from "Frank Leslie's Illustrated Newspaper," containing three or four full-length figures of imaginary ladies, in the widest expansion of crinoline which fashion at that time prescribed. The poor Korak said he had often wondered what those curious objects could be; and now, as I was an American, perhaps I could tell him. He evidently had not the most remote suspicion that they were intended to represent human beings. I told him that those curious objects, as he called them, were American women. He burst out into a "tyée-ē-ē-ē" of amazement, and asked with a wondering look, "Are *all* the women in your country as big as that at the bottom?" It was a severe reflection upon our ladies' dress, and I did not venture to tell him that the bigness was artificial, but merely replied sadly that they were. He looked curiously down at my feet, and then at the picture, and then again at my feet, as if he were trying to trace some resemblance between the American man and the American woman; but he failed to do it, and wisely concluded that they must be of widely different species.

The pictures from these papers are sometimes put to curious uses. In the hut of a christianized but ignorant native near Anadyrsk, I once saw an engraved portrait cut from "Harper's Weekly," of Maj. Gen. Dix, posted up in a corner of the room and worshipped as a Russian saint! A gilded candle was burning before his smoky features, and every night and morning a dozen natives said their prayers to a major-general in the United States Army! It is the only instance I believe on record, where a major-general has been raised to the dignity of a saint without even being dead. St. George of England, we are told, was originally a corrupt army contractor of Cappadocia, but he was not canonized until long after his death, when the memory of his contracts was no more. For Maj.-Gen. Dix was reserved the peculiar privilege of being at the same time a United States Minister in Paris and a saint in Siberia!

CHAPTER XXX.

AN ARCTIC AURORA.

AMONG the few pleasures which reward the traveller for the hardships and dangers of life in the far north, there are none which are brighter or longer remembered than the magnificent Auroral displays which occasionally illumine the darkness of the long polar night, and light up with a celestial glory the whole blue vault of heaven. No other natural phenomenon is so grand, so mysterious, so terrible in its unearthly splendor as this; the veil which conceals from mortal eyes the glory of the eternal throne seems drawn aside, and the awed beholder is lifted out of the atmosphere of his daily life into the immediate presence of God.

On the 26th of February, while we were all yet living together at Anadyrsk, there occurred one of the grandest displays of the Arctic Aurora which had been observed there for more than fifty years, and which exhibited such unusual and extraordinary brilliancy that even the natives were astonished. It was a cold, dark, but clear winter's night, and the sky in the earlier part of the evening showed no signs of the magnificent illumination which was already being prepared. A few streamers wavered now and then in the North, and a faint radiance like that of the rising moon shone above the dark belt of shrubbery which bordered the river; but this was a common occurrence, and it excited no notice or remark. Late in the evening, just as we were preparing to go to bed, Dodd happened to go out of doors for a moment to look after his dogs ; but no sooner had he reached the outer door of the entry than he came rushing back, his face ablaze with excitement, shouting " Kennan ! Robinson ! Come out, quick ! " With a vague impression that the village must be on fire, I sprang up, and without stopping to put on any furs, ran hastily out, followed closely by Robinson, Harder, and Smith. As we emerged into the open air there burst suddenly upon our startled eyes the grandest exhibition of vivid dazzling light and color of which the mind can conceive. The whole universe seemed to be on fire. A broad arch of brilliant prismatic colors spanned the heavens from east to west like a gigantic rainbow, with a long fringe of crimson and yellow streamers stretching up from its convex edge to the very zenith. At short intervals of one or two seconds, wide, luminous bands, parallel with the arch, rose suddenly out of the northern horizon and swept with a swift, steady majesty across the whole heavens, like long breakers of phosphorescent light rolling in from some limitless ocean of space.

Every portion of the vast arch was momentarily wavering, trembling, and changing color, and the brilliant streamers which fringed its edge swept back and forth in great curves, like the fiery sword of the angel at the gate of Eden. In a moment the vast Auroral rainbow, with all its wavering streamers, began to move slowly up toward the zenith, and a second arch of equal brilliancy

formed directly under it, shooting up another long serried
row of slender colored lances toward the North Star, like
a battalion of the celestial host presenting arms to its
commanding angel. Every instant the display increased
in unearthly grandeur. The luminous bands revolved
swiftly, like the spokes of a great wheel of light across
the heavens; the streamers hurried back and forth with
swift, tremulous motion from the ends of the arches to
the centre, and now and then a great wave of crimson
would surge up from the north and fairly deluge the
whole sky with color, tingeing the white snowy earth far
and wide with its rosy reflection. But as the words of
the prophecy, " And the heavens shall be turned to blood,"
formed themselves upon my lips, the crimson suddenly
vanished, and a lighting flash of vivid orange startled us
with its wide, all-pervading glare, which extended even
to the southern horizon, as if the whole volume of the
atmosphere had suddenly taken fire. I even held my
breath a moment, as I listened for the tremendous crash
of thunder which it seemed to me must follow this sudden
burst of vivid light; but in heaven or earth there was not
a sound to break the calm silence of night, save the has-
tily-muttered prayers of the frightened native at my side,
as he crossed himself and kneeled down before the visible majesty of God. I could not imagine any possible
addition which even Almighty power could make to the
grandeur of the Aurora as it now appeared. The rapid
alternations of crimson, blue, green, and yellow in the
sky were reflected so vividly from the white surface of
the snow, that the whole world seemed now steeped in

blood, and then quivering in an atmosphere of pale, ghastly green, through which shone the unspeakable glories of the mighty crimson and yellow arches. But the end was not yet. As we watched with upturned faces the swift ebb and flow of these great celestial tides of colored light, the last seal of the glorious revelation was suddenly broken, and both arches were simultaneously shivered into a thousand parallel perpendicular bars, every one of which displayed in regular order, from top to bottom, the seven primary colors of the solar spectrum. From horizon to horizon there now stretched two vast curving bridges of colored bars, across which we almost expected to see, passing and repassing, the bright inhabitants of another world. Amid cries of astonishment and exclamations of "God have mercy!" from the startled natives, these innumerable bars began to move, with a swift dancing motion, back and forth along the whole extent of both arches, passing each other from side to side with such bewildering rapidity, that the eye was lost in the attempt to follow them. The whole concave of heaven seemed transformed into one great revolving kaleidoscope of shattered rainbows. Never had I even dreamed of such an aurora as *this*, and I am not ashamed to confess that its magnificence at that moment overawed and frightened me. The whole sky, from zenith to horizon, was "one molten mantling sea of color and fire, crimson and purple, and scarlet and green, and colors for which there are no words in language and no ideas in the mind, —things which can only be conceived while they are visible." The "signs and portents" in the heavens were grand enough to herald the destruction of a world: flashes of rich quivering color, covering half the sky for an instant and then vanishing like summer lightning; brilliant green streamers shooting swiftly but silently up across the zenith; thousands of variegated bars sweeping past each other in two magnificent arches, and great luminous waves rolling in from the inter-planetary spaces and breaking in long lines of radiant glory upon the shallow atmosphere of a darkened world.

With the separation of the two arches into component bars it reached its utmost magnificence, and from that time its supernatural beauty slowly but steadily faded. The first arch broke up, and soon after it the second; the flashes of color appeared less and less frequently; the luminous bands ceased to revolve across the zenith; and in an hour nothing remained in the dark starry heavens to remind us of the Aurora, except a few faint Magellan clouds of luminous vapor.

I am painfully conscious of my inability to describe as they should be described the splendid phenomena of a great polar Aurora; but such magnificent effects cannot be expressed in a mathematical formula, nor can an inexperienced artist reproduce, with a piece of charcoal, the brilliant coloring of a Turner landscape. I have given only faint hints, which the imagination of the reader must fill up. But be assured that no description, however faithful, no flight of the imagination, however exalted, can begin to do justice to a spectacle of such unearthly grandeur. Until man drops his vesture of flesh and stands in the presence of Deity, he will see no more striking manifestation of the "glory of the Lord, which is terrible," than that presented by a brilliant exhibition of the Arctic Aurora.

The month of February wore slowly away, and March found us still living in Anadyrsk, without any news from the Major, or from the missing men, Arnold and Macrae. Fifty-seven days had now elapsed since they left their camp on the lower Anadyr, and we began to fear that they would never again be seen. Whether they had starved, or frozen to death on some great desolate plain south of Behring's Straits, or been murdered by the Chookchees, we could not conjecture, but their long absence was a proof that they had met with some misfortune.

I was not at all satisfied with the route over which we had passed from Shestakova to Anadyrsk, on account of its barrenness, and the impossibility of transporting heavy telegraph poles over its great snowy steppes from the few wooded rivers by which it was traversed. I accordingly started from Anadyrsk with five dog-sledges on March 4th, to try and find a better route between the Anadyr and the head-waters of the Penzhina River. Three days after our departure we met, on the road to Penzhina, a special messenger from Geezhega, bringing a letter from the Major dated Okhotsk, Jan. 19th. Enclosed were letters from Col. Bulkley, announcing the landing of the Anadyr River party under Lieut Macrae, and a map showing the location of their camp. The Major wrote as follows: "In case—what God forbid—Macrae and party have not arrived at Anadyrsk, you will immediately, upcn

the receipt of this letter, do your utmost to deliver them
from their too long winter-quarters at the mouth of the
Anadyr, where they were landed in September. I was
told that Macrae would be landed *only in case of perfect
certainty* to reach Anadyrsk in boats, and I confess I don't
like such surprises as Colonel Bulkley has made me now.
For the present our duty consists in doing our utmost to
extricate them from where they are, and you must get
every dog-sledge you can, stuff them with dog-food and
provisions, and go at once in search of Macrae's camp."
These directions I had already anticipated and carried
out, and Macrae's party, or at least all I could find of it,
was now living in Anadyrsk. When the Major wrote this
letter, however, he did not suppose that Dodd and I
would hear of the landing of the party through the Wandering Chookchees, or that we would think of going in
search of them without orders. He knew that he had
told us particularly not to attempt to explore the Anadyr
River until another season, and did not expect that we
would go beyond the last settlement. I wrote a hasty
note to Dodd upon the icy runner of my overturned
sledge—freezing two fingers in the operation—and sent
the courier on to Anadyrsk with the letters. The mail
also included letters to me from Capt. Scammon, comman-
der of the Company's fleet, and one from my naturalistic
friend Dall, who had returned with the vessels to San
Francisco, and had written me while stopping a few days
at Petropavlovski. He begged me, by all the sacred interests of Science, not to let a single bug or living thing
of any kind escape my vigilant eye; but, as I read his

letter that night by the camp-fire, I thought with a smile
that snowy Siberian steppes and temperatures of 30° and
40° below zero were not very favorable to the growth and
dispersion of bugs, nor to efforts for their capture and
preservation.

I will not weary the reader with a detailed account of
the explorations which Lieut. Robinson and I made in
search of a more practicable route for our line between
the Penzhina River and Anadyrsk. We found that the
river system of the Anadyrsk was divided from that of the
Penzhina only by a low mountain ridge, which could be
easily passed, and that, by following up certain tributaries
of the latter, crossing the water-shed, and descending one
of the branches of the Anadyr, we should have almost
unbroken water-communication between the Okhotsk Sea
and Behring's Straits. Along these rivers timber was generally abundant, and where there was none, poles could
be distributed easily in rafts. The route thus indicated
was everything which could be desired ; and, much gratified by the results of our labors, we returned on March
13th to Anadyrsk.

We were overjoyed to learn from the first man who
met us after we entered the settlement that Macrae and
Arnold had arrived, and in five minutes we were shaking
them by the hand, congratulating them upon their safe
arrival, and overwhelming them with questions as to their
travels and adventures, and the reasons of their long absence.

For sixty-four days they had been living with the Wandering Chookchees, and making their way slowly and by a

circuitous route toward Anadyrsk. They had generally
been well treated, but the band with whom they travelled
had been in no hurry to reach the settlement, and had
been carrying them at the rate of ten or twelve miles a
day all over the great desolate steppes which lie south of
the Anadyr River.   They had experienced great hardships;
had lived upon reindeer's entrails and tallow for weeks at
a time; had been alive almost constantly with vermin;
had spent the greater part of two long months in smoky
Chookchee pologs, and had despaired, sometimes, of ever
reaching a Russian settlement or seeing again a civilized
human being; but hope and courage had sustained them
through it all, and they had finally arrived at Anadyrsk
safe and well. The sum total of their baggage when
they drove into the settlement was a quart bottle of whiskey
wrapped up in an American flag! As soon as we were
all together, we raised the flag on a pole over our little
log-house, made a whiskey punch out of the liquor which
had traversed half Northeastern Siberia, and drank it in
honor of the men who had lived sixty-four days with the
Wandering Chookchees, and carried the stars and stripes
through the wildest, least known region on the face of the
globe.

Having now accomplished all that could be done in the
way of exploration, we began making preparations for a
return to Geezhega. The Major had directed me to meet
him there with Macrae, Arnold, Robinson, and Dodd, as
soon as the first of April, and the month of March was
now rapidly drawing to a close.

On the 20th we packed up our stores, and bidding good-by to the kind-hearted, hospitable people of Anadyrsk, we set out with a long train of sledges for the coast of the Okhotsk Sea.

Our journey was monotonous and uneventful, and on the second of April, late at night, we left behind us the white desolate steppe of the Paren, and drew near the little flat-topped yourt on the Malmofka, which was only twenty-five versts from Geezhega. Here we met fresh men, dogs, and sledges, sent out to meet us by the Major, and, abandoning our loaded sledges and tired dogs, we took seats upon the light "narts" of the Geezhega Cossacks, and dashed away by the light of a brilliant Aurora toward the settlement.

About one o'clock we heard the distant barking of dogs, and in a few moments we rushed furiously into the silent village, and stopped before the house of the Russian merchant Vorrebeoff, where we had lived the previous fall, and where we expected to find the Major. I sprang from my sledge, and groping my way through the entry into a warm dark room, I shouted "Fstavaitia" to arouse the sleeping inmates. Suddenly some one rose up from the floor at my feet, and grasping me by the arm, exclaimed in a strangely familiar voice, "Kennan, is that you?" Startled and bewildered with half-incredulous recognition, I could only reply "Bush, is that you?" and, when a sleepy boy came in with a light, he was astonished to find a man dressed in heavy frosty furs embracing another who was clad only in a linen shirt and drawers.

There was a joyful time in that log-house when the Major, Bush, Macrae, Arnold, Robinson, Dodd, and I gath-

ered around a steaming "samovar" or tea-urn which stood
on a pine table in the centre of the room, and discussed
the adventures, haps, and mishaps of our first Arctic
winter. Some of us had come from the extremity of Kamtchatka, some from the frontier of China, and some from
Behring's Straits, and we all met that night in Geezhega,
and congratulated ourselves and each other upon the successful exploration of the whole route of the proposed
Russo-American Telegraph, from Anadyr Bay to the
Amoor River. The different members of the party there
assembled had, in seven months, travelled in the aggregate almost ten thousand miles.

The results of our winter's work were briefly as follows:
Bush and Mahood, after leaving the Major and me at
Petropavlovski, had gone on to the Russian settlement
of Nikolaevsk, at the mouth of the Amoor River, and had
entered promptly upon the exploration of the west coast
of the Okhotsk Sea. They had travelled with the
Wandering Tongoos through the densely-timbered region
between Nikolaevsk and Aian, ridden on the backs of
reindeer over the rugged mountains of the Stanavoi range
south of Okhotsk, and had finally met the Major at the
latter place on the 22d of February. The Major had
explored the whole north coast of the Okhotsk Sea
alone, and had made a visit to the Russian city of Yakootsk, six hundred versts west of Okhotsk, in quest of
laborers and horses. He had ascertained the possibility
of hiring a thousand Yakoot laborers in the settlements
along the Lena River, at the rate of sixty dollars a year
for each man, and of purchasing there as many Siberian

horses as we should require at very reasonable prices.
He had located a route for the line from Geezhega to
Okhotsk, and had superintended generally the whole
work of exploration. Macrae and Arnold had explored
nearly all the region lying south of the Anadyr and along
the lower Myan, and had gained much valuable information concerning the little-known tribe of Wandering
Chookchees. Dodd, Robinson, and I had explored two
routes from Geezhega to Anadyrsk, and had found a
chain of wooded rivers connecting the Okhotsk Sea with the
Pacific Ocean near Behring's Straits. The natives we had
everywhere found to be peaceable and well disposed, and
many of them along the route of the line were already
engaged in cutting poles. The country, although by no
means favorable to the construction of a telegraph, presented no obstacles which energy and perseverance
could not overcome ; and, as we reviewed our winter's
work, we felt satisfied that the enterprise in which we
were engaged, if not altogether an easy one, held out at
least a fair prospect of success.

CHAPTER XXXI.

SOCIAL LIFE AT GEEZHEGA—MAJOR ABASA'S EXPEDITION
—SUDDEN TRANSFORMATION FROM WINTER TO SUMMER
—CUSTOMS OF THE PEOPLE, ETC.

THE months of April and May, owing to the great length of the days and the comparative mildness of the weather, are the most favorable months in North-eastern Siberia for out-door work and travel; and as the Company's vessels could not be expected to arrive at Geezhega before the early part of June, Major Abasa determined to make the most of the intervening time. As soon as he had recovered a little, therefore, from the fatigue of his previous journey, he started with Bush, Macrae, and the Russian Governor, for Anadyrsk, intending to engage there fifty or sixty native laborers and begin at once the construction of station-houses and the cutting and distribution of poles along the Anadyr River. My own efforts to that end, owing to the laziness of the Anadyrsk people, had been unsuccessful; but it was hoped that through the influence and co-operation of the civil authority something might perhaps be done.

Major Abasa returned by the very last winter road in May. His expedition had been entirely successful; Mr. Bush had been put in command of the Northern District from Penzhina to Behring's Straits, and he, together with

Macrae, Harder, and Smith, had been left at Anadyrsk for the summer. As soon as the Anadyr River should open, this party was directed to descend it in canoes to its mouth, and there await the arrival of one of the Company's vessels from San Francisco, with reinforcements and supplies. In the mean time fifty native laborers from Anadyrsk, Osolkin, and Pokorookof, had been hired and placed at their disposal, and it was hoped that by the time the ice should be out of the river they would have six or eight station-houses prepared, and several thousand poles cut, ready for distribution in rafts between the settlements of Anadyrsk and the Pacific Coast. Having thus accomplished all that it was possible to accomplish with the limited means and force at his disposal, Major Abasa returned to Geezhega, to await the arrival of the promised vessels from America, with men, material, and supplies, for the prosecution of the work.

The season for dog-sledge travel was now over; and as the country afforded no other means of interior transportation, we could not expect to do any more work, or have any further communication with our outlying parties at Anadyrsk and Okhotsk until the arrival of our vessels. We therefore rented ourselves a little log-house overlooking the valley of the Geezhega River, furnished it as comfortably as possible with a few plain wooden chairs and tables, hung up our maps and charts over the rough log walls, displayed our small library of two books— Shakespeare and the New Testament—as advantageously as possible in one corner, and prepared for at least a month of luxurious idleness.

It was now June. The snow was rapidly disappearing under the influence of the warm long-continued sunshine, the ice in the river showed unmistakable signs of breaking up, patches of bare ground appeared here and there along the sunny hill-sides, and everything foretold the speedy approach of the short but hot Arctic summer. Winter in most parts of Northeastern Siberia begins to break up in May, and summer advances with rapid strides upon its retreating footsteps, covering instantly with grass and flowers the ground which it reclaims from the melting snow-drifts of winter. Hardly is the snow off the ground before the delicate wax-like petals of the blueberry and star-flower, and the great snowy clusters of Labrador tea begin to whiten the mossy plains; the birches, willows, and alders burst suddenly into leaf, the river banks grow green with a soft carpet of grass, and the warm still air is filled all day with the trumpet-like cries of wild swans and geese, as they come in great triangular flocks from the sea and pass high overhead toward the far North. In three weeks after the disappearance of the last snow all Nature has put on the garments of midsummer and rejoices in almost perpetual sunshine. There is no long, wet, lingering spring, no gradual unfolding of buds and leaves one by one as with us. The vegetation, which has been held in icy fetters for eight long months, bursts suddenly its bonds, and with one great irresistible sweep takes the world by storm. There is no longer any night; one day blends almost imperceptibly into another, with only a short interval of twilight, which has all the coolness and repose of night without its darkness. You may sit by your open window and read until twelve o'clock, inhaling the fragrance of flowers which is brought to you on the cool night wind, listening to the murmur and flash of the river in the valley below, and tracing the progress of the hidden sun by the flood of rosy light which streams up in the North from behind the purple mountains. It is broad daylight, and yet all Nature is asleep, and a strange mysterious stillness pervades heaven and earth like that which accompanies a solar eclipse. You can even hear the faint roar of the surf on the rocky coasts ten miles away. Now and then a little song-sparrow hidden in the alder thicket by the river-bank dreams that it is morning and breaks out into a quick unconscious trill of melody; but as he wakes he stops himself suddenly and utters a few "peeps" of perplexity, as if not quite sure whether it be morning, or only last evening, and whether he ought to sing or go to sleep again. He finally seems to decide upon the latter course, and all becomes silent once more save the murmur of the river over its rocky bed and the faint roar of the distant sea. Soon after one o'clock a glittering segment of the sun appears between the cloud-like peaks of the distant mountains, a sudden flash of golden light illumines the green dewy landscape, the little sparrow in the alder thicket triumphantly takes up again his unfinished song, the ducks, geese, and aquatic birds renew their harsh discordant cries from the marshy flats along the river, and all animated nature wakes suddenly to a consciousness of daylight as if it were a new thing. There has been no night—but it is another day.

The traveller who has never before experienced an

Arctic summer, and who has been accustomed to think of
Siberia as a land of eternal snow and ice, cannot help
being astonished at the sudden and wonderful development of animal and vegetable life throughout that country
in the month of June, and the rapidity of the transition
from winter to summer in the course of a few short weeks.
In the early part of June it is frequently possible to travel
in the vicinity of Geezhega upon dog-sledges, while by
the last of the same month the trees are all in full leaf,
primroses, cowslips, buttercups, valerian, cinque-foil, and
Labrador tea, blossom everywhere upon the higher plains
and river-banks, and the thermometer at noon frequently
reaches 70° Fahr. in the shade. There is no spring, in the
usual acceptation of the word, at all. The disappearance
of snow and the appearance of vegetation are almost
simultaneous; and although the "toondras" or moss-
steppes continue for some time to hold water like a saturated sponge, they are covered with flowers and blos-
soming blueberry bushes, and show no traces of the long,
cold winter which has so recently ended. In less than a
month after the disappearance of snow in 1866, I collected from one high plain about five acres in extent, near
the mouth of the Geezhega River, more than sixty species
of flowers. Animal life of all kinds is equally prompt in
making its appearance. Long before the ice is out of the
gulfs and bays along the coast, migratory birds begin to
come in from the sea in immense numbers. Innumerable
species of ducks, geese, and swans—many of them unknown to the American ornithologist—swarm about every
little pool of water in the valleys and upon the lower plains;

gulls, fish-hawks, and eagles, keep up a continual scream·
ing about the mouths of the numerous rivers, and the
rocky precipitous coast of the sea is literally alive with
countless millions of red-beaked puffin or sea-parrots,
which build their nests in the crevices and upon the ledges
of the most inaccessible cliffs, and at the report of a pis·
tol fly out in clouds which fairly darken the air. Besides
these predatory and aquatic birds, there are many others
which are not as gregarious in their habits, and which,
consequently, attract less notice. Among these are the
common barn and chimney swallows, crows, ravens, mag·
pies, thrushes, plover, ptarmigan, and a kind of grouse
known to the Russians as "teteer." Only one singing-
bird, as far as I know, is to be found in the country, and
that is a species of small ground sparrow which frequents
the drier and more grassy plains in the vicinity of the Russian settlements.

The village of Geezhega, where we had temporarily established our head-quarters, was a small settlement of perhaps fifty or sixty plain log-houses, situated upon the left
bank of the Geezhega River, eight or ten miles from the
gulf. It was at that time one of the most important and
flourishing settlements upon the coast of the Okhotsk Sea,
and controlled all the trade of Northeastern Siberia as
far north as the Anadyr and as far west as the village of
Okhotsk. It was the residence of a local governor, the
head-quarters of four or five Russian merchants, and was
visited annually by a government supply steamer, and several trading-vessels belonging to wealthy American houses.
Its population consisted principally of Siberian Cossacks

and the descendants of compulsory emigrants from Russia proper, who had received their freedom as compensation for forcible expatriation. Like all other *settled* inhabitants of Siberia and Kamtchatka, they depended for their subsistence principally upon fish; but as the country abounded in game, and the climate and soil in the valley of the Geezhega River permitted the cultivation of the hardiest kinds of garden vegetables, their condition was undoubtedly much better than it would have been in Russia proper. They were perfectly free, could dispose of their time and services as they chose, and by hiring themselves and their dog-sledges to Russian traders in the winter, they earned money enough to keep themselves supplied with the simpler luxuries, such as tea, sugar, and tobacco, throughout the year. Like all the inhabitants of Siberia, and indeed like all Russians, they were extremely hospitable, good-natured, and obliging, and contributed not a little to our comfort and amusement during the long months which we were obliged to spend in their far away isolated settlement.

The presence of Americans in a village so little frequented by strangers as Geezhega had a very enlivening influence upon society, and as soon as the inhabitants ascertained by experiment that these distinguished sojourners did not consider it beneath their dignity to associate with the "prostoi narod," or common people, they overwhelmed us with invitations to tea-parties and evening dances. Anxious to see more of the life of the people, and glad to do anything which would diversify our monotonous existence, we made it a point to accept every

such invitation which we received, and many were the
dances which Arnold and I attended during the absence
of the Major and the Russian Governor at Anadyrsk.
We had no occasion to ask our Cossack Yagor when
there was to be another dance. The question was rather,
" Where is the dance to be to-night ? " because we knew to
a certainty that there would be one somewhere, and wished only to know whether the house in which it was to be
held had a ceiling high enough to insure the safety of our
heads.   It would seem like a preposterous idea to invite
people to dance the Russian jig in a room which was too
low to permit a man of average stature to stand upright ;
but it did not seem at all so to these enthusiastic pleas-
ure-seekers in Geezhega, and night after night they would
go hopping around a seven-by-nine room to the music of
a crazy fiddle and a two-stringed guitar, stepping on each
other's toes and bumping their heads against the ceiling
with the most cheerful equanimity imaginable.   At these
dancing parties the Americans always received a hearty
welcome, and were fed with berries, black bread, and tea,
until they could eat and dance no more.   Occasionally,
however, Siberian hospitality took a form which, to say
the least, was not altogether pleasant.   For instance,
Dodd and I were invited one evening to some kind of an
entertainment at the house of one of the Cossacks, and,
as was customary in such cases, our host set before us a
plain lunch of black bread, salt, raw frozen fish, and a
small pepper-sauce bottle about half full of some liquid
which he declared to be "vodka."   Knowing that there
was no liquor in the settlement except what we had, Dodd

inquired where he had obtained it. He replied with evi
dent embarrassment that it was some which he had
bought from a trading-vessel the previous fall, and which
he had reserved for cases of emergency! I didn't believe
that there was a Cossack in all Northeastern Siberia who
was capable of *reserving* a bottle of liquor for any such
length of time, and in view of his evident uneasiness we
thought best to decline to partake of the liquid refreshments and to ask no further questions. It might be
"vodka," but it was not free from suspicion. Upon our
return home I called our boy and inquired if he knew
anything about the Cossack's liquor—how he obtained it,
and where it came from at that season of the year, when
none of the Russian merchants had any for sale. The
boy hesitated a moment, but upon being questioned closely he explained the mystery. It appears that the liquor
was ours. Whenever any of the inhabitants of the village
came to call upon us, as they frequently did, especially
upon holidays, it was customary to give each one of them
a drink. Taking advantage of this custom, our friend the
Cossack used to provide himself with a small bottle, hang
it about his neck with a string, conceal it under his fur
coat, and present himself at our house every now and
then for the ostensible purpose of congratulating us upon
some Russian holiday. Of course we were expected to
reward this disinterested sociability with a drink. The
Cossack would swallow all he could of the fiery stuff, and
then holding as much as possible in his mouth he would
make a terrible grimace, cover his face with one hand as
if the liquor were very strong, and start hurriedly for the

kitchen to get some water.   As soon as he was secure
from observation he would take out his bottle, deposit in
it the last mouthful of liquor which he had *not* swallow-
ed, and return in a few moments to thank us for our hospitality—and our "vodka."   This manœuvre he had
been practising at our expense for an unknown length of
time, and had finally accumulated nearly a pint.   He then
had the unblushing audacity to set this half-swallowed
"vodka" before us in an old pepper-sauce bottle, and
pretend that it was some which he had reserved since the
previous fall for cases of emergency!   Could human impudence go farther?

I will relate one other incident which took place during
the first month of our residence at Geezhega, and which
illustrates another phase of the popular character, viz. :
extreme superstition.   As I was sitting alone in the house
one morning, drinking tea, I was interrupted by the sudden entrance of a Russian Cossack named Kolmagorof.
He seemed to be unusually sober and anxious about
something, and as soon as he had bowed and bade me
good morning, he turned to our Cossack, Vushine, and
began in a low voice to relate to him something which
had just occurred, and which seemed to be of great interest to them both.   Owing to my imperfect knowledge
of the language, and the low tone in which the conversation was carried on, I failed to catch its purport; but it
closed with an earnest request from Kolmagorof that Vushine should give him some article of clothing, which I
understood to be a scarf or tippet.   Vushine immediately
went to a little closet in one corner of the room, where

he was in the habit of storing his personal effects, dragged out a large seal-skin bag, and began searching in it for the desired article.   After pulling out three or four pair of fur boots, a lump of tallow, some dog-skin stockings, a hatchet, and a bundle of squirrel-skins, he finally produced and held up in triumph one-half of an old, dirty, moth-eaten woollen tippet, and handing it to Kolmagorof, he resumed his search for the missing piece.   This also he presently found, in a worse state of preservation, if possible, than the other.   They looked as if they had been discovered in the bag of some poor rag-picker who had fished them up out of a gutter in the Five Points.   Kolmagorof tied the two pieces together, wrapped them up carefully in an old newspaper, thanked Vushine for his trouble, and, with an air of great relief, bowed again to me and went out.   Wondering what use he could make of such a worn, dirty, dilapidated article of clothing as that which he had received, I applied to Vushine for a solution of the mystery.

"What did he want that tippet for?" I inquired; "it isn't good for anything."

"I know," replied Vushine, "it is a miserable old thing; but there is no other in the village, and his daughter has got the 'Anadyrski bol' (Anadyrsk sickness)."

"Anadyrski bol!" I repeated in astonishment, never having heard of the disease in question; "what has the 'Anadyrski bol' got to do with an old tippet?"

"Why, you see, his daughter has asked for a tippet, and as she has the Anadyrsk sickness, they must get one for her.   It don't make any difference about its being old."

This struck me as being a very singular explanation of a very curious performance, and I proceeded to question Vushine more closely as to the nature of this strange disease, and the manner in which an old moth-eaten tippet could afford relief. The information which I gathered was briefly as follows: The "Anadyrski bol," so called from its having originated at Anadyrsk, was a peculiar form of disease, resembling very much the modern spiritual "trance," which had long prevailed in Northeastern Siberia, and which defied all ordinary remedies and all usual methods of treatment. The persons attacked by it, who were generally women, became unconscious of all surrounding things, acquired suddenly a faculty of speaking languages which they had never heard, particularly the Gakout language, and were gifted temporarily with a sort of second-sight or clairvoyance which enabled them to describe accurately objects which they could not see and never had seen. While in this state they would frequently ask for some particular thing, whose appearance and exact location they would describe, and unless it was brought to them they would apparently go into convulsions, sing in the Gakout language, utter strange cries, and behave generally as if they were insane. Nothing could quiet them until the article for which they had asked should be produced. Thus Kolmagorof's daughter had imperatively demanded a woollen tippet, and as the poor Cossack had nothing of the sort in the house, he had started out through the village to find one. This was all the information which Vushine could give me. He had never seen one of these possessed persons himself, and had only heard of the disease from others; but he said that Paderin, the Chief of the Geezhega Cossacks, could undoubtedly tell me all about it, as his daughter had been similaily afflicted. Surprised to find among the ignorant peasantry of Northeastern Siberia a disease whose symptoms resembled so closely the phenomena of modern spiritualism, I determined to investigate the subject as far as possible, and as soon as the Major came in, I persuaded him to send for Paderin. The Chief of the Cossacks—a simple, honest old fellow, whom it was impossible to suspect of intentional deception—confirmed all that Vushine had told me, and gave us many additional particulars. He said that he had frequently heard his daughter talk the Gakout language while in one of these trances, and had even known her to relate events which were occurring at a distance of several hundred miles. The Major inquired how he knew that it was the Gakout language which his daughter spoke. He said he did not know certainly that it was; but it was not Russian, nor Korak, nor any other native language with which he was familiar, and it sounded very much like Gakout. I inquired what was done in case the sick person demanded some article which it was impossible to obtain. Paderin replied that he had never heard of such an instance; if the article asked for was an uncommon one, the girl always stated where it was to be found—frequently describing with the greatest minuteness things which, so far as he knew, she had never seen. On one occasion, he said his daughter asked for a particular spotted dog which he was accustomed to drive in his team. The dog was brought into the

room, and the girl at once became quiet; but from that
time the dog itself became so wild and restless as to be
almost unmanageable, and he was finally obliged to kill
him.   "And do you believe in all this stuff?" broke in
the Major impatiently, as Paderin hesitated for a moment.

"I believe in God and in our Saviour Jesus Christ,"
replied the Cossack, as he crossed himself devoutly.

"That's all right, and so you ought," rejoined the
Major; "but that has nothing whatever to do with the
'Anadyrsk bol.' Do you really believe that these women
talk in the Gakout language, which they have never
heard, and describe things which they have never seen?"

Paderin shrugged his shoulders expressively and said
that he believed what he saw. He then proceeded to relate
to us further and still more incredible particulars as to
the symptoms of the disease, and the mysterious powers
which it developed in the persons attacked, illustrating his
statements by reference to the case of his own daughter.
He was evidently a firm believer in the reality of the
sickness, but would not say to what agency he ascribed
the phenomena of second-sight and the ability to
speak strange languages, which were its most remarkable
symptoms.

During the day we happened to call upon the Ispravnik
or Russian Governor, and in course of conversation mentioned the "Anadyrsk bol," and related some of the
stories which we had heard from Paderin. The Ispravnik
—skeptical upon all subjects, and especially upon this—
said that he had often heard of the disease, and that his
wife was a firm believer in it, but that in his opinion it

was a humbug, which deserved no other treatment than severe corporal punishment. The Russian peasantry, he said, were very superstitious and would believe almost any-thing, and the "Anadyrsk bol" was partly a delusion and partly an imposition practised by the women upon their male relatives to further some selfish purpose. A woman who wanted a new bonnet, and who could not obtain it by the ordinary method of teasing, found it very conve-nient as a "dernier ressort" to fall into a trance state and demand a bonnet as a physiological necessity. If the husband still remained obdurate, a few well-executed con-vulsions and a song or two in the so-called Gakout lan-guage were generally sufficient to bring him to terms. He then related an instance of a Russian merchant whose wife was attacked by the "Anadyrsk bol," and who actually made a winter journey from Geezhega to Gamsk—a distance of 300 versts—to procure a silk dress for which she had asked and which could not be elsewhere obtained ! Of course the women do not always ask for articles which they might be supposed to want in a state of health. If they did, it would soon arouse the suspicions of their deluded husbands, fathers, and brothers, and lead to inconvenient inquiries, if not to still more unpleasant experiment, upon the character of the mysterious disease. To avoid this, and to blind the men to the real nature of the deception, the women frequently ask for dogs, sledges, axes, and other similar articles of which they can make no possible use, and thus persuade their credulous male relatives that their demands are governed only by diseased caprice and have in view no definite object. Such was

the rationalistic explanation which the Ispravnik gave of
the curious delusion known as the "Anadyrsk bol;" and
although it argued more subtlety on the part of the women
and more credulity on the part of the men than I had
supposed either sex to be capable of, I could not but
admit that the explanation was a plausible one, and
accounted satisfactorily for most of the phenomena.

In view of this remarkable piece of feminine strategy,
our strong-minded women in America must admit that
their Siberian sisters show greater ingenuity in obtaining
their rights and throwing dust in the eyes of their lords
and masters than has yet been exhibited by all the
Women's Rights Associations in Christendom.   To invent
an imaginary disease with such peculiar symptoms, cause
it to prevail as an epidemic throughout a whole country,
and use it as a lever to open the masculine pocket-books
and supply feminine wants, is the greatest triumph which
woman's craft has ever achieved over man's stupidity!

The effect of the Ispravnik's revelation upon Dodd was
very singular.   He declared that he felt the premonitory
symptoms of the "Anadyrsk bol" coming on, and was
sure that he was destined to be a victim to the insidious
disease.   He therefore requested the Major not to be
surprised if he should come home some day and find him
in strong convulsions, singing "Yankee Doodle" in the
Gakout language, and demanding his back pay!   The
Major assured him that, in a case of such desperate emergency, he should be compelled to apply the Ispravnik's
remedy, viz., twenty lashes on the bare back, and advised
him to postpone his convulsions until the exchequer of

the Siberian Division should be in a condition to meet his demands.

Our life at Geezhega during the early part of June was a very decided improvement upon the experience of the previous six months. The weather was generally warm and pleasant, the hills and valleys were green with luxuriant vegetation, daylight had become perpetual, and we had nothing to do but ramble about the country in pursuit of game, row down to the mouth of the river occasionally to look for vessels, and plan all sorts of amusements to pass away the time.

The nights were the most glorious parts of the days, but the perpetual light seemed even more strange to us at first than the almost perpetual darkness of winter. We could never decide to our own satisfaction when one day ended and another began, or when it was time to go to bed. It seemed ridiculous to make any preparations for retiring before the sun had set ; and yet, if we did not, it was sure to rise again before we could possibly get to sleep, and then it seemed just as preposterous to lie in bed as it did in the first place. We finally compromised the matter by putting tight wooden shutters over all our windows, and then, by lighting candles inside, succeeded in persuading our unbelieving senses that it was night, although the sun outside was shining with noon-day brilliancy. When we awoke, however, another difficulty presented itself. Did we go to bed to-day ? or was it yesterday ? And what time is it now ? To-day, yesterday, and to-morrow were all mixed up, and we found it almost impossible to distinguish one from the other. I caught myself repeatedly making two entries in my journal in the course of twenty-four hours, with the mistaken impression that two days had passed.

As soon as the ice was fairly out of Geezheginsk Gulf, so that vessels might be expected to enter, Major Abasa caused a number of Cossacks to be stationed at the mouth of the river, with orders to watch night and day for sails and warn us at once if any appeared.

On the 18th of June the trading brig "Hallie Jackson," belonging to W. H. Bordman, of Boston, entered the gulf, and as soon as the tide permitted, ran into the mouth of the river to discharge her cargo. This vessel brought us the first news from the great outside world which we had received in more than eleven months, and her arrival was hailed with the greatest enthusiasm by both Russians and Americans. Half the population of the village came hurrying down to the mouth of the river as soon as it became known that a ship had arrived, and the landing-place for several days was a scene of unwonted activity and excitement. The "Jackson" could give us no information with regard to the vessels of our Company, except that when she sailed from San Francisco in March they were being rapidly loaded and fitted for sea. She brought, however, all the stores which we had left at Petropavlovski the previous fall, as well as a large cargo of tea, sugar, tobacco, and sundries for the Siberian trade.

We had found by our winter's experience that money could not be used to advantage in payment for native labor, except in the settlements of Okhotsk, Geezhega, and Anadyrsk ; and that tea, sugar, and tobacco were in every way preferable, on account of the universal consumption of those articles throughout the country and the high price which they commanded during the winter months. A laborer or teamster who would demand *twenty* roubles *in money* for a month's work, was entirely satisfied if we gave him eight pounds of tea and ten pounds of sugar in its stead ; and as the latter cost us only *ten* roubles, we made a saving of one-half in all our expenditures. In view of this fact Major Abasa determined to use as little money as possible, and pay for labor in merchandise at current rates. He accordingly purchased from the " Jackson " 10,000 lbs. of tea and 15 or 20,000 lbs. of white loaf-sugar, which he stored away in the Government magazines, to be used during the coming winter instead of money.

The " Jackson " discharged all the cargo which she intended to leave at Geezhega, and as soon as the tide was sufficiently high to enable her to cross the bar at the mouth of the river, she sailed for Petropavlovski and left us again alone.

CHAPTER XXXII.

AFTER the departure of the " Jackson " we began to look forward with eager anticipation to the arrival of our own vessels and the termination of our long imprisonment at Geezhega. Eight months of nomadic camp-life had given us a taste for adventure and excitement which nothing but constant travel could gratify, and as soon as the first novelty of idleness wore off we began to tire of our compulsory inactivity, and became impatient for work. We had exhausted all the amusements of Geezhega, read all the newspapers which had been brought by the " Jackson," discussed their contents to the minutest details, explored every foot of ground in the vicinity of the settlement, and tried everything which our ingenuity could devise to pass away the time, but all to no avail. The days seemed interminable, the long-expected ships did not come, and the mosquitoes and gnats made our life a burden.

About the tenth of July the mosquito—that curse of the northern summer—rises out of the damp moss of the lower plains, and winds his shrill horn to apprise all animated nature of his triumphant resurrection and his willingness to furnish musical entertainment to man and beast upon extremely reasonable terms. In three or four days, if the weather be still and warm, the whole atmosphere will be literally filled with clouds of mosquitoes, and from that time until the 10th of August they persecute every living thing with a bloodthirsty eagerness which knows no rest and feels no pity. Escape is impossible and defence useless; they follow their unhappy victims everywhere, and their untiring perseverance overcomes every obstacle which human ingenuity can throw in their way. Smoke of any ordinary density they treat with contemptuous indifference; mosquito-bars they either evade or carry by assault, and only by burying himself alive can man hope to finally escape their relentless persecution. In vain we wore gauze veils over our heads and concealed ourselves under calico " pologs." The multitude of our tiny assailants was so great that some of them sooner or later were sure to find an unguarded opening, and just when we thought ourselves most secure we were suddenly surprised and driven out of our shelter by a fresh and unexpected attack. Mosquitoes, I know, do not enter into the popular conception of Siberia; but never in any tropical country have I seen them prevail in such immense numbers as in Northeastern Siberia during the month of July. They make the great moss "toondras" in some places utterly uninhabitable, and force even the fur-clad reindeer to seek the shelter and the cooler atmosphere of the mountains. In the Russian settlements they torment dogs and cattle until the latter run furiously about in a perfect frenzy of pain, and fight desperately for a place to stand in the smoke of a fire. As far north as the settlement of Kolyma, on the coast of the Arctic Ocean, the natives are compelled, in still, warm weather, to surround their houses with a circle of "smudges," to protect themselves and their domestic animals from the ceaseless persecution of mosquitoes.

Early in July all the inhabitants of Geezhega, with the exception of the Governor and a few Russian merchants, closed their winter-houses, and removed to their "letovas" or summer fishing-stations along the banks of the river, to await the arrival of the salmon. Finding the deserted village rather dull, Dodd, Robinson, Arnold, and I removed to the mouth of the river, and took up our quarters once more in the empty government storehouse which we had occupied during the stay of the "Hallie Jackson."

I will not dwell long upon the monotonous discomfort of the life which we led for the next month. It may all be comprised in four words—inactivity, disappointment, mosquitoes, and misery. Looking for vessels was our only duty, fighting mosquitoes our only diversion ; and as the former never appeared and the latter never disappeared, both occupations were equally unprofitable and unsatisfactory. Twenty times a day we put on our gauze veils, tied our clothing down at the wrists and ankles, and climbed laboriously to the summit of a high bluff to look for vessels ; but twenty times a day we returned disappointed to our bare, cheerless rooms, and vented our indignation indiscriminately upon the country, the Company, the ships, and the mosquitoes. We could not help feeling as if we had dropped out of the great current of human affairs, as if our places in the distant busy world had been filled and our very existence forgotten.

The chief engineer of our enterprise had promised faithfully that ships with men, material, and supplies for the immediate prosecution of the work, should be at Geezhega and at the mouth of the Anadyr River as early in the season as ice would permit them to enter ; but it was now August, and they had not yet made their appearance. Whether they had been lost, or whether the whole enterprise had been abandoned, we could only conjecture ; but as week after week passed away without bringing any news, we gradually lost all hope and began to discuss the advisability of sending some one to the Siberian capital to inform the Company by telegraph of our situation.

It is but justice to Major Abasa to say that during all these long weary months of waiting he never entirely gave up to discouragement, nor allowed himself to doubt the perseverance of the Company in the work which it had undertaken.   The ships might have been belated or have met with some misfortune, but he did not think it possible that the work had been abandoned, and he continued throughout the summer to make such preparations as he could for another winter's campaign.

Early in August, Dodd and I, tired of looking for vessels which never came, and which we firmly believed never would come, returned on foot to the settlement, leaving Arnold and Robinson to maintain the watch at the mouth of the river.

Late in the afternoon of the 14th, while I was busily engaged in drawing maps to illustrate the explorations of the previous winter, our Cossack servant came rushing furiously into the house, breathless with haste and excite-

ment, crying out: "Pooshka! soodna!"—a cannon! a
ship! Knowing that three cannon shots were the signals which Arnold and Robinson had been directed to
make in case a vessel was seen entering the gulf, we ran
hurriedly out of doors and listened eagerly for a second
report. We had not long to wait. Another faint, dull
explosion was heard in the direction of the light-house, followed at an interval of a moment by a third, leaving no
room for a doubt that the long-expected ships had arrived.
Amid great excitement a canoe was hastily prepared and
launched, and taking our seats upon bear-skins in the bottom, we ordered our Cossack rowers to push off. At
every "letova" or fishing-station which we passed in our
rapid descent of the river, we were hailed with shouts of:
"Soodna!" "soodna!"—a ship! a ship! and at the last
one—Volynkina—where we stopped for a moment to rest
our men, we were told that the vessel was now in plain
sight from the hills, and that she had anchored near an
island known as the Matooga, about twelve miles distant
from the mouth of the river. Assured that it was no false
alarm, we pushed on with redoubled speed, and in fifteen
minutes more landed at the head of the gulf. Arnold
and Robinson, with the Russian pilot, Kerrillof, had already gone off to the vessel in the government whale-
boat, so that there remained nothing for us to do but
climb to the summit of light-house bluff and watch impatiently for their return.

It was late in the afternoon when the signal of a vessel
in sight had been given, and by the time we reached the
mouth of the river it was nearly sunset. The ship, which

was a good-sized barque, lay quietly at anchor near the middle of the gulf, about twelve miles distant, with a small American flag flying at her peak. We could see the government whale-boat towing astern, and knew that Arnold and Robinson must be on board; but the ship's boats still hung at the davits, and no preparations were apparently being made to come ashore. The Russian Governor had made us promise when we left the settlement, that if the reported vessel turned out a reality and not a delusion, we would fire three more guns. Frequent disappointment had taught him the fallibility of human testimony touching the arrival of ships at that particular port, and he did not propose to make a journey to the light-house in a leaky canoe, unless further intelligence should fully justify it. As there could no longer be any doubt about the fact, we loaded up the old rusty cannon once more, stuffed it full of wet grass to strengthen its voice, and gave the desired signals, which echoed in successive crashes from every rocky promontory along the coast, and died away to a faint mutter far out at sea.

In the course of an hour the Governor made his appearance, and as it was beginning to grow dark, we all climbed once more to the summit of the bluff to take a last look at the ship before she should be hidden from sight. There was no appearance of activity on board, and the lateness of the hour made it improbable that Arnold and Robinson would return before morning. We went back therefore to the empty government house, or "kazarme," and spent half the night in fruitless conjectures as to the cause of the vessel's late arrival and the nature of the news which she would bring.

With the earliest morning twilight Dodd and I clambered again to the crest of the bluff, to assure ourselves by actual observation that the ship had not vanished like the Flying Dutchman under cover of darkness, and left us to mourn another disappointment. There was little ground for fear. Not only was the barque still in the position which she had previously occupied, but there had been another arrival during the night. A large three-masted steamer, of apparently 2,000 tons, was lying in the offing, and three small boats could be seen a few miles distant pulling eagerly toward the mouth of the river. Great was the excitement which this discovery produced. Dodd rushed furiously down the hill to the kazarme, shouting to the Major that there was a steamer in the gulf, and that boats were within five miles of the light-house. In a few moments we were all gathered in a group on the highest point of the bluff, speculating upon the character of the mysterious steamer which had thus taken us by surprise, and watching the approach of the boats. The largest of these was now within three miles, and our glasses enabled us to distinguish in the long, regular sweep of its oars, the practised stroke of a man-of-war's crew, and in its stern sheets the peculiar shoulder-straps of Russian officers. The steamer was evidently a large ship-of-war, but what had brought her to that remote, unfrequented part of the world we could not conjecture.

In half an hour more two of the boats were abreast of

light-house bluff, and we descended to the landing-place
to meet them in a state of excitement not easily imagined.
Fourteen months had elapsed since we had heard from
home, and the prospect of receiving letters and of getting
once more to work was a sufficient excuse for unusual excitement. The smallest boat was the first to reach the
shore, and as it grated on the sandy beach an officer in
blue naval uniform sprang out and introduced himself as
Captain Sutton, of the Russo-American Telegraph Company's barque "Clara Bell," two months from San Francisco, with men and material for the construction of the
line. "Where have you been all summer?" demanded
the Major as he shook hands with the Captain; "we have
been looking for you ever since June, and had about come
to the conclusion that the work was abandoned." Captain Sutton replied that all of the Company's vessels had
been late in leaving San Francisco, and that he had also
been detained some time in Petropavlovski by circumstances explained in his letters. "What steamer is that
lying at anchor beyond the "Clara Bell," inquired the
Major. "That is the Russian corvette 'Varag,' from
Japan."—"But what is she doing up here?"—"Why,"
said the Captain with a quizzical smile, "you ought to
know, sir; I understand that she reports to you for
orders; I believe she has been detailed by the Russian
Government to assist in the construction of the line; at
least that was what I was told when we met her at Petropavlovski. She has a Russian Commissioner on board,
and a correspondent of the *New York Herald*." This
was unexpected news. We had heard that the Russian

and American Naval Departments had been instructed to send ships to Behring's Sea to assist the Company in making soundings and laying down the cable between the American and Siberian coasts, but we had never expected to see either of these vessels at Geezhega. The simultaneous arrival of a loaded barque, a steam corvette, a Russian Commissioner, and a correspondent of the *New York Herald*, certainly looked like business, and we congratulated ourselves and each other upon the improving prospects of the Siberian Division.

The corvette's boat by this time had reached the shore, and after making the acquaintance of Mr. Anossof, Col. Knox, the *Herald* correspondent, and half a dozen Russian officers who spoke English with the greatest fluency, we proceeded to open and read our long-delayed mail.

The news, as far as it related to the affairs of the Company and the prospects of the enterprise, was very satisfactory. Col. Bulkley, the Engineer-in-Chief, had touched at Petropavlovski on his way north, and had written us from there by the "Varag" and the "Clara Bell" full particulars as to his movements and dispositions. Three vessels—the "Clara Bell," "Palmetto," and "Onward"—had been sent from San Francicso to Geezhega with a force of about sixty men, and large assorted cargoes to the value of sixty thousand dollars. One of these, the "Clara Bell," loaded with brackets and insulators, had already arrived ; and the other two, with commissary stores, wire, instruments and men, were en route. A fourth vessel with thirty officers and workmen, a small river steamer, and a full supply of tools and provisions, had also been sent to the mouth

of the Anadyr River, where it would be received by Lieut.
Bush. The corvette " Varag " had been detailed by the
Russian Naval Department to assist in laying the cable
across Behring's Straits ; but as the cable, which was ordered in England, had not arrived, there was nothing in
particular for the " Varag " to do, and Col. Bulkley had
sent her with the Russian Commissioner to Geezhega.
Owing to her great draught of water—twenty-two feet—
she could not safely come within less than fifteen or
twenty miles of the Okhotsk Sea coast, and could not of
course give us much assistance ; but her very presence,
with a special Russian Commissioner on board, invested
our enterprise with a sort of governmental authority and
sanction, which enabled us to deal more successfully with
the local authorities and people than would otherwise
have been possible.

It had been Major Abasa's intention, as soon as one of
the Company's vessels should arrive, to go to the Russian
city and province of Yakoutsk, on the Lena River, engage
there five or six hundred native laborers, purchase three
hundred horses, and make arrangements for their distribution along the whole route of the line. The peculiar
state of affairs, however, at the time the " Varag " and the
" Clara Bell " reached Geezhega, made it almost impossible for him to leave. Two vessels—the " Onward " and
the " Palmetto "—were yet to arrive with large and valuable cargoes, whose distribution along the coast of the
Okhotsk Sea he wished to superintend in person. He decided therefore to postpone his trip to Yakoutsk until
later in the fall, and to do what he could in the mean time

with the two vessels already at his disposal. The "Clara Bell," in addition to her cargo of brackets and insulators, brought a foreman and three or four men as passengers, and these Major Abasa determined to send under command of Lieut. Arnold to Yamsk, with orders to hire as many native laborers as possible and begin at once the work of cutting poles and preparing station-houses. The "Varag" he proposed to send with stores and despatches to Mahood, who had been living alone at Okhotsk almost five months without news, money, or provisions, and who it was presumed must be nearly discouraged.

On the day previous to the "Varag's" departure, we were all invited by her social and warm-hearted officers to a last complimentary dinner; and although we had not been and should not be able with our scanty means to reciprocate such attentions, we felt no hesitation in accepting the invitation and tasting once more the pleasures of civilized life. Nearly all the officers of the "Varag," some thirty in number, spoke English with the greatest fluency; the ship itself was luxuriously fitted up; a fine military band welcomed us with "Hail Columbia" when we came on board, and played selections from Martha, Traviata, and Der Freischütz while we dined, and all things contributed to make our visit to the "Varag" a bright spot in our Siberian experience.

On the following morning at ten o'clock we returned to the "Clara Bell" in one of the latter's small-boats, and the corvette steamed slowly out to sea, her officers waving their hats from the quarter-deck in mute farewell, and her band playing the Pirate's Chorus—"Ever be happy and blest as thou art"—as if in mockery of our lonely, cheerless exile ! It was a gloomy party of men which returned that afternoon to a supper of reindeer-meat and cabbage in the bare deserted rooms of the government store-house at Geezhega ! We realized then, if never before, the difference between *life* in " God's country " and *existence* in Northeastern Asia.

As soon as possible after the departure of the " Varag," the " Clara Bell" was brought into the mouth of the river, her cargo of brackets and insulators discharged, Lieut. Arnold and party sent on board, and with the next high tide, August 26th, she sailed for Yamsk and San Francisco, leaving no one at Geezhega but the original Kamtchatkan party, Dodd, the Major, and myself.

CHAPTER XXXIII.

ARRIVAL OF SUPPLY-SHIPS—LAST JOURNEY TO THE ARC-
TIC CIRCLE—KORAK DRIVERS—FAMINE AT ANADYRSK.

THE brief excitement produced by the arrival of the *Varag* and the *Clara Bell* was succeeded by another long, dreary month of waiting, during which we lived as before in lonely discomfort at the mouth of the Geezhega River. Week after week passed away without bringing any tidings from the missing ships, and at last the brief northern summer closed, snow appeared upon the mountains, and heavy long-continued storms announced the speedy approach of another winter. More than three months had now elapsed since the supposed departure of the *Onward* and *Palmetto* from San Francisco, and we could only account for their non-appearance by the supposition that they had either been disabled or lost at sea. On the 18th of September Major Abasa determined to send a messenger to the Siberian capital, to telegraph the Company for instructions. Left as we were at the beginning of a second winter without men, tools, or materials of any kind, except 50,000 insulators and brackets, we could do nothing toward the construction of the line, and our only resource was to make our unpleasant situation known to the Company. On the 19th, however, before this reso-

lution could be carried into effect, the long-expected
barque *Palmetto* arrived, followed closely by the Russian supply-steamer *Saghalin*, from Nikolaevsk. The
latter, being independent of wind and drawing very little
water, had no difficulty in crossing the bar and gaining the
shelter of the river ; but the *Palmetto* was compelled
to anchor outside and await a higher tide. The weather,
which for several days had been cold and threatening,
grew momentarily worse, and on the 22d the wind was
blowing a close-reefed topsail gale from the southeast, and
rolling a tremendous sea into the unprotected gulf. We
felt the most serious apprehensions for the safety of the
unfortunate barque ; but as the water would not permit
her to cross the bar at the mouth of the river, nothing
could be done until another high tide. On the 23d it
became evident that the *Palmetto*—upon which now
rested all our hopes—must inevitably go ashore. She had
broken her heaviest anchor, and was drifting slowly but
surely against the rocky, precipitous coast on the east side
of the river, where nothing could prevent her from being
dashed to pieces. As there was now no other alternative,
Capt. Arthur slipped his cable, got his ship under way,
and stood directly in for the mouth of the river. He could
no longer avoid going ashore somewhere, and it was better to strike on a yielding bar of sand than to drift help-
lessly against a black perpendicular wall of rock, where
destruction would be certain. The barque came gallantly
in until she was only half a mile distant from the light-
house, and then grounded heavily in about seven feet of
water. As soon as she struck she began pounding with

tremendous violence against the bottom, while the seas broke in great white clouds of spray entirely over her quarter-deck. It did not seem probable that she would live through the night. As the tide rose, however, she drove farther and farther in toward the mouth of the river, until, at full flood, she was only a quarter of a mile distant. Being a very strongly built ship, she suffered less damage than we supposed, and, as the tide ran out, she lay high and dry on the bar, with no more serious injury than the loss of her false keel and a few sections of her copper sheathing.

As she was lying on her beam-ends, with her deck careened at an angle of forty-five degrees, it was impossible to hoist anything out of her hold, but we made preparations at once to discharge her cargo in boats as soon as another tide should raise her into an upright position. We felt little hope of being able to save the ship, but it was all-important that her cargo should be discharged before she should go to pieces. Capt. Tobezin, of the Russian steamer *Saghalin*, offered us the use of all his boats and the assistance of his crew, and on the following day we began work with six or seven boats, a large lighter, and about fifty men. The sea still continued to run very high; the barque recommenced her pounding against the bottom; the lighter swamped and sank with a full load about a hundred yards from shore, and a miscellaneous assortment of boxes, crates, and flour-barrels went swimming up the river with the tide. Notwithstanding all these misfortunes, we kept perseveringly at work with the boats as long as there was water enough around the barque to float them, and by the time the tide ran out we could congratulate ourselves upon having saved provisions enough to insure us against starvation, even though the ship should go to pieces that night. On the 25th the wind abated somewhat in violence, the sea went down, and as the barque did not seem to be seriously injured we began to entertain some hope of saving both ship and cargo. From the 25th until the 29th of September, all the boats of the *Saghalin* and of the *Palmetto*, with the crews of both vessels, were constantly engaged in transporting stores from the barque to the shore, and on the 30th at least half of the *Palmetto's* cargo was safely discharged. So far as we could judge, there would be nothing to prevent her from going to sea with the first high tide in October. A careful examination proved that she had sustained no greater injury than the loss of her false keel, and this, in the opinion of the *Saghalin's* officers, would not make her any the less seaworthy, or interfere to any extent with her sailing. A new difficulty, however, presented itself. The crew of the *Palmetto* were all negroes ; and as soon as they learned that Major Abasa intended to send the barque to San Francisco that fall, they promptly refused to go, declaring that the vessel was unseaworthy, and that they preferred to spend the winter in Siberia rather than risk a voyage in her to America. Major Abasa immediately called a commission of the officers of the *Saghalin*, and requested them to make another examination of the bark and give him their opinion in writing as to her seaworthiness. The examination was made, and the opinion given that she was entirely fit for a voyage to Petropavlovski, Kamtchatka, and probably to San Francisco. This decision was read to the negroes, but they still persisted in their refusal. After warning them of the consequences of mutiny, the Major ordered their ring-leader to be put in irons, and he was conveyed on board the *Saghalin* and imprisoned in the "black hole ;" but his comrades still held out. It was of vital importance that the *Palmetto* should go to sea with the first high tide, because the season was already far advanced, and she must inevitably be wrecked by ice if she remained in the river later than the middle of October.

Besides this, Major Abasa would be compelled to leave for Yakoutsk on the steamer *Saghalin*, and the latter was now ready to go to sea.   On the afternoon of the 1st, just as the *Saghalin* was getting up steam to start, the negroes sent word to the Major that if he would release the man whom he had caused to be put in irons, they would do their best to finish unloading the *Palmetto* and to get her back to San Francisco. The man was promptly released, and two hours afterwards Major Abasa sailed on the *Saghalin* for Okhotsk, leaving us to do the best we could with our half-wrecked stranded ship and her mutinous crew.

The cargo of the barque was still only half discharged, and we continued for the next five days to unload in boats ; but it was hard, discouraging work, as there were only six hours in the twenty-four during which boats could reach the ship, and those six hours were from eleven o'clock P. M. to five in the morning. At all other times the ship lay on her beam-ends, and the water around her was too shallow

to float even a plank. To add, if possible, to our difficul
ties and to our anxiety, the weather became suddenly
colder, the thermometer fell to zero, masses of floating
ice came in with every tide and tore off great sheets of
the vessel's copper as they drifted past, and the river soon
became so choked up with icy fragments that we were
obliged to haul the boats back and forth with ropes. In
spite of weather, water, and ice, however, the vessel's
cargo was slowly but steadily discharged, and by the 10th
of October nothing remained on board except a few hogs-
heads of flour, some salt beef and pork which we did not
want, and seventy-five or a hundred tons of coal. These
we determined to let her carry back to San Francisco as
ballast. The tides were now getting successively higher
and higher every day, and on the 11th the *Palmetto* floated
for the first time in almost three weeks. As soon as her
keel cleared the bar she was swung around into the channel, head to sea, and moored with light kedge-anchors,
ready for a start on the following day. Since the intensely-
cold weather of the previous week, her crew of negroes
had expressed no further desire to spend a winter in Siberia; and unless the wind should veer suddenly to the
southward, we could see nothing to prevent her from getting safely out of the river. The wind for once proved
favorable, and at 2 P.M. on the 12th of October the *Palmetto* shook out her long-furled courses and topsails, cut
the cables of her kedge-anchors, and with a light breeze
from the northeast, moved slowly out into the gulf. Never
was music more sweet to my ears than the hearty "Yo
heave ho!" of her negro crew as they sheeted home the

topgallant sails outside the bar !   The barque was safely
at sea.   She was not a day too soon in making her escape.
In less than a week after her departure, the river and the
upper part of the gulf were so packed with ice that it
would have been impossible for her to move or to avoid
total wreck.

The prospects of the enterprise at the opening of the
second winter were more favorable than they had been
at any time since its inception.   The Company's vessels,
it is true, had been very late in their arrival, and one of
them, the *Onward*, had not come at all ; but the *Palmetto* had brought twelve or fourteen more men and a
full supply of tools and provisions, Major Abasa had gone
to Yakoutsk to hire six or eight hundred native laborers
and purchase three hundred horses, and we hoped that
the first of February would find the work progressing rapidly along the whole extent of the line.

As soon as possible after the departure of the *Palmetto*
I sent Lieut. Sandford and the twelve men whom she had
brought into the woods on the Geezhega River above the
settlement, supplied them with axes, snow-shoes, dog-
sledges, and provisions, and set them at work cutting
poles and building houses, to be distributed across the
steppes between Geezhega and Penzhinsk Gulf.   I also
sent a small party of natives under Mr. Wheeler to Gamsk,
with five or six sledge-loads of axes and provisions for
Lieut. Arnold, and despatches to be forwarded to Maj.
Abasa.   For the present nothing more could be done on
the coast of the Okhotsk Sea, and I prepared to start
once more for the North.   We had heard nothing whatever

from Lieut. Bush and party since the first of the previous
May, and we were of course anxious to know what success
he had met with in cutting and rafting poles down the
Anadyr River, and what were his prospects and plans for
the winter. The late arrival of the *Palmetto* at Geezhega
had led us to fear that the vessel destined for the Anadyr
might also have been detained, and have placed Lieut.
Bush and party in a very unpleasant, if not dangerous
situation. Major Abasa had directed me therefore, when
he sailed for Okhotsk, to go by the first winter road to
Anadyrsk and ascertain whether the Company's vessels
had been at the mouth of the river, and whether Bush
needed any assistance. As there was no longer anything to
detain me at Geezhega, I packed up my camp equipage
and extra fur clothes, loaded five sledges with tea, sugar,
tobacco, and provisions, and on November 2d started
with six Cossacks for my last journey to the Arctic
Circle.

In all my Siberian experience I can recall no expedition
which was so lonely and dismal as this. For the sake of
saving transportation, I had decided not to take any of my
American comrades with me ; but by many a silent camp-
fire did I regret my self-denying economy, and long for
the hearty laugh and good-humored raillery of my " fidus
Achates"—Dodd. During twenty-five days I did not meet
a civilized being or speak a word of my native language,
and at the end of that time I would have been glad to
talk to an intelligent American dog. " Aloneness," says
Beecher, " is to social life what rests are to music ;" but a
journey made up entirely of " aloneness " is no more en-

tertaining than a piece of music made up entirely of rests —only a vivid imagination can make anything out of either.

At Kooeel, on the coast of Penzhinsk Gulf, I was compelled to leave my good-humored Cossacks and take for drivers half a dozen stupid, sullen, shaven-headed Koraks, and from that time I was more lonesome than ever. I had been able to talk a little with the Cossacks, and had managed to pass away the long winter evenings by the camp-fire in questioning them about their peculiar beliefs and superstitions, and listening to their characteristic stories of Siberian life; but now, as I could not speak the Korak language, I was absolutely without any resource for amusement.

My new drivers were the ugliest, most villanous-looking Koraks that it would have been possible to select in all the Penzhinsk Gulf settlements, and their obstinacy and sullen stupidity kept me in a chronic state of ill-humor from the time we left Kooeel until we reached Penzhina. Only by threatening them periodically with a revolver could I make them go at all. The art of camping out comfortably in bad weather they knew nothing whatever about, and in vain did I try to teach them. In spite of all my instructions and illustrations, they would persist night after night in digging a deep narrow hole in the snow for a fire, and squatting around the top of it like frogs around the edge of a well, while I made a camp for myself. Of the art of cooking they were equally ignorant, and the mystery of canned provisions they could never fathom. Why the contents of one can should be boiled, while the contents of another precisely similar can should be fried—why one turned into soup and another into a cake—were questions which they gravely discussed night after night, but about which they could never agree. Astounding were the experiments which they occasionally tried upon the contents of these incomprehensible tin boxes. Tomatoes they brought to me fried into cakes with butter, peaches they mixed with canned beef and boiled for soup, green corn they sweetened, and desiccated vegetables they broke into lumps with stones. Never by any accident did they hit upon the right combination, unless I stood over them constantly and superintended personally the preparation of my own supper. Ignorant as they were, however, of the nature of these strange American eatables, they always manifested a great curiosity to taste them, and their experiments in this way were sometimes very amusing. One evening, soon after we left Shestakova, they happened to see me eating a pickled cucumber, and as this was something which had never come within the range of their limited gastronomical experience, they asked me for a piece to taste. Knowing well what the result would be, I gave the whole cucumber to the dirtiest, worst-looking vagabond in the party, and motioned to him to take a good bite. As he put it to his lips his comrades watched him with breathless curiosity to see how he liked it. For a moment his face wore an expression of blended surprise, wonder, and disgust which was irresistibly ludicrous, and he seemed disposed to spit the disagreeable morsel out; but with a strong effort he controlled himself, forced his features into a ghastly imitation of satisfaction, smacked his lips, declared it was

" akhmel nemélkhin "—very good, and handed the pickle
to his next neighbor. The latter was equally astonished and disgusted with its unexpected sourness, but,
rather than admit his disappointment and be laughed at
by the others, he also pretended that it was delicious, and
passed it along. Six men in succession went through
with this transparent farce with the greatest solemnity ; but
when they had all tasted it, and all been victimized, they
burst out into a simultaneous " ty-e-e-e " of astonishment,
and gave free expression to their long-suppressed emotions of disgust. The vehement spitting, coughing, and
washing out of mouths with snow, which succeeded this
outburst, proved that the taste for pickles is an acquired
one, and that man in his aboriginal state does not possess
it. What particularly amused me, however, was the way
in which they imposed on one another. Each individual
Korak, as soon as he found that he had been victimized,
saw at once the necessity of getting even by victimizing
the next man, and not one of them would admit that
there was anything bad about the pickle until they had all
tasted it. " Misery loves company," and human nature
is the same all the world over. Dissatisfied as they were
with the result of this experiment, they were not at all
daunted, but still continued to ask me for samples of
every tin can I opened. Just before we reached Penzhina,
however, a catastrophe occurred which relieved me from
their importunity, and inspired them with a superstitious
reverence for tin cans which no subsequent familiarity
could ever overcome. We were accustomed, when we
came into camp at night, to set our cans into a bed of hot

ashes and embers to thaw out, and I had cautioned my drivers repeatedly not to do this until after the cans had been opened. I could not of course explain to them that the accumulation of steam would cause the cans to burst; but I did tell them that it would be "atkin"—bad— if they did not make a hole in the cover before putting the can on the fire. One evening, however, they forgot or neglected to take this precaution, and while they were all squatting in a circle around the fire, absorbed in meditation, one of the cans suddenly blew up with a tremendous explosion, set free an immense cloud of steam, and scattered fragments of boiling hot mutton in every direction. Had a volcano opened suddenly under the camp-fire, the Koraks could not have been more dismayed. They had not time to get up and run away, so they rolled over backward with their heels in the air, shouted "Kammuk!"—the Devil—and gave themselves up for lost. My hearty laughter finally reassured them, and made them a little ashamed of their momentary panic; but from that time forward they handled tin cans as if they were loaded percussion shells, and could never again be induced to taste a morsel of their contents.

Our progress toward Anadyrsk after we left the coast of the Okhotsk Sea was very slow, on account both of the shortness of the days, and the depth and softness of the freshly fallen snow. Frequently, for ten or fifteen miles at a stretch, we were compelled to break a road on snow-shoes for our heavily loaded sledges, and even then our tired dogs could hardly struggle through the soft powdery drifts. The weather, too, was so intensely cold that my mercurial thermometer, which indicated only —23°, was almost useless. For several days the mercury never rose out of the bulb, and I could only estimate the temperature by the rapidity with which my supper froze after being taken from the fire. More than once soup turned from a liquid to a solid in my hands, and geren corn froze to my tin plate before I could finish eating it.

On the fourteenth day after leaving Geezhega we reached the native settlement of Penzhina, two hundred versts from Anadyrsk. Ours was the first arrival at that place since the previous May, and the whole population of the village—men, women, children, and dogs—turned out *en masse* to meet us, with the most joyful demonstrations. Six months had elapsed since they last saw a strange face or heard from the outside world, and they proceeded to fire a salute from half a dozen rusty old muskets, as a faint expression of their delight.

I had confidently expected when I left Geezhega that I would meet somewhere on the road a courier with news and despatches from Bush; and I was very much disappointed and a little alarmed when I reached Penzhina to find that no one had arrived at that place from Anadyrsk, and that nothing had been heard from our party since the previous spring. I felt a presentiment that something was wrong, because Bush had been expressly directed to send a courier to Geezhega by the first winter road, and it was now late in November.

On the following day my worst anticipations were realized. Late in the evening, as I was sitting in the house of one of the Russian peasants drinking tea, the cry was raised that "Anadyrski yaydoot"—some one was coming from Anadyrsk ; and running hastily out of the house I met the long-haired Anadyrsk priest just as he stepped from his sledge in front of the door.   My first question of course was, "Where's Bush?"   But my heart sank as the priest replied, "Bokh yevo zniet"—God only knows. "But where did you see him last—where did he spend the summer?" I inquired.   "I saw him last at the mouth of the Anadyr River, in July," said the priest, "and since that time nothing has been heard from him."   A few more questions brought out the whole dismal story. Bush, Macrae, Harder, and Smith, had gone down the Anadyr River in June with a large raft of station-houses, intended for erection along its banks.   After putting up these houses at necessary points, they had gone on in canoes to Anadyr Bay, to await the arrival of the Company's vessels from San Francisco.   Here the priest had joined them and had lived with them several weeks ; but late in July their scanty supply of provisions had given out, the expected ships had not come, and the priest returned to the settlement, leaving the unfortunate Americans in a half-starving condition at the mouth of the river. Since that time nothing whatever had been heard from them, and as the priest mournfully said, "God only knew" where they were and what had happened to them. This was bad news, but it was not the worst.   In consequence of the entire failure of the salmon fisheries of the Anadyr River that season, a terrible famine had broken out at Anadyrsk, part of the inhabitants and nearly all the dogs had died of starvation, and the village was

almost deserted. Everybody who had dogs enough to
draw a sledge had gone in search of the Wandering
Chookchees, with whom they could live until another summer ; and the few people who were left in the settlement
were eating their boots and scraps of reindeer-skin to
keep them alive. Early in October a party of natives
had gone in search of Bush and his comrades on dog-
sledges, but more than a month had now elapsed since
their departure and they had not yet returned. In all
probability they had starved to death on the great desolate plains of the Lower Anadyr, as they had been compelled to start with only ten days' provisions, and it was
doubtful whether they would meet Wandering Chookchees who would supply them with more.

Such was the first news which I heard from the Northern District — a famine at Anadyrsk, Bush and party
missing since July, and eight natives and dog-sledges
since the middle of October. I did not see how the
state of affairs could be any worse, and I spent a sleep-
less night in thinking over the situation and trying to
decide upon some plan of operations. Much as I dreaded
another journey to the mouth of the Anadyr in midwinter, I saw no way of avoiding it. The fact that nothing
had been heard from Bush in four months proved that he
had met with some misfortune, and it was clearly my duty
to go to Anadyr Bay in search of him if there was a possibility of doing so. On the following morning, therefore,
I began buying a supply of dog-food, and before night I
had collected 2,000 dried fish and a quantity of seals'
blubber, which I felt sure would last five dog-teams at

least forty days. I then sent for the chief of a band of Wandering Koraks who happened to be encamped near Penzhina, and prevailed upon him to drive his herd of reindeer to Anadyrsk, and kill enough to supply the starving inhabitants with food until they could get other help. I also sent two natives back to Geezhega on dog-sledges, with a letter to the Russian Governor, apprising him of the famine, and another to Dodd, directing him to load every dog-sledge he could get with provisions and send them at once to Penzhina, where I would make arrangements for their transportation to the famine-stricken settlement.

I started myself for Anadyrsk on November 20th, with five of the best men and an equal number of the best dog-teams in Penzhina. These men and dogs I intended to take with me to the mouth of the Anadyr River if I heard nothing from Bush before I reached Anadyrsk.

CHAPTER XXXIV.

BUSH REDIVIVUS---SERIOUS DILEMMA---STARVATION THREAT-
ENED — EIGHT HUNDRED LABORERS HIRED——ENTERPRIS-
ING AMERICAN——A WILDERNESS.

AVAILING ourselves of the road which had been broken
by the sledges of the priest, we made more rapid progress
toward Anadyrsk than I had anticipated, and on November 22d we camped at the foot of a range of low mountains known as the "Rooske Krebet," only thirty versts
south of the settlement. With the hope of reaching our
destination before the next morning, we had intended to
travel all night; but a storm sprang up most inopportunely
just before dark and prevented us from getting over the
pass. About midnight the wind abated a little, the moon
came out occasionally through rifts in the clouds, and,
fearing that we should have no better opportunity, we
roused up our tired dogs and began the ascent of the
mountain. It was a wild, lonely scene. The snow was
drifting in dense clouds down the pass, half hiding from
sight the bare white peaks on either side, and blotting out
all the landscape behind us as we ascended. Now and
then the misty moonbeams would struggle faintly through
the clouds of flying snow and light up for a moment the
great barren slope of the mountain above our heads; then

they would be suddenly smothered in dark vapor, the wind would come roaring down the ravine again, and everything would vanish in clouds and darkness. Blinded and panting for breath, we finally gained the summit, and as we stopped for a moment to rest our tired dogs, we were suddenly startled by the sight of a long line of dark objects passing swiftly across the bare mountain-top only a few yards away, and plunging down into the ravine out of which we had just come. I caught only a glimpse of them, but they seemed to be dog-sledges, and with a great shout we started in pursuit. Dog-sledges they were, and as we drew nearer I recognized among them the old seal-skin covered "pavoska" which I had left at Anadyrsk the previous winter, and which I knew must be occupied by an American. With heart beating fast from excitement I sprang from my sledge, ran up to the "pavoska," and demanded in English, "Who is it?" It was too dark to recognize faces, but I knew well the voice that answered "Bush!" and never was that voice more welcome. For more than three weeks I had not seen a countryman nor spoken a word of English; I was lonely and disheartened by constantly accumulating misfortunes, when suddenly at midnight, on a desolate mountain-top, in a storm, I met an old friend and comrade whom I had almost given up as dead. It was a joyful meeting. The natives who had gone to Anadyr Bay in search of Bush and his party had returned in safety, bringing Bush with them, and he was on his way to Geezhega to carry the news of the famine and get provisions and help. He had been stopped by the storm as we had, and when it abated

a little at midnight we had both started from opposite
sides to cross the mountain. and had thus met upon the
summit.

We went back together to my deserted camp on the
south side of the mountain, blew up the embers of my
still smouldering fire, spread down our bear-skins, and sat
there talking until we were as white as polar bears with
the drifting snow, and day began to break in the East.

Bush brought more bad news. They had gone down
to the mouth of the Anadyr, as the priest had already
informed me, in the early part of June, and had waited
there for the Company's vessels almost four months.
Their provisions had finally given out, and they had been
compelled to subsist themselves upon the few fish which
they were able to catch from day to day, and to go
hungry when they could catch none. For salt they
scraped the staves of an old pork barrel which had been
left at Macrae's camp the previous winter, and for coffee
they drank burned rice water. At last, however, salt and
rice both failed, and they were reduced to an unvarying
and often scanty diet of boiled fish, without coffee, bread,
or salt. Living in the midst of a great moss swamp fifty
miles from the nearest tree, dressing in skins for the want
of anything else, suffering frequently from hunger, tormented constantly by mosquitoes, from which they had
no protection, and looking day after day and week after
week for vessels which never came, their situation was
certainly miserable. The Company's barque *Golden
Gate* had finally arrived in October, bringing twenty-five
men and a small steamer ; but winter had already set in,

and five days afterwards, before they could finish discharging the vessel's cargo, she was wrecked by ice. Her crew and nearly all her stores were saved, but by this misfortune the number of the party was increased from twenty-five to forty-seven, without any corresponding increase in the quantity of provisions for their subsistence. Fortunately, however, there were bands of Wandering Chookchees within reach, and from them Bush succeeded in buying a considerable number of reindeer, which he caused to be frozen and stored away for future use. After the freezing over of the Anadyr River, Bush was left as Macrae had been the previous winter, without any means of getting up to the settlement, a distance of 250 miles; but he had foreseen this difficulty, and had left orders at Anadyrsk that if he failed to return in canoes before the river closed, dog-sledges should be sent to his assistance. Notwithstanding the famine the dog-sledges were sent, and Bush, with two men, had returned on them to Anadyrsk. Finding that settlement famine-stricken and deserted, he had started without a moment's delay for Geezhega, his exhausted and starving dogs dying along the road.

The situation of affairs, then, when I met Bush on the summit of the Rooski Krebet, was briefly as follows :—

Forty-four men were living at the mouth of the Anadyr River, 250 miles from the nearest settlement, without provisions enough to last them through the winter, and without any means whatever of getting away. The village of Anadyrsk was deserted, and with the exception of a few teams at Penzhina, there were no available dogs in all the

Northern District, from the Okhotsk Sea to Behring's
Straits. Under such circumstances, what could be done?
Bush and I discussed the question all night beside our lonely
camp-fire under the Rooski Krebet Mountains, but could
come to no decision, and after sleeping three or four hours
we started for Anadyrsk. Late in the afternoon we drove
into the settlement—but it could be called a settlement no
longer. The two upper villages—"Osolkin" and "Pokorookof," which on the previous winter had presented so
thriving an appearance, were now left without a single inhabitant, and Markova itself was only occupied by a few
starving families whose dogs had all died, and who were
therefore unable to get away. No chorus of howls announced our arrival; no people came out to meet us; the
windows of the houses were closed with wooden shutters,
and half buried in drifts; the snow was unbroken by
paths, and the whole village was silent and desolate. It
looked as if one-half of the inhabitants had died and the
other half had gone to the funeral! We stopped at a
small log-house where Bush had established his head-
quarters, and spent the remainder of the day in talking
over our respective experiences.

The unpleasant situation in which we found ourselves
placed was due almost entirely to the famine at Anadyrsk.
The late arrival and consequent wreck of the *Golden
Gate* was of course a great misfortune; but it would not
have been irretrievable had not the famine deprived us of
all means of transportation. The inhabitants of Anadyrsk,
as well as of all the other Russian settlements in Siberia,
are dependent for their very existence upon the fish

which enter the rivers every summer to spawn, and are
caught by thousands as they make their way up stream
toward the shallow water of the tributary brooks in the interior of the country.   As long as these migrations of the
fish are regular the natives have no difficulty in providing
themselves with an abundance of food ; but once in every
three or four years, for some unexplained reason, the fish
fail to come, and the following winter brings precisely such
a famine as the one which I have described at Anadyrsk,
only frequently much worse.   In 1860 more than a hundred and fifty natives died of starvation in four settlements
on the coast of Penzhinsk Gulf, and the peninsula of
Kamtchatka has been swept by famines again and again
since the Russian conquest, until its population has been
reduced more than one-half.   Were it not for the Wandering Koraks, who come to the relief of the starving people
with their immense herds of reindeer, I firmly believe that
the *settled* population of Siberia, including the Russians,
Chooances, Gookaghiris, and Kamtchadals, would become
extinct in less than fifty years.   The great distance of the
settlements one from another, and the absence of any
means of intercommunication in summer, make each village entirely dependent upon its own resources, and prevent any mutual support and assistance, until it is too
late to be of any avail.   The first victims of such famines
are always the dogs ; and the people, being thus deprived
of their only means of transportation, cannot get away
from the famine-stricken settlement, and after eating their
boots, seal-skin thongs, and scraps of untanned leather,
they finally die of pure starvation.   For this, however,

their own careless improvidence is primarily responsible. They might catch and dry fish enough in one year to last them three ; but instead of doing this, they provide barely food enough to last them through one winter, and take the chances of starvation on the next. No experience, however severe—no suffering, however great, ever teaches them prudence. A man who has barely escaped starvation one winter, will run precisely the same risk on the next, rather than take a little extra trouble and catch a few more fish. Even when they see that a famine is inevitable, they take no measures to mitigate its severity or to obtain relief, until they find themselves absolutely without a morsel to put in their mouths.

A native of Anadyrsk once happened to tell me, in the course of conversation, that he had only five days' dog-food left. " But," said I, " what do you intend to do at the end of those five days ?"—" Bokh gevo zniet "—God only knows !—was the characteristic response, and the native turned carelessly away as if it were a matter of no consequence whatever. If God only knew, he seemed to think that it made very little difference whether anybody else knew or not. After he had fed his dogs the last dried fish in his store-house, it would be time enough to look about for more ; but until then he did not propose to borrow any unnecessary trouble. This well-known recklessness and improvidence of the natives finally led the Russian Government to establish at several of the North-eastern Siberian settlements a peculiar institution which may be called a Fish Savings Bank, or Starvation Insurance Office. It was organized at first by the gradual pur-

chase from the natives of about a hundred thousand dried
fish, or "gookala," which constituted the capital stock of
the bank. Every male inhabitant of the settlement was
then obliged by law to pay into this bank annually one-
tenth of all the fish which he caught, and no excuse
was admitted for a failure. The surplus fund thus created
was added every year to the capital, so that as long as
the fish continued to come regularly, the resources of
the bank were constantly accumulating. When, however,
the fish for any reason failed and a famine was threatened,
every depositor—or, more strictly speaking, tax-payer—
was allowed to borrow from the bank enough fish to supply his immediate wants, upon condition of returning the
same on the following summer, together with the regular
annual payment of ten per cent. It is evident that an
institution once thoroughly established upon such a basis,
and managed upon such principles, could never fail, but
would constantly increase its capital of dried fish until the
settlement would be perfectly secure against even the possibility of famine. At Kolyma, a Russian post on the
Arctic Ocean, where the experiment was first tried, it
proved a complete success. The bank sustained the inhabitants of the village through severe famines during
two consecutive winters, and its capital in 1867 amounted
to 300,000 dried fish, and was accumulating at the rate of
20,000 a year. Anadyrsk not being a Russian military post,
had no bank of this kind; but had our work been continued
another year, we intended to petition the Government for
the organization of such institutions at all the settlements,
Russian and native, along the whole route of our line.

In the mean time, however, the famine was irremedi
able, and on December 1st, 1867, poor Bush found himself in a deserted settlement 600 versts from Geezhega,
without money, without provisions, and without means of
transportation—but with a helpless party of forty-four men,
at the mouth of the Anadyr River, dependent upon him
for support. Building a telegraph line under such circumstances was out of the question. All that he could hope
to do would be to keep his parties supplied with provisions
until the arrival of horses and men from Yakootsk should
enable him to resume work.

On November 29th, finding that I could be of no further
assistance at Anadyrsk, and that I was only helping to
eat up more rapidly Bush's scanty supply of provisions, I
started with two Penzhina sledges for Geezhega. As I did
not again visit the Northern District, and shall have no
further occasion to refer to it, I will relate briefly here
the little which I afterward learned by letter with regard
to the misfortunes and unhappy experiences of the Company's employés in that region. The sledges which I had
ordered from Geezhega reached Penzhina late in December, with about 3,000 pounds of beans, rice, hard bread,
and assorted stores. As soon as possible after their
arrival Bush sent half a dozen sledges and a small quantity
of provisions to the party at the mouth the Anadyr
River, and in February they returned, bringing six men.
Determined to accomplish something, however little, Bush
sent these six men to a point on the Myan River, about
seventy-five versts from Anadyrsk, and set them at work
putting poles on snow-shoes along the route of the line.

Later in the winter another expedition was sent to Anadyr Bay, and on the 4th of March it also returned, bringing Lieut. Macrae and seven more men. This party experienced terrible weather on its way from the mouth of the river to Anadyrsk, and one of its members—a man named Robinson—died in a storm about 150 versts east of the settlement. His body was left unburied in one of the houses which Bush had erected the previous summer and his comrades pushed on. As soon as they reached the Anadyrsk they were sent to the Myan, and by the middle of March the two parties together had cut and distributed along the banks of that river about 3,000 poles. In April, however, their provisions began again to run short, and they were gradually reduced to the verge of starvation, and Bush started a second time for Geezhega with a few miserable half-starved and exhausted dog-teams, to get more provisions. During his absence the unfortunate parties on the Myan were left to take care of themselves, and after consuming their last morsel of food and eating up three horses which had previously been sent to them from Anadyrsk, they organized themselves into a forlorn hope, and started on snow-shoes for the settlement. It was a terrible walk for half-starving men; and although they reached their destination in safety, they were entirely exhausted, and when they approached the village could hardly go a hundred yards at a time without falling down. At Anadyrsk they succeeded in obtaining a small quantity of reindeer meat, upon which they lived until the return of Lieut. Bush from Geezhega with provisions, some time in May. Thus ended the second winter's work in the

Northern District.　As far as practicable results were concerned, it was an almost complete failure; but it developed in our officers and men a courage, a perseverance, and a patient endurance of hardships which deserved, and which under more favorable auspices would have achieved, the most brilliant success.　In the month of February, while Mr. Norton and his men were at work on the Myan River, the thermometer indicated more than forty degrees below zero during sixteen days out of twenty-one, sank five times to —60° and once to —68°, or one hundred degrees below the freezing-point of water.　Cutting poles on snow-shoes, in a temperature ranging from 40° to 60°. below zero, is in itself no slight trial of men's hardihood; but when to this are added the sufferings of hunger and the peril of utter starvation in a perfect wilderness, it passes human endurance, and the only wonder is that Norton and Macrae could accomplish as much as they did.

Returning from Anadyrsk, I reached Geezhega on the 15th of December, after a hard and lonely journey of sixteen days.　A special courier had just arrived there from Yakootsk, bringing letters and orders from Major Abasa.

He had succeeded, with the sanction and co-operation of the Governor of that Province, in hiring for a period of three years a force of eight hundred Yakoot laborers, at a fixed rate of sixty roubles, or about forty dollars a year for each man.　He had also purchased three hundred Yakoot horses and pack-saddles, and an immense quantity of material and provisions of various kinds for the equipment and subsistence of horses and work men. A portion of these men were already on their way to Okhotsk, and the whole force would be sent thither in successive detachments as rapidly as possible, and distributed from there along the whole route of the line. It would be necessary, of course, to put this large force of native laborers under skilled American superintendence; and as we had not foremen enough in all our parties to oversee more than five or six gangs of men, Major Abasa had determined to send a courier to Petropavlovski for the officers who had sailed from San Francisco in the barque *Onward*, and who he presumed had been landed by that vessel in Kamtchatka. He directed me, therefore, to make arrangements for the transportation of these men from Petropavlovski to Geezhega, to prepare immediately for the reception of fifty or sixty Yakoot laborers, to send six hundred army rations to Gamsk for the subsistence of our American party there, and three thousand pounds of rye flour for a party of Yakoots who would reach there in February. To fill all these requisitions I had at my disposal about fifteen dog-sledges, and even these had gone with provisions to Penzhina for the relief of Lieut. Bush. With the assistance of the Russian Governor I succeeded in getting two Cossacks to go to Petropavlovski after the Americans who were presumed to have been left there by the *Onward*—and half a dozen Koraks to carry provisions to Gamsk, while Lieut. Arnold himself sent sledges for the six hundred rations. I thus retained my own fifteen sledges to supply Lieut. Sandford and party, who were now cutting poles on the Tilghai River, north of Penzhinsk Gulf. One day late in December, while Dodd and I were out on the river above the settlement training a team of dogs, word was brought to us that an American had arrived from Kamtchatka, bringing news from the long-missing barque *Onward* and the party of men whom she landed at Petropavlovski. Hurrying back to the village with all possible speed, we found Mr. Lewis, the American in question, seated comfortably in our house drinking tea. This enterprising young man—who, by the way, was a telegraph operator, wholly unaccustomed to rough life—without being able to speak a word of Russian, had traversed alone, in midwinter, the whole wilderness of Kamtchatka from Petropavlovski to Geezhega. He had been forty-two days on the road, and had travelled on dog-sledges nearly twelve hundred miles, with no companions except a few natives and a Cossack from Tigil. He seemed disposed to look upon this achievement very modestly, but in some respects it was one of the most remarkable journeys ever made by the Company's employés.

The *Onward*, as we had supposed, being unable to reach Geezhega, on account of the lateness of the season, had discharged her cargo and landed most of her passengers at Petropavlovski ; and Mr. Lewis had been sent by the chief of the party to report their situation to Major Abasa, and find out what they should do.

After the arrival of Mr. Lewis nothing of special importance occurred until March. Arnold at Gamsk, Sandford on the Tilghai, and Bush at Anadyrsk, were trying with the few men which they had to accomplish some

work ; but, owing to deep snow-storms, intensely cold
weather, and a general lack everywhere of provisions and
dogs, their efforts were mostly fruitless. In January I
made an excursion with twelve or fifteen sledges to Sandford's camp on the Tilghai, and attempted to move his
party to another point thirty or forty versts nearer Gee-
zheega ; but in a severe storm on the Kooeel steppe we
were broken up, dispersed, and all lost separately, and af
ter wandering around four or five days in clouds of drifting snow which hid even our dogs from sight, Sandford
with a portion of his party returned to the Tilghai, and I
with the balance to Geezhega.

Late in February the Cossack Kolmagorof arrived from
Petropavlovski, Kamtchatka, bringing three of the men
who had been landed there by the *Onward.*

In March I received by a special courier from Yakootsk
another letter and more orders from Major Abasa. The
eight hundred laborers whom he had engaged were being
rapidly sent forward to Okhotsk, and more than a hundred and fifty were already at work at that place and at
Gamsk. The equipment and transportation of the remainder still required his personal supervision, and it
would be impossible, he wrote, for him to return that
winter to Geezhega. He could come, however, as far as
the Korak settlement of Gamsk, three hundred versts west
of Geezhega, and requested me to meet him at that place
within twelve days after the receipt of his letter. I started
at once with one American companion named Leet, taking twelve days' dog-food and provisions.

The country between Geezhega and Gamsk was entire

ly different in character from anything which I had previous
ly seen in Siberia.   There were no such great desolate plains
as those between Geezhega and Anadyrsk and in the northern part of Kamtchatka.   On the contrary, the whole coast
of the Okhotsk Sea, for nearly six hundred miles west of
Geezhega, was one wilderness of rugged, broken, almost
impassable mountains, intersected by deep valleys and
ravines, and heavily timbered with dense pine and larch
forests.   The Stanavoi range of mountains, which sweeps
up around the Okhotsk Sea from the Chinese frontier, keeps
everywhere near the coast line, and sends down between its
lateral spurs hundreds of small rivers and streams which
run through deep wooded valleys to the sea.   The road, or
rather the travelled route from Geezhega to Gamsk cros-
ses all these streams and lateral spurs at right angles, keeping about midway between the great mountain range and
the sea.   Most of the dividing ridges between these
streams are nothing but high, bare water-sheds, which
can be easily crossed ; but at one point, about a hundred
and fifty versts west of Geezhega, the central range sends
out to the sea-coast a great spur of mountains 2,500 and
3,000 feet in height, which completely blocks up the road.
Along the bases of these mountains runs a deep gloomy
valley known as the " Viliga," whose upper end pierces
the central Stanavoi range and affords an outlet to the
winds pent up between the steppes and the sea.   In winter,
when the open water of the Okhotsk Sea is warmer than
the frozen plains north of the mountains, the air over the
former rises, and a colder atmosphere rushes through the
valley of the Viliga to takes its place.   In summer, while

the water of the sea is still chilled with masses of unmelt-
ed ice, the great steppes behind the mountains are covered
with vegetation and warm with almost perpetual sunshine,
and the direction of the wind is consequently reversed.
This valley of the Viliga, therefore, may be regarded as a
great natural breathing-hole, through which the interior
steppes respire once a year. At no other point does the
Stanavoi range afford an opening through which the air can
pass back and forth between the steppes and the sea, and
as a natural consequence this ravine is swept by one almost uninterrupted storm. While the weather everywhere
else is calm and still, the wind blows through the Viliga in
a perfect hurricane, tearing up great clouds of snow from
the mountain sides and carrying them far out to sea. For
this reason it is dreaded by all natives who are compelled
to pass that way, and is famous throughout Northeastern
Siberia as "the stormy gorge of the Viliga!"

On the fifth day after leaving Geezhega our small party,
increased by a Russian "pochtillion" and three or four
sledges carrying the annual Kamtchatkan mail, drew near
the foot of the dreaded Viliga Mountains. Owing to
deep snow our progress had not been so rapid as we had
anticipated, and we were only able to reach on the fifth
night a small yourt built to shelter travellers, near the
mouth of a river called the Topollofka, thirty versts from
the Viliga. Here we camped, drank tea, and stretched
ourselves out on the rough plank floor to sleep, knowing
that a hard day's work awaited us on the morrow.

CHAPTER XXXV.

JOURNEY TO GAMSK—VALLEY OF THE VILIGA—A STORM
—A PERILOUS PASS.

"KENNAN! Oh Kennan! Turn out! It's daylight."
A sleepy grunt and a still more drowsy "Is it?" from the
pile of furs lying on the rough plank floor betrayed no
very lively interest on the part of the prostrate figure in
the fact announced, while the heavy, long-drawn breathing
which soon succeeded this momentary interruption proved that more active measures must be taken to recall
him from the land of dreams. "I say! Kennan! Wake
up! Breakfast has been ready this half-hour." The magic
word breakfast appealed to a stronger feeling than drow-
siness, and thrusting my head out from beneath its covering of furs, I took a sleepy blinking view of the situation,
endeavoring in a feeble sort of way to recollect where I
was and how I came there. A bright crackling fire of
resinous pine boughs was burning on the square log altar
in the centre of the hut, radiating a fierce heat to its re-
motest corner, and causing the perspiration to stand in
great beads on its mouldy logs and rough board ceiling.
The smoke rose lazily up through the square hole in the
roof toward the white, solemn-looking stars which winked
soberly at us between the dark overhanging branches of
the larches. Mr. Leet, who acted as the Soyer of our

campaign, was standing over me with a slice of bacon impaled on a bowie-knife in one hand, and a poker in the other—both of which insignia of office he was brandishing furiously, with the intention of waking me up more effectually. His frantic gesticulations had the desired result. With a vague impression that I had been shipwrecked on the Cannibal Islands and was about to be sacrificed to the tutelary deities, I sprang up and rubbed my eyes until I gathered together my scattered senses. Mr. Leet was in high glee. Our travelling companion, the postilion, had manifested for several days an inclination to shirk work and allow us to do all the road-breaking, while he followed comfortably in our tracks, and by this strategic manœuvre had incurred Mr. Leet's most implacable hatred. The latter, therefore, had waked the unfortunate man up before he had been asleep five hours, and had deluded him into the belief that the Aurora Borealis was the first flush of daylight. He had accordingly started off at midnight and was laboriously breaking a road up the steep mountain side through three feet of soft snow, relying upon Mr. L.'s promise that we would be along before sunrise. At five o'clock, when I got up, the voices of the postilion's men could still be heard shouting to their exhausted dogs near the summit of the mountain. We all breakfasted as leisurely as possible, in order to give them plenty of time to break a road for us, and did not finally start until after six o'clock.

It was a beautifully clear, still morning when we crossed the mountain above the yourt, and wound around through bare open valleys, among high hills, toward the sea-coast.

The sun had risen over the eastern hill-tops, and the snow
glittered as if strewn with diamonds, while the distant
peaks of the Viliga appeared—

"Bathed in the tenderest purple of distance
Tinted and shadowed by pencils of air"—

as calm and bright in their snowy majesty as if the suspicion of a storm had never attached to their smooth white
slopes and sharp pinnacles. The air, although intensely
cold, was clear and bracing ; and as our dogs bounded at
a gallop over the hard, broken road, the exhilarating
motion caused the very blood in our veins

———"to dance"
"Blithe as the sparkling wine of France."

About noon we came out of the mountains upon the
sea-beach and overtook the postilion, who had stopped to
rest his tired dogs. Our own being fresh, we again took
the lead, and drew rapidly near to the valley of the Viliga.
I was just mentally congratulating myself upon our
good fortune in having clear weather to pass this dreaded
point, when my attention was suddenly attracted by a
curious white cloud or mist, extending from the mouth of
the Viliga ravine far out over the black open water of
the Okhotsk Sea. Wondering what it could be, I pointed
it out to our guide, and inquired if it were fog. His face
clouded up with anxiety as he glanced at it, and replied
laconically, "Viliga dooreet," or "the mountains are
fooling." This oracular response did not enlighten me
very much, and I demanded an explanation. I was then
told, to my astonishment and dismay, that the curious
white mist which I had taken to be fog was a dense driv-

ing cloud of snow, hurled out of the mouth of the ravine by a storm, which had apparently just begun in the upper gorges of the Stanavoi range. It would be impossible, our guide said, to cross the valley, and dangerous to attempt it until the wind should subside. I could not see either the impossibility or the danger, and as there was another "yourt" or shelter-house on the other side of the ravine, I determined to go on and make the attempt at least to cross. Where we were the weather was perfectly calm and still; a candle would have burned in the open air without flickering, and I could not realize the tremendous force of the hurricane which, only a mile ahead, was vomiting snow out of the mouth of that ravine and carrying it four miles to sea. Seeing that Leet and I were determined to cross the valley, our guide shrugged his shoulders expressively, as much as to say, "You will soon regret your haste," and we went on.

As we gradually approached the white curtain of mist, we began to feel sharp intermittent puffs of wind and little whirlwinds of snow, which increased constantly in strength and frequency as we drew nearer and nearer to the mouth of the ravine. Our guide once more remonstrated with us upon the folly of going deliberately into such a storm as this evidently would be; but Leet laughed him to scorn, declaring in broken Russian that he had seen storms in the Sierra Nevadas to which this was not a circumstance—"Col-shoi storms, you bet!" But in five minutes more Mr. Leet himself was ready to admit that this storm on the Viliga would not compare unfavorably with anything of the kind which he had ever seen in California.

As we rounded the end of a protecting bluff on the edge of the ravine, the gale burst upon us in all its fury, blinding and suffocating us with dense clouds of driving snow, which blotted out instantly the sun and the clear blue sky, and fairly darkened the whole earth. The wind roared as it sometimes does through the cordage of a ship at sea. There was something almost supernatural in the suddenness of the change from bright sunshine and calm still air to this howling, blinding tempest, and I began to feel doubtful myself as to the practicability of crossing the valley. Our guide turned with a despairing look to me, as if reproaching me with my obstinacy in coming into the storm against his advice, and then urged on with shouts and blows his cowering dogs. The sockets of the poor brutes' eyes were completely plastered up with snow, and out of many of them were oozing drops of blood; but blind as they were they still struggled on, uttering at intervals short mournful cries, which alarmed me more than the roaring of the storm. In a moment we were at the bottom of the ravine; and before we could check the impetus of our descent we were out on the smooth glare ice of the " Propadschina," or " River of the Lost," and sweeping rapidly down toward the open water of the Okhotsk Sea, only a hundred yards below. All our efforts to stop our sledges were at first unavailing against the force of the wind, and I began to understand the nature of the danger to which our guide had alluded. Unless we could stop our sledges before we should reach the mouth of the river we must inevitably be blown off the ice into three or four fathoms of water. Precisely such a disaster had given the river its ominous name. Leet and the Cossack Paderin, who were alone upon their respective sledges, and who did not get so far from the shore in the first place, finally succeeded with the aid of their spiked sticks in getting back; but the old guide and I were together upon one sledge, and our voluminous fur clothes caught so much wind that our spiked sticks would not stop or hold us, and our dogs could not keep their feet. Believing that the sledge must inevitably be blown into the sea if we both clung to it, I finally relinquished my hold and tried to stop myself by sitting down, and then by lying down flat upon my face on the ice; but all was of no avail; my slippery furs took no hold of the smooth treacherous surface, and I drifted away even faster than before. I had already torn off my mittens, and as I slid at last over a rough place in the ice I succeeded in getting my finger-nails into the little corrugations of the surface and in stopping my perilous drift; but I hardly dared breathe lest I should lose my hold. Seeing my situation, Leet slid to me a sharp iron-spiked "oerstel," which is used to check the speed of a sledge in descending hills, and by digging this into the ice at short intervals I crept back to shore only a short distance above the open water at the mouth of the river, into which my mittens had already gone. Our guide was still sliding slowly and at intervals down stream, but Paderin went to his assistance with another "oerstel," and together they brought his sledge once more to land. I would have been quite satisfied now to turn back and get out of the storm; but our guide's blood was up, and cross the valley he would if we lost all our sledges in the sea. He had warned us of the danger and we had insisted upon coming on ; we must now take the consequences.

As it was evidently impossible to cross the river at this point, we struggled up its left bank in the teeth of the storm almost half a mile, until we reached a bend which put land between us and the open water. Here we made a second attempt, and were successful. Crossing a low ridge on the west side of the " Propadschina," we reached another small stream, known as the Viliga, at the foot of the Viliga Mountains. Along this there extended a narrow strip of dense timber, and in this timber, somewhere, stood the yourt of which we were in search. Our guide seemed to find the road by a sort of instinct, for the drifting clouds of snow hid even our leading dogs from sight, and all that we could see of the country was the ground on which we stood. About an hour before dark, tired and chilled to the bone, we drew up before a little log-hut in the woods, which our guide said was the Viliga yourt. The last travellers who had occupied it had left the chimney-hole open, and it was nearly filled with snow, but we cleared it out as well as we could, built a fire on the ground in the centre, and, regardless of the smoke, crouched around it to drink tea. We had seen nothing of the " postilion " since noon, and hardly thought it possible that he could reach the yourt ; but just as it began to grow dark we heard the howling of his dogs in the woods, and in a few moments he made his appearance. Our party now numbered nine men—two Americans, three Russians, and four Koraks—and a wild-looking crowd it

was, as it squatted around the fire in that low smoke-
blackened hut, drinking tea and listening to the howling
wind. As there was not room enough for all to sleep inside the yourt, the Koraks camped out doors on the snow,
and before morning were half buried in a drift.

All night the wind roared a deep, hoarse bass through
the forest which sheltered the yourt, and at daylight on the
following morning there was no abatement of the storm.
We knew that it might blow without intermission in that
ravine for two weeks, and we had only four days' dog-food
and provisions left. Something must be done. The Viliga Mountains which blocked up the road to Gamsk were
cut by three gaps or passes, all of which opened into the
valley, and in clear weather could be easily found and
crossed. In such a storm, however, as the one which had
overtaken us, a hundred passes would be of no avail,
because the drifting snow hid everything from sight at a
distance of thirty feet, and we were as likely to go directly
up the side of a peak. * * * We were making very
fair progress when we found ourselves suddenly confronted
by an entirely unexpected and apparently insurmountable obstacle. The beach, as far as we could see to the
westward, was completely filled up from the water's edge
to a height of seventy-five or a hundred feet by enormous
drifts of snow, which had been gradually accumulating
there throughout the winter, and which now masked the
whole face of the precipice, and left no room for passage
between it and the sea. These snow-drifts, by frequent alternations of warm and cold weather, had been rendered
almost as hard and slippery as ice, and as they sloped up-

ward toward the tops of the cliffs at an angle of seventy
five or eighty degrees, it was impossible to stand upon
them without first cutting places for the feet with an axe
Along the face of this smooth, snowy escarpment, which
rose directly out of two or three fathoms of water, lay our
only route to Gamsk. The prospect of getting over it
without meeting with some disaster seemed very faint, for
the slightest caving away of the snow would tumble us all
into the open sea ; but as there was no alternative, we
fastened our dogs to cakes of ice, distributed our axes and
hatchets, threw off our heavy fur coats, and began cutting
out a road.

We worked hard all day, and by six o'clock in the evening had cut a deep trench three feet in width along the
face of the escarpment to a point about a mile and a
quarter west of the mouth of the Viliga. Here we were
again stopped, however, by a difficulty infinitely worse
than any which we had surmounted. The beach, which
had previous extended in one unbroken line along the
foot of the cliffs, here suddenly disappeared, and the mass
of snow over which we had been cutting a road came to
an abrupt termination. Unsupported from beneath, the
whole escarpment had caved away into the sea, leaving a gap of open water about thirty-five feet in width,
out of which rose the black perpendicular wall of the
coast. There was no possibility of getting across without
the assistance of a pontoon bridge. Tired and disheartened, we were compelled to camp on the slope of the escarpment for the night, with no prospect of being able to
do anything in the morning except return with all possible

speed to the Viliga, and abandon entirely the idea of reaching Gamsk.

A wilder, more dangerous location for a camp than that which we occupied could hardly be found in Siberia, and I watched with the greatest uneasiness the signs of the weather as it began to grow dark. The huge sloping snow-drift upon which we stood rose directly out of the water, and, as far as we knew, it might have no other foundation than a narrow strip of ice. If so, the faintest breeze from any direction except north would roll in waves high enough to undermine and break up the whole escarpment, and either precipitate us with an avalanche of snow into the open sea, or leave us clinging like barnacles to the bare face of the precipice, seventy-five feet above it. Neither alternative was pleasant to contemplate, and I determined, if possible, to find a place of greater security. Leet, with his usual recklessness, dug himself out what he called a "bed-room" in the snow, about fifty feet above the water, and promised me "a good night's sleep" if I would accept his hospitality and share his cave; but under the circumstances I thought best to decline. His "bed-room," bed, and bedding, might all tumble into the sea before morning, and his "good night's sleep" be indefinitely prolonged. Going back a short distance in the direction of the Viliga, I finally discovered a place where a small stream had once fallen over the summit of the cliff, and had worn out a steep narrow channel in its face. In the rocky, uneven bed of this little ravine the natives and I stretched ourselves out for the night—our bodies inclined at an angle of forty-five degrees —our heads, of course, up-hill.

If the reader can imagine himself camping out on the steep sloping roof of a great cathedral, with a precipice a hundred feet high over his head and three or four fathoms of open water at his feet, he will be able, perhaps, to form some idea of the way in which we spent that dismal night.

With the first streak of dawn we were up. While we were gloomily making preparations to return to the Viliga, one of the Koraks who had gone to take a last look at the gap of open water came hurriedly running back, shouting joyfully, " Mozhno perryékat, mozhno perryékat ! "—It is possible to cross. The tide which had risen during the night had brought in two or three large cakes of broken ice, and had jammed them into the gap in such a manner as to make a rude bridge. Fearing, however, that it would not support a very heavy weight, we unloaded all our sledges, carried the loads, sledges, and dogs across separately, loaded up again on the other side, and went on. The worst of our difficulties was past. We still had some road-cutting to do through occasional snow-drifts ; but as we went farther and farther to the westward the beach, as the Koraks had predicted, became wider and higher, the ice disappeared, and by night we were thirty versts nearer to our destination. The sea on one side, and the cliffs on the other, still hemmed us in ; but on the following day we succeeded in making our escape through the valley of the Kananaga River.

The twelfth day of our journey found us on a great steppe called the Malcachán, only thirty miles from Gamsk ; and although our dog-food and provisions were

both exhausted, we hoped to reach the settlement late in
the night. Darkness came on, however, with another
blinding snow-storm, in which we again lost our way ; and
fearing that we would drive over the edges of the precipices
into the sea, by which the steppe was bounded on the east,
we were finally compelled to stop. We could find no
wood for a fire ; but even had we succeeded in making a
fire, it would have been instantly smothered by the clouds
of snow which the furious wind drove across the plain.
Spreading down our canvas tent upon the ground, and
capsizing a heavy dog-sledge upon one edge of it to hold
it fast, we crawled under it to get away from the suffocating snow. Lying there upon our faces, with the canvas
flapping furiously against our backs, we scraped our bread-
bag for the last few frozen crumbs which remained, and ate
a few scraps of raw meat which Mr. Leet found on one of
the sledges. In the course of fifteen or twenty minutes
we noticed that the flappings of the canvas were getting
shorter and shorter, and that it seemed to be tightening
across our bodies, and upon making an effort to get out
we found that we were fastened down. The snow had
drifted in such masses upon the edges of the tent and had
packed there with such solidity that it could not be moved, and after trying once or twice to break out we concluded to lie still and make the best of our situation. As
long as the snow did not bury us entirely, we were better
off under the tent than anywhere else, because we were
protected from the wind. In half an hour the drift had
increased to such an extent that we could no longer turn
over, and our supply of air was almost entirely cut off.

We must either get out or be suffocated. I had drawn my sheath-knife fifteen minutes before in expectation of such a crisis, and as it was already becoming difficult to breathe, I cut a long slit in the canvas above my head and we crawled out. In an instant eyes and nostrils were complete-ly plastered up with snow, and we gasped for breath as if the stream of a fire-engine had been turned suddenly in our faces. Drawing our heads and arms into the bodies of our fur coats, we squatted down upon the snow to wait for daylight. In a moment I heard Mr. Leet shouting down into the neck-hole of my fur coat, " What would our mothers say if they could see us now ? " I wanted to ask him how this would compare with a gale in his boasted Sierra Nevadas, but he was gone before I could get my head out, and I heard nothing more from him that night. He went away somewhere in the darkness and squatted down alone upon the snow, to suffer cold and hunger and anxiety until morning. For more than ten hours we sat in this way on that desolate storm-swept plain, without fire, food, or sleep, becoming more and more chilled and ex-hausted, until it seemed as if day-light would never come.

Morning dawned at last through gray drifting clouds of snow, and getting up with stiffened limbs, we made feeble attempts to dig out our buried sledges. But for the un-wearied efforts of Mr. Leet we should hardly have suc-ceeded, as my hands and arms were so benumbed with cold that I could not hold an axe or a shovel, and our drivers, frightened and discouraged, seemed unable to do anything. By Mr. Leet's individual exertions the sledges were dug out and we started. His brief spasm of energy was the last effort of a strong will to uphold a sinking and exhausted body, and in half an hour he requested to be tied on his sledge. We lashed him on from head to foot with seal-skin thongs, covered him up with bear-skins, and drove on. In about an hour his driver, Padarin, came back to me with a frightened look in his face, and said that Mr. Leet was dead; that he had shaken him and called him several times, but could get no reply. Alarmed and shocked, I sprang from my sledge and ran up to the place where he lay, shouted to him, shook him by the shoulder, and tried to uncover his head, which he had drawn down into the body of his fur coat. In a moment, to my great relief, I heard his voice, saying that he was all right and could hold out, if necessary, until night; that he had not answered Padarin because it was too much trouble, but that I need not be alarmed about his safety; and then I thought he added something about "worse storms in the Sierra Nevadas," which convinced me that he was far from being used up yet. As long as he could insist upon the superiority of Californian storms, there was certainly hope.

Early in the afternoon we reached the Gamsk River, and, after wandering about for an hour or two in the timber, came upon one of Lieut. Arnold's Yakoot working-parties and were conducted to their camp, only a few miles from the settlement. Here we obtained some rye bread and hot tea, warmed our benumbed limbs, and partially cleared the snow out of our clothing. When I saw Mr. Leet undressed I wondered that he had not died. While squatting out on the ground during the storm of the previous night, snow in great quantities had blown in at his neck, had partially melted with the warmth of his body, and had then frozen again in a mass of ice along his whole spine, and in that condition he had lived to be driven twenty versts. Nothing but a strong will and the most intense vitality enabled him to hold out during these last six dismal hours. When we had warmed, rested, and dried ourselves at the camp fire of the Yakoots, we resumed our journey, and late in the afternoon we drove into the settlement of Gamsk, after thirteen days of as hard experience as usually falls to the lot of Siberian travellers. Mr. Leet so soon recovered his strength and spirits that three days afterwards he started for Okhotsk, where the Major wished him to take charge of a gang of Yakoot laborers. The last words which I remember to have ever heard him speak were those which he shouted to me in the storm and darkness of that gloomy night on the Malcachan steppe: "What would our mothers say if they could see us now?" The poor fellow was afterwards driven insane by excitements and hardships such as these which I have described, and probably to some extent by this very expedition, and finally committed suicide by shooting himself at one of the lonely Siberian settlements on the coast of the Okhotsk Sea.

I have described somewhat in detail this trip to Gamsk because it illustrates the darkest side of Siberian life and travel. It is not often that one meets with such an experience, or suffers so many hardships in any one journey; but in a country so wild and sparsely populated as Siberia, winter travel is necessarily attended with more or less suffering and privation.

CHAPTER XXXVI.

RETURN TO GEEZHEGA—ARRIVAL OF THE "ONWARD"—
ORDERS TO "CLOSE UP"—BEATEN BY THE ATLANTIC
CABLE—SUMMARY—START FOR ST. PETERSBURG—A
TRIP OF MORE THAN 5,000 MILES.

THE trip to Gamsk described in the previous chapter
was the last journey which I ever made in Northeastern
Siberia. On the 18th of March Major Abasa returned to
Yakootsk, to complete the organization and equipment
of our Yakoot laborers, and I to Geezhega to await once
more the arrival of vessels from America. From that
time until the opening of navigation little was done in
any part of the Siberian Division. Gregorie Zinovief, the
Cossack who had been sent to Petropavlovski, returned
in March with the remainder of the officers who had been
left at that place by the *Onward*, and I sent them on,
as the Major had directed, to Gamsk. Sandford and
party finished cutting poles on the Tilghai, and I forwarded them to Penzhina ; but the time for which his
men had agreed to serve the Company expired, and they
refused to renew their contracts, leaving me with only
five men to carry on the work.

Late in May the ice in the Gulf of Geezhega began
to disappear, and on the first of June we boarded a whal-

ing vessel off Matooga Island. It was the barque *Sea Breeze*, from New Bedford, Mass., with American news to the first of March. The Atlantic cable had proved to be an entire success, and from the *San Francisco Bulletin* we learned that in consequence of this success " all work on the Russian American Telegraph line had been stopped and the enterprise abandoned."

On the 15th of July the Company's barque *Onward* arrived from San Francisco, bringing orders to close up the business, discharge our native laborers, gather up our men, and return to America. The Atlantic cable was a complete success, and the Western Union Telegraph Company, after sinking nearly $3,000,000, had decided to abandon the project of an overland line to Russia. It seemed hard to give up at once the object to which we had devoted three years of our lives, and for whose attainment we had suffered all possible hardships of cold, exile, and starvation; but we had no alternative, and began at once to make preparations for our final departure.

The situation of affairs at the time the work was abandoned was briefly as follows. We had explored and located the whole route of the line, from the Amoor River to Behring's Straits. We had prepared altogether about 15,000 telegraph poles, built between forty and fifty station-houses and magazines, cut nearly fifty miles of road through the forests in the vicinity of Gamsk and Okhotsk, and accomplished a great deal of preparatory work along the whole extent of the line. Our resources for another season would have been ample. Besides seventy-five Americans, we had a force of a hundred and fifty natives

already at work between Gamsk and Okhotsk, and six
hundred more were on their way from Yakootsk : our
facilities for transportation another year would have been
almost unlimited. We had a small steamer on the Anadyr
River, and had ordered another for the Penzhina ; we
owned a hundred and fifty dogs and several hundred
reindeer at Gamsk, Okhotsk, and Geezhega, and had purchased three hundred Siberian horses at Yakootsk, with
an immense amount of material for their equipment and
subsistence. By the first of September we would have
been able to take the field with a force of nearly a thousand men. The success of the Atlantic cable, however,
rendered all our preparations unavailing. We might
build the line, but there was no Company in the world
which would undertake to sustain and work it a single
year in competition with the cable.

In itself, the route of the Russo-American Telegraph
Company from Behring's Straits to the Amoor River presented no insurmountable obstacles to the construction
of a line. The work would have been difficult, but it
could have been accomplished, and I believe that this is a
much more practical route for a line to China than the
one recently proposed by Mr. Collins, via the Aleutian
Islands, Kamtchatka, and Japan. Labor in Siberia is very
cheap, and almost any desired number of men can be engaged at Yakootsk for about forty dollars a year and subsistence. Horses can also be purchased at Yakootsk and
Kolyma to the number of five or six hundred, at prices
varying from fifteen to twenty-five dollars. Nothing
need be brought from America except wire, insulators,

and tools, and a small quantity of provisions for a limited
number of American foremen.   If there were any call for
it, I believe that a line could be successfully built from
Behring's Straits to the Amoor River in two years, at an
expense not exceeding $250,000.

The remainder of the summer of 1867, after the arrival
of the *Onward*, was almost entirely consumed in picking
up our scattered parties along the coast of the Okhotsk
Sea, selling off our stores to Russian merchants, and
making preparations for departure.   A separate vessel
had been sent to the mouth of the Anadyr after Bush and
his comrades, so that we did not have another opportunity
of seeing them.   On the 6th of August Major Abasa left
for St. Petersburg, overland, and early in October the
Onward sailed for San Francisco, carrying back all
but four of the employés of the unfortunate Russo-
American Telegraph Expedition.   Leet, Price, Mahood,
and I—the "rear-guard of the grand army"—remained
at Okhotsk, with the intention of going home in winter
across Asia and Europe, around the world.

It was a lonely time in that dreary settlement after all
our comrades had gone ; but winter soon set in, and on
the 24th of October Price and I started on dog-sledges
for a journey of more than 5,000 miles to St. Petersburg.
I will not add another to the number of descriptions which
have already been written of overland trips from the
Pacific Ocean to Russia.

Suffice it to say, that, taking government post-horses
at Yakootsk, and travelling night and day, we passed
Irkootsk, the capital of Eastern Siberia, on December

6th. On the 30th we crossed the Russian frontier, and on January 3d, after ten weeks of incessant travel, we caught sight of the glittering domes of Moscow, and closed forever the book of our Siberian Experience.